West German Foreign Policy:
1949-1979

Other Titles in This Series

Westview Special Studies in West European Politics and Society

West German Foreign Policy: 1949-1979
edited by Wolfram F. Hanrieder

This collection of original papers by prominent political and academic figures from both sides of the Atlantic focuses on the political, economic, military-strategic, and domestic dimensions of West Germany's foreign policy.

The authors first consider the changing constraints and opportunities that have shaped West German foreign policy. Succeeding chapters examine Germany's relationship with the United States, the Soviet Union, Eastern Europe, and the Third World; the evolution and development of Germany's Eastern European policy; the role of Germany in a changing political, strategic, and economic environment; arms proliferation and control; and prospects for the future.

Wolfram F. Hanrieder is professor of political science at the University of California at Santa Barbara.

West German Foreign Policy: 1949-1979

edited by Wolfram F. Hanrieder

Westview Press / Boulder, Colorado

Westview Special Studies in West European Politics and Society

Copyright © 1980 by Westview Press, Inc.

Published in 1980 in the United States of America by
  Westview Press, Inc.
  5500 Central Avenue
  Boulder, Colorado 80301
  Frederick A. Praeger, Publisher

Library of Congress Cataloging in Publication Data
Main entry under title:
  West German foreign policy, 1949-1979.
  (Westview special studies in West European politics and society)
  Papers presented at a January 1979 conference sponsored by the Konrad Adenauer Foundation and the University of California, Santa Barbara.
  1.Germany, West—Foreign relations—Congresses. I. Hanrieder, Wolfram F. II. Konrad-Adenauer—Stiftung für Politische Bildung und Studienförderung. III. California. University, Santa Barbara.
DD259.4.W426   327.43   79-18169
ISBN 0-89158-579-6

Printed and bound in the United States of America

Contents

Acknowledgments

The essays in this collection were initially presented as papers at a conference held in Santa Barbara, California, January 4-6, 1979. The conference, intended to mark the thirtieth anniversary of the Federal Republic of Germany, was sponsored by the Konrad-Adenauer-Stiftung and the University of California, Santa Barbara. The financial support of the Konrad-Adenauer-Stiftung, which made it possible to bring the participants to Santa Barbara, is gratefully acknowledged. Special thanks are due to Mr. Larry Buel, then my assistant, for his untiring and cheerful labors before and during the conference.

Wolfram F. Hanrieder

Contributors

David P. Calleo is professor of European studies and director of the European Studies Program, Johns Hopkins University School of Advanced International Studies, Washington, D.C.

Ernst-Otto Czempiel is professor of political science at the University of Frankfurt, West Germany.

Wolfram F. Hanrieder is professor of political science at the University of California, Santa Barbara.

Martin J. Hillenbrand, formerly U.S. ambassador to the Federal Republic of Germany, is currently director-general of the Atlantic Institute for International Affairs, Paris, and a consultant to the U.S. Department of State.

William G. Hyland is an associate in the office of Dr. Henry A. Kissinger and a senior fellow at the Center for Strategic and International Studies at Georgetown University.

Karl Kaiser is director of the Research Institute of the German Society for Foreign Affairs, Bonn, and professor of political science at the University of Cologne, West Germany.

Catherine McArdle Kelleher is professor of political science at the Graduate School of International Studies, University of Denver.

Peter Merkl is professor of political science at the University of California, Santa Barbara.

Hans J. Morgenthau is professor of political science at the New School for Social Research, Albert A. Michelson Distinguished Service Professor of Political Science and Modern History, Emeritus, at the University of Chicago, and Leonard Davis Distinguished Professor of Political Science, Emeritus, at City College of the City University of New York.

Julia Dingwort-Nusseck is president of the Landeszentralbank of Niedersachsen, West Germany.

Jan Reifenberg is political correspondent for the *Frankfurter Allgemeine Zeitung* in Washington, D.C.

J. Robert Schaetzel is a former U.S. ambassador to the European Community.

Hans-Peter Schwarz is professor of political science at the University of Cologne, West Germany.

F. Roy Willis is professor of history at the University of California, Davis.

Manfred Wörner is chairman of the Armed Services Committee of the West German *Bundestag*.

Gerhard Zeitel is a member of the West German *Bundestag* and a professor of economics at the University of Mannheim.

West German Foreign Policy:
1949-1979

1

Germany and the Balance of Power

David Calleo

The modern history of all European nation-states has been bound intimately to the continent's balance of power. Germany's relation to that European balance has passed through three phases. In the early modern era, as Europe's great powers fought out their rivalries over a fragmented German nation, Germany was, in effect, the balance's principal victim. While Habsburg Spain was ascendant, Germany's division was essential to equilibrium. Hence, Germans suffered the protracted agony of the Thirty Years' War, ended by the Treaty of Westphalia that sealed Germany's failure to develop a centralized national state like France or Britain. With Spain's eclipse, Germany remained the principal continental battleground to check French power, until the Congress of Vienna established a new equilibrium.

Bismarck's creation of the imperial *Reich* opened a new role for Germany. Once consolidated and then united in "organic" alliance with Austria-Hungary, the German *Reich*, by its very existence, became a serious threat to the post-Napoleonic balance. Imperial Germans, indeed, came to reject that balance as obsolescent. Their reasoning was based on three major developments during the nineteenth century that, they believed, profoundly changed the framework of international equilibrium. These were the evolution of Britain into the world's first industrial, world-imperial power and the gradual consolidation of the Russian empire and the American Republic into modern, continental-sized nation-states. Henceforth, they maintained, balance would have to be achieved on a global rather than continental scale. And global equilibrium required German hegemony over Europe.

World War II ended the *Reich*'s challenge and Germany reverted to the old status of victim. Europe's continental balance now depends upon Germany's permanent partition, while global balance requires each German fragment to remain within the sphere of its respective superpower.

This brief historical sketch suggests that any model of Germany in the balance of power should incorporate four fundamental variables. The first set of two are needed to depict Germany itself — either united or divided into several states. The other set of two are needed to describe the balance of power itself, whether a European or a world balance. Bismarck's *Reich* changed the first set of variables — Germany's own scale. The rise of Britain, Russia, the United States, Japan, and the *Reich* itself radically changed the second set — the context within which the balance of power had to be calculated.

Germany's career as an aggressor can be traced in terms of our model. By uniting Germany, Bismarck created the prospect of German hegemony over Europe. Bismarck, it might be said, had no desire to assert that hegemony. He merely wished to unite the country, or rather the non-Austrian parts of it, into a modern nation-state. He was fearful from the start of the combined vengeance of Europe's other great powers. Hence his elaborate system of alliances was aimed essentially at keeping the others perpetually off balance and at odds with each other. Bismarck encouraged the other powers in their extra-European ambitions. He thus hoped to exacerbate their rivalries, prevent their combination, and insulate the continent and Germany from any direct confrontations. Bismarck's strategy required that his *Reich* be seen as a satisfied power, with no desire to alter further Europe's territorial arrangements, or to challenge Britain, France, or Russia in the extra-European imperial sphere. Hence, in his triumphs of 1866 and 1870, he vehemently rejected ambitions for a Big Germany that would encompass Austria. Thereafter, he did his best to avoid colonial adventures. But whatever Germany's diplomatic restraint under Bismarck, it was difficult to see the new *Reich* as a static power. For it was rapidly becoming Europe's most dynamic economy — by 1870 already more industrially advanced than France and gaining fast on Britain. Thus, in the economic sphere, an aggressively commercial Germany could not help but appear threatening to the established positions of others. But Bismarck gambled that Germany's encroaching economic power could somehow be protected from political retribution so long as the regime carefully avoided further territorial ambitions. He became, in effect, a disciple of Richard Cobden. His international strategy depended upon the continuation of Cobden's liberal world, an open international economy where an industrial Germany could easily obtain the raw materials that it needed and sell the goods that it produced. Germany would leave to Britain the task of managing that world system politically. Germany would merely skim off the economic cream.

Bismarck's strategy was undone by the Great Depression that plagued the world economy from the early 1870s into the 1890s. Protectionism was the natural reaction. Widespread domestic bankruptcy and unemployment forced all industrial powers into an intense competition for markets. The liberal age of Cobden was succeeded by the Darwinian age of cartels. Political imperialism was the natural accompaniment to economic protectionism. For once political power began to regulate economic intercourse; a nation whose political unit or military reach did not extend to the markets and the vital resources upon which its industrial prosperity depended might be fatally handicapped. The future would belong to those powers with either vast external empires, like Britain, or vast continental hinterlands, like Russia and the United States. Traditional European powers, unsustained by imperial empires, would prosper only on sufferance. These geopolitical views grew commonplace in imperial Germany, and indeed everywhere else. Various German interests began promoting German colonialism and a fleet, on the one hand, and a big German territorial sphere in Europe, *Mitteleuropa*, on the other. This logic of protectionism began to push even Bismarck toward that Great German policy he had once resolutely rejected. By the late 1870s, he had become a protectionist, abandoned his old liberal allies, and built a new conservative domestic coalition. At the same time, his organic Austrian alliance, portending German hegemony on the continent, signaled the demise of his old diplomatic strategy. Later imperial governments promoted colonies and fleet-building. In short, from a Little Germany respecting a European balance, the *Reich* evolved into a Big Germany demanding hegemony in Europe and a major place in a global balance. To act otherwise, as the imperial Germans saw it, was to be condemned to domination by powers less fatally constrained.

Imperial Germany's external policies were powerfully shaped by its domestic economic and political character. Unlike Britain, which became an industrial nation in the age of textiles, Germany achieved its modern economic majority in the era of heavy industry—first iron, steel, and machine tools, then chemicals, optics, and electrical goods. Compared with textiles, industries in this later phase required massive concentrations of capital investment. And with a huge capital at stake, such industries were highly vulnerable to sharp fluctuations in market conditions. Hence, they naturally tended toward consolidation. A vertically integrated firm could more easily assure itself of adequate supplies at favorable prices. A large firm, tied closely to a large bank, could garner the financial resources to weather hard times and keep abreast of technological innovation. The formation of cartels was expedient for these heavy industries. In iron and steel, for example, the huge capital investment, as well as the special features of steel technology, made it essential to keep the mills in operation to cover overhead costs. A firm that could assure for itself a certain level of demand through a protected domestic market was in a far better competitive position than a firm that could not. Once basic costs were met, moreover, the low marginal cost of additional production permitted highly competitive pricing. Thus, if overhead were covered by guaranteed domestic demand, a firm could afford to dump in markets abroad.

Protection was also encouraged by a series of related political and social developments of the imperial era. Bismarck's was a new regime, eager to legitimize itself through its modernity. Hence, it sought to identify itself with industry and with the national prosperity and power that came with industrialization. Prolonged depression, however, threatened the legitimacy of the new imperial order. Thus some sort of counter cyclical policy to counteract the depression was vitally important. With imperial fiscal policy hemmed in by a federal constitution and imperial monetary policy subject to the rigors of the gold standard, foreign trade offered the most readily available possibilities for government manipulation. In an economy dominated by heavy industries, possibilities were limited for any sort of Keynesian "demand management," that is, any countercyclical stimulation of the domestic market through domestic government expenditure or income redistribution. That sort of countercyclical policy required consumer industries aimed at a mass domestic market, like automobiles. Thus foreign trade offered the principal new markets for the heavy industry that dominated the imperial economy. For as the railroad boom subsided in Europe itself, the market for iron and steel had shifted increasingly to developing regions beyond Europe's core. Hence, the interests of heavy industry and the Bismarckian state came together around protectionist policy.

The protectionist coalition was powerfully reinforced by the conversion of the agriculturalists, traditionally favorable to free trade. By the 1880s, thanks to railroads and steamships, German grain farming (preserve of the *Junkers*) was beginning to face competition from the vast new areas of Russia and the Americas. In short, the later Bismarckian alliance of *Junker* agriculture, heavy industry, and the imperial state flowed naturally from the dominant societal interests of the time. The Bismarckian domestic coalition, in turn, powerfully affected the *Reich*'s foreign policy. The agricultural protectionism of the *Junkers* fanned enmity with Russia while the aggressive expansion of the industrialists alienated Britain. Thus France was gradually able to put together the diplomatic coalition Bismarck had feared. When the showdown came in 1914, Germany was isolated. Bismarck's nightmare became a reality. His upstart *Reich* was defeated and the European balance restored at Germany's expense.

The fragility of that restoration was all too apparent when Hitler renewed the German challenge in the 1930s. For all his crazy racial ideas, Hitler was a careful student of geopolitics. Imperial Germany's failure, he decided, was predetermined by the flaws in its basic strategy. It was an illusion, Hitler believed, to suppose that Germany's position as a great political and economic power could be consolidated, or even maintained, without a decisive war. The problem for Germany was to choose a coherent goal. Geopolitically, Germany had two options. She could imitate Britain or she could imitate the United States. If she followed her first option, Germany would remain territorially limited and become an export machine for the world. This would require an empire beyond Europe, since in a highly competitive world, a country dependent upon world trade needed secure access to foreign markets and raw materials. To sustain such a system beyond Europe meant having colonies and a fleet, as well as the rest of the apparatus required for an internationalist world policy. For Germany to follow such a policy inevitably meant conflict with Britain, and beyond Britain, with America. Imperial strategists, according to Hitler, had naively believed that economic competition could be separated from military confrontation. But history made abundantly clear that when a challenger's commercial success began seriously to undermine the position of its rival, force would be used to reverse the market. Britain had built her world economic position with power and would, if necessary, seek to maintain it by power. Behind Britain, moreover, was America. Britain had created the world system, but the United States was expecting to inherit it. America would therefore never let a declining Britain be replaced by a dynamic Germany.

Germany's other option, according to Hitler, lay in building an autarchic continental political economy with enough territory to sustain its strength and prosperity from its own resources. Germany would thus imitate the United States. Such a goal meant destroying the great Russian empire and gaining sway over a European system stretching from the Atlantic to the Caucasus. Such a Germany could eschew involvement in a world economy, and therefore pose no threat to the Anglo-Saxon world system.

Imperial Germany's failure, according to Hitler, lay in its inability to choose one option decisively over the other. On the one hand, the *Reich* pursued a continental policy by allying itself with the Habsburg monarchy and dreaming of *Mitteleuropa*. On the other, it pursued a world policy through aggressive international commercial expansion and fleet-building. The results were foreordained. The *Reich* fought not one enemy but two. An ocean of precious German blood was spilled in pursuit of an ill-conceived policy. Hitler's resolution (proposed as early as the writing of *Mein Kampf*) was to choose decisively the continental option, to become an autarchic continental power at Russia's expense. Such a choice, he believed, could avoid a simultaneous conflict with Britain. Indeed, a Germany that had renounced its world ambitions might expect to strike an alliance with

Britain against America. For Britain's world position was threatened far more by the nascent superpowers, the United States in particular, than by an autarchic Germany resolutely determined to remain continental.

Some twenty years later, in his *Last Testament*, Hitler reflected upon his own failure. He had overestimated British intelligence, he decided. Who would have imagined Britain fighting with such blind tenacity to destroy herself and deliver the world to the Americans? Britain's true interest did lie in abandoning the continental balance and letting Germany triumph over Russia. A genuine world balance would then have emerged to contain the otherwise overweening power of the United States. Like his imperial predecessors, Hitler was, in effect, arguing for a united and expanded Germany, with continental hegemony, as an essential element in a new world balance. European balance had to be sacrificed because European unity was essential to any world balance.

If Hitler's defeat ended the second phase of Germany's role in the balance of power, postwar Germany is, nevertheless, as much embroiled in the balance of power as ever. Indeed, Germany is at the center of the postwar balance, that is to say, the balance between the Russian and American superpowers. And as that balance has evolved, it has required the division of Europe into two hegemonic blocs, the boundaries of which run down the middle of the old *Reich*. In short, the balance of power in the postwar era has been achieved at the expense of the historic ambitions of Germany and the autonomy of Europe as a system. In the new world system, as long as Germany remains divided, the local European balance is preserved. But the European balance no longer serves its classic function; it no longer merely preserves the independence of Europe's major states of each other. Instead, it makes them all subject to the hegemony of world powers from beyond Europe. In a sense, of course, this merely enacts the scenario feared by German geopoliticians from the late nineteenth century. As the system of power has expanded from Europe to the world, preservation of the European continental balance has become the ideology of European subjection. Looked at from this perspective, the defeat of Hitler was, as he himself claimed, the defeat of Europe.

Other Europeans, of course, can hardly be blamed for failing to identify with Nazi Germany. German claims to speak for Europe presumed that subjection to the United States or the Soviet Union would be more alien and intolerable to other Europeans than subjection to Germany. The issue may never have been clearly posed, but the aversion of most other Europeans to German hegemony was clear in both world wars. The Germans have never been very talented at hegemony. Hitler's racial program, of course, gravely hamstrung his geopolitical ambitions. A Germany whose hegemony held out the prospect of exploitation and slavery, if not extermination, was hardly calculated to encourage European solidarity.

To say that the Europeans rejected German hegemony in World Wars I and II is not to say, however, that they chose the present Russian-American hegemonies or that they can be expected to tolerate the postwar status quo indefinitely. Although conditions and relations in the American sphere have been very much more favorable than in the Soviet, Western European states nonetheless have grown increasingly restive under American hegemony—hence the persistent strength of the postwar European movement. In it, the European states have sought both to find the unity needed to eject the superpowers and to maintain the balance needed to avoid German hegemony. The European Community, originally based on and still sustained by a sort of Franco-German organic alliance, has proved the most promising formula. European coalescence has been enough to make American hegemony increasingly ineffective and unstable, notably in the economic, and particularly in the monetary, sphere. But, as the uncertain progress of the communities indicates, European cleavages and vulnerabilities have been sufficient to inhabit any heroic efforts at Western European independence. Thus, the postwar order has endured a sort of low-grade crisis—a stalemate leading to gradual deterioration, but as yet without a dramatic breakdown. Such systems can, of course, last for a long time—as anyone familiar with the Hapsburg empire, or indeed much of European history, cannot help but be aware.

Assessing the stability of the postwar balance, or Germany's place in it, requires weighing European restiveness against European inhibitions and vulnerabilities. Such calculations may also be strongly affected by changes in the world system because of extra-European factors, like the gradual rise of new powers difficult to contain within the bipolar postwar order, or a deterioration in relations between the superpowers. Each topic is obviously large and complex and is sketched here only to set the proper perspective for viewing Germany's present relation to the balance of power.

To begin with, why are West European states dissatisfied with the postwar system? In many respects, they are not dissatisfied with the system as a whole. Despite the alarms and excursions of the Cold War, the *Pax Americana* has given Western Europe a period of military security with few parallels in modern times. Along with military security has come a great and sustained economic boom, providing the West with a degree of prosperity and growth without historical precedent. American hegemony, moreover, has not been burdensome in other respects—particularly by comparison with the present Soviet or former Nazi influence. Certainly the smaller European countries have had no pressing incentive to replace American leadership with that of any of the more traditional candidates nearer to home.

Among Europe's own great powers, the British, despite bursts of anti-American temper, have resolutely pursued the mirage of the "special relationship." The Federal Republic, because of its geographical and historical vulnerabilities, has, of course, not been in any real position to challenge the United States directly. Only France has consistently displayed dissatisfaction with the postwar order. Yet the French have often spoken for Europe, which has given them an influence and authority beyond their national strength. In particular, they have articulated many feelings that the Germans have felt unable to express directly.

Why have the French apparently been dissatisfied? Part of their restiveness stems simply from their own historical ambition to remain a major world power. Unlike the British, they were defeated and occupied in World War II, and only with great difficulty did they squeeze into the victors' circle at the war's end. After the war, they were forced out of their old colonial empire, but without either the pragmatism or the illusions that sustained the British. In the postwar period, as in the interwar decades, the loss of their old ally, Russia, deprived them of the leverage that formerly had sustained their own great power position. They were forced to depend upon the "Anglo-Saxons." But their experiences during the war, and especially in the interwar period, left their leadership skeptical about how well a junior partnership with the Anglo-Saxons would preserve France's national interests. Old suspicions revived particularly as the Americans began in the fifties to cultivate a new special relationship with the Federal Republic — a relationship that, in effect, further isolated the French. French diplomacy countered, particularly after the Suez debacle, with a special relationship of its own with Germany. Hence, the Common Market.

French dissatisfaction with the postwar American hegemony has extended to several major spheres, military security among them. With the advances of Soviet nuclear and missile technology pointing toward a growing American vulnerability to direct attack, French strategists began openly to question the reliability of the American nuclear protectorate for Europe. Hence, in the mid-fifties the French developed a nuclear capability, which de Gaulle greatly enhanced. Hence, too, the French developed reservations about integration in NATO.

In the diplomatic sphere, the French have accused the Americans of seeking "condominium" over Europe in partnership with the Soviet Union. Thus détente for the Americans has meant stabilizing a status quo that leaves Europe partitioned. By contrast, de Gaulle envisaged détente as withdrawal of both Americans and Russians from their Central European confrontation and from hegemony over their respective blocs. An autonomous European system was then supposed to emerge — a "Europe from the Atlantic to the Urals." Among the attractions of such a European order, it was argued, were its possibilities for resolving Germany's postwar division within some new all-European system. A Europe partitioned by the superpowers, by contrast, offered no prospect for any real improvement in the German situation. Instead, such a European order would continue indefinitely to base itself upon Germany's division.

French discontent has also been strong in the economic sphere. In the mid-sixties, de Gaulle launched a major attack against American management of the international monetary system. The dollar's role as a reserve currency, in his view, was both unjust and inflationary for Europe's domestic economies. The French have been no less dissatisfied with the floating system that has evolved since 1971. Continual dollar fluctuations, they argue, make European economies unstable and promote both inflation and unemployment.

Finally, France has grown increasingly critical of American positions toward the Third World. Whereas the American interest is said to lie in perpetuating a neocolonial international order that denies economic self-determination and security to Third World states, Europe's interest lies in a new partnership with these countries, leading to a more just and stable world system. Beneath the rhetoric lies Europe's greater dependence on trade with the Third World and renewed hopes for displacing American predominance in the old colonial regions.

All these various French positions, modified but not abandoned by de Gaulle's successors, together constitute a coherent European revisionist ideology toward the postwar status quo. French policy points toward a European bloc independent of either superpower, in effect a new world balance in which Europe would play a major autonomous role. Whether the French would ultimately find such an arrangement in their national interest is an intriguing question. In any event, they have shrewdly preserved their Atlantic options, while carefully promoting the European alternative. Whereas French dissatisfaction has been vocal and articulate, French policy has, in fact, been prudently restrained. France has clearly separated herself from American leadership in all spheres, yet she has taken care not to disrupt the system seriously enough to cause a major breakdown. In effect, France has played the role of a dissident but loyal ally, skillfully enjoying the advantages of selective independence while continuing to participate within the Western system sustained by American power.

By themselves, the French lack the power to create and lead an independent Europe. De Gaulle was too realistic to believe in the strength of federal institutions and too nationalist to want them. But he did hope for the gradual coalescence of Europe's great powers around a common perception of mutual interest. Central to his hopes was the revival of German dissatisfaction with the postwar balance—a dissatisfaction he hoped to channel into an organic partnership with France. In this respect, de Gaulle was only following the policy of his predecessors in the Fourth Republic, who, disillusioned with Britain, had built the various European Communities around a Franco-German core. And like them he also was careful to remain a loyal, if exasperating, American ally.

Whatever the differences in rhetoric, the differences between actual French and German policies can easily be exaggerated. Not surprisingly, both share a common discontent as well as a common reluctance to upset the status quo. In many respects, their varying approaches represent a division of labor as much as a difference of view. In a sense, each speaks for the silent half of the other. Whereas France's position encouraged her to feel and express the dissatisfactions of all Europeans with the postwar order, the Federal Republic's situation prompts it to feel and express the inhibitions felt by all Europeans in trying to change that order. Of all the West European states, the Federal Republic has been both the most prosperous and the most vulnerable.

German well-being, despite the nation's division, has been increasingly blatant in the seventies. Whatever its long-range economic problems, the Federal Republic has achieved the highest standard of living of any major European state. Its prosperity, moreover, has weathered the various systemic shocks of recent years with the least disruption. Despite the appreciating deutsche mark (DM), Germany has sustained a substantial export surplus, in part because so many of its exports are high-quality capital goods less sensitive to fluctuations in price than most consumer items. Similarly, Germany's specialization in capital goods has made it a special beneficiary of the rapid industrialization of Eastern and various Third World countries, as well as less vulnerable to competition from such countries as they industrialize. Germany, in effect, sells the capital machinery that puts other European industries out of business. And thanks to its still huge coal reserves and lesser dependence on oil, the Federal Republic has been less directly affected by the oil crisis than her European competitors. Germany, moreover, has captured a large share of the new demand for capital goods that has sprung from the increased income of the oil states. And with its appreciating currency, the Federal Republic has benefited more than its competitors from oil prices tied to the dollar. Even unemployment in Germany, although relatively severe, is softened by the presence of large numbers of foreign workers who can be sent home as the economy stagnates. In short, Germany's economic situation is very comfortable, a state of affairs that naturally promotes caution. Even if American policies increasingly seem to threaten Germany's long-range position, hopes come naturally that the United States can be induced to reform rather than be compelled by more heroic but hazardous European policies. In this respect, of course, Germans only reflect, even if in an advanced degree, the situation and attitude of other comfortable Europeans, the French included.

German caution is also encouraged by Europe's real military weakness in the face of the Soviet Union. Not only would a more independent Europe probably require a notable increase in conventional defense forces, and an improbable degree of coordination among them, but Germany would have to face the dread question of nuclear arms. Although some Franco-German nuclear arrangement is not inconceivable, Germany would very likely have to pay a heavy price, perhaps heavier than the present inconveniences with the Americans. In any event, a Germany moving toward a nuclear capacity would easily risk arousing the old anti-German European coalition. And even with an independent nuclear force — European or German — certain basic vulnerabilities would remain. Europe is geographically smaller and its population more concentrated than the two superpowers. European states could not enter for long into the more elaborate scenarios for nuclear exchanges without risking their very lives as nations. Although some may doubt whether nuclear exchanges can ever be less than life-and-death affairs for the nations involved, the Europeans clearly have fewer theoretical options than others.

These military vulnerabilities, shared by all in Europe, are nevertheless most keenly felt by the Germans. The Federal Republic is the frontier. Any Russian thrust will very likely be on its territory. It is the smallest of the major Western states and its population the most highly concentrated. It could hardly survive nuclear war. Hence, it remains particularly sensitive to the advantages of the American military alliance and cautious about exploring European alternatives.

For all these reasons, the Federal Republic, despite its separation from the East, has not been an active revisionist power. So long as the U.S. protectorate in Europe has been credible and the U.S.-sponsored world economic system open to Germany, the *Pax Americana* has suited the Federal Republic very well. This is not to say, however, that the Federal Republic has therefore shed Germany's traditional geopolitical situation and its problems. On the contrary, the old options are clearly reflected in postwar German foreign policy. Today's Federal Republic is the Little German model to an exaggerated degree. West Germany is an export machine. It has not needed its own empire because the *Pax Americana* has provided one gratis. The Americans have given the Germans what the British refused: access to their world imperial system. In this respect, Germany, like Japan, has gained more from losing the war than she might have expected from winning it.

At the same time, the Great German continental option has been reborn in the more subtle form of the European Community. That community has consolidated a European economic system and sought, moreover, to extend its influence to the Third World—in particular to areas with traditional European connections. Within the Atlantic system, the European Community has greatly strengthened the Europeans collectively for economic competition and political bargaining with the Americans. Should the American-sponsored international system deteriorate to the point of a serious general breakdown, the community obviously has the potential to become a major unit in a restructured world economy.

The Federal Republic's Atlantic and continental policies have also been balanced by a more national policy looking toward eventual German reunification. Hence various forms of *Ostpolitik* have evolved over the years, the latest and most imaginative being that which, by formally accepting the status quo in the East, greatly increases opportunities for gradually undermining it. At the very least, *Ostpolitik* has greatly increased the Federal Republic's diplomatic maneuverability.

From this perspective of Germany's traditional geopolitical options, the Federal Republic's foreign policy seems a balancing act. Like Britain, postwar Germany has lived in three circles. More successfully than Britain, the Federal Republic has tried to pursue one goal only insofar as it would not seriously compromise the others. The oscillations between Konrad Adenauer's Europeanism and Ludwig Erhard's Atlanticism in the sixties, for example, suggest a sort of self-correcting mechanism in German policy. The unwillingness to chose between France and the United States can be seen as an unwillingness to choose between Germany's traditional continental and world options. In any event, in practice these opposite policies have been mutually reinforcing. The Federal Republic's efforts in the East have strengthened its position in Western Europe and with the Americans. Its capacity to play off European and Atlantic systems has strengthened its role in each. And its growing salience in the Third World similarly strengthens its position in European and transatlantic relationships.

In balancing its foreign policies, the Federal Republic is no different from any other European power. But it would be disingenuous to count the Federal Republic a power like any other. Germany has been the center of the last two great revolutions against the status quo. And Germany is unlikely to avoid being at the center of any great changes in the future. No one can divine that future with assurance, but any realistic assessment of the potential for change in the present-day world cannot overlook the anomalous dependency of the major Western European states. So far it has served their interests to remain part of an American-led system. Increasingly, however, that system seems to be suffering from a steady deterioration both internally and in its relations with the Third World. Hence, a return to the economic conditions of the twenties and thirties, scarcely imaginable a decade ago, is now a commonplace fear. Should a major breakdown of the world economy occur, the incentives for a more independent Europe will rise dramatically. Germany cannot avoid being at the center of that issue. Nor, of course, is it realistic to take for granted the continuing stability of the Soviet sphere.

Germans would perhaps do well to prepare themselves for a more adventurous future by a more careful study of their own past. In recent years, however, a sort of consensus has grown up among historians blaming Germany's past aggression on the immoral or atavistic quality of its domestic political culture. In effect, Germany's "crimes" are seen as the result of an inherent German "badness." Although no one should presume to deny modern Germans their guilt for some of the more barbaric occurrences of this century, no service is done either the past or the future by analyzing international politics with a simpleminded, provincial, and facile moralism. Germans were aggressors not because history had endowed them with some singularly vicious domestic economy, society, polity, or culture. Like all the other modernizing powers, Germany was dynamically expansive, but in a geographical and historical context that inevitably pitted it against the rest of Europe. In retrospect, Ludwig Dehio's judgment that the European balance became an ideology to preserve the world hegemony of the Anglo-Saxon powers seems rather self-evident. For that matter, Hitler's judgment that his own defeat meant a new world balance that would subject Europe to outsiders also seems valid.

How then to explain the fashionable self-abnegation among historians of modern Germany? No one can impugn their moral sincerity. Their view, nevertheless, does have an ideological use in the current German situation. If the aggression of the past can be blamed on the badness of past generations, then the "good" or "reborn" new generation can claim it has nothing to do with that past. Thus Germans will no longer trouble the world because nowadays they are economic liberals, like Ludwig Erhard—or Social Democrats, like Willy Brandt. What is uncomfortable for today's West Germans about a view of the past like Dehio's is its implication that the German problem is not settled. Once German aggression against the status quo is assumed to be the consequence of a historical situation—when the similar ambitions of great powers were almost inevitably colliding—then the uncomfortable thought arises that such circumstances may recur. And in particular, the issue suggested by Dehio and Hitler, namely the relation of Germany, and Europe, to a world system, may very well arise yet again. Such may be, indeed, the real significance of the systemic shocks of recent years. If so, the past thirty years will prove not so much a new departure in modern history, as a vacation from old problems.

2

West German Foreign Policy, 1949-1979: Necessities and Choices

Wolfram F. Hanrieder

Politics is the art of the necessary as well as the art of the possible. From the very beginning of the Federal Republic, the interplay of necessity and possibility has been unusually intriguing. The defeat of Nazi Germany, the years of political impotence and economic deprivation during the occupation, and the Cold War not only raised West Germany's foreign policy issues but also apparently mapped or foreclosed the paths toward their resolution. The Federal Republic owes its very existence to the East-West disagreements that prevented the joint administration of Germany after World War II and made control of Germany the pivot and most coveted prize of the Cold War. The "German problem" was cause as well as effect in the origins of the Cold War, and the creation of the two German states in 1949 seems, in retrospect, a logical conclusion to the East-West contest over the nature of the postwar European order.

The context of necessity is reflected in the continuity that has characterized the foreign policy preoccupations of West Germany. Throughout the thirty-year history of the Federal Republic, its foreign policy aims — security, political and economic reconstruction in the context of Europe and the Atlantic alliance, and reunification — have remained remarkably constant even though they have been modified (especially the goal of unification) in the light of failures and successes and in response to changes in international and domestic politics.

Over the years, necessities became coupled with possibilities. As the political, strategic, and economic configurations of power changed during the last three decades, so did the mix of restraints and opportunities confronting German foreign policy. In retrospect, three distinct phases emerge. In the first, the formative years from 1949 to the late 1950s, the Cold War contest between the two power blocs (as well as the burdens of the past) presented the Federal Republic with the most severe restraints and led to fundamental contradictions between West German foreign policy goals, above all between Bonn's aims in the West and its aims in the East.

During the second phase, from the late fifties to the late sixties, a different set of contradictions was placed on German policy. As the Soviet Union began to reach for nuclear parity and sought to legitimize the status quo in Europe, Gaullism, determined to gain a global role for a French-led Europe, even at the expense of the Atlantic alliance, compelled Bonn to make choices between Washington and Paris, between its central security interests in the Atlantic alliance and its central political interests in Western Europe.

In the third phase, the last decade, the restraints and contradictions affecting German foreign policy goals were less clear-cut, for several reasons. First, in the seventies the elements of international power and its overall configuration changed considerably, making for a much more complicated international system that lacked stark alternatives and thus demanded less clear-cut choices from German foreign policymakers. Second, West German foreign policy goals themselves became more muted, in part because of the dynamics of German domestic politics and in part because Willy Brandt's *Ostpolitik* settled the last "classical" foreign policy issue of the Federal Republic. Third, while the emerging primacy of economic-monetary matters and the ramification of global economic interdependence significantly increased Germany's power, they also made German foreign policy projects more prosaic both because of their technical nature and because they reflected the confluence of domestic and foreign policy.

I

In the first phase of West German foreign policy—from 1949 to the late 1950s—the necessities and contradictions affecting West German foreign policy goals were the most visible. The period is characterized by the sharp contrast betwen the failure of Bonn's reunification policy and the remarkable success the Federal Republic achieved in the area of security and political and economic recovery. This contrast developed from the impossiblity of pursuing these goals simultaneously in a Cold War setting in which the cross-purposes and power relations between East and West were sharply polarized. The very success of Bonn's pro-Western security and recovery policy, through which the Federal Republic became the bulwark of Washington's containment policy in Europe, solidified the Cold War alliances in Central Europe and further deepened the division of Germany.

It is doubtful whether the Federal Republic, faced with a hostile Eastern bloc and restrained by political and contractual commitments to the Western alliance, had a genuine choice of incompatible alternatives. For although the Western powers were ready to make political and economic concessions in return for West Germany's willingness to rearm, these concessions did not allow Bonn to pursue an independent or flexible foreign policy because the diplomatic-political, economic, and military instruments of policy were securely embedded within the Western alliance structure. In the Bonn Conventions and Paris Agreements, Bonn traded rearmament for the restoration of legal sovereignty and the Western commitment to recognize the Bonn government as the only legitimate spokesman for all of Germany. But the elements of sovereignty that were being restored were immediately frozen in the international organizations Germany joined. When this happened — as in the cases of the Organization for European Economic Cooperation (OEEC), the European Payments Union, NATO, the Western European Union, the European Coal and Steel Community — the primary payoff for Bonn was in terms of equality rather than of independence.

From Chancellor Adenauer's perspective, "diluting" gains of sovereignty by joining integrative organizations was intrinsically unobjectionable. His sense of priorities was shaped by choice as well as by necessity. Adenauer's version of the goal of political recovery — the integration of the Federal Republic in a tightly knit Western European community — could be achieved even with the curtailing of Germany's freedom of action, so long as it brought gains of equality. In fact, it would have been much more difficult for Bonn to extract concessions from the Western powers if the restored elements of sovereignty had not been subject to international surveillance. The creation of integrative West European and Atlantic structures had a decisive influence on the speedy political recovery of West Germany. They provided mechanisms for controlling Germany and they made the restoration of sovereignty less risky for the Western powers, especially France. In turn, the mounting pressures to grant West Germany political and economic concessions provided a powerful impetus for establishing integrative structures that could supervise the Federal Republic. In this two-way interaction, Adenauer's Europe-oriented policy was an essential precondition for successful political and economic recovery.

The pursuit of the goal of security — implemented as it was by close alignment with the West and the decision to rearm — thus not only was compatible with the goal of political recovery but was its prerequisite. The quest for security and the aim of political recovery, with the meaning attached to recovery by Adenauer, were mutually reinforcing.

Economic and political recovery were also complementary. A weak West German economy would have been a liability for the Western alliance, undermining political stability and opening up opportunities for Soviet maneuvers. Because of the integrative features of the Western alliance, the faltering economy of one alliance partner would have weakened the bloc, with negative consequences for military preparedness. The tensions of the

Cold War created an atmosphere in the West that was generally in sympathy with German aspirations to restore a viable economy.

The achievement of economic recovery was skillfully complemented and underpinned by Bonn's policy on political recovery, and by extension, its policy on security and rearmament. In such mixed political-economic ventures as the Schuman Plan (and later, the EEC), political and economic gains went hand in hand and were achieved through a coordinated strategy that advanced German demands in the name of European and Atlantic unity rather than in the name of a discredited German nationalism. The German government's determination to liberalize domestic and international trade was in the long run advantageous politically as well as economically, since it underlined Bonn's commitment to political internationalism. By forgoing traditional protectionism, Bonn rejected the economic corollary to political nationalism, an attitude appreciated especially in Washington. In sum, the Federal Republic's foreign policy goals of security-rearmament, political recovery, and economic recovery were interdependent, complementary, and mutually reinforcing—as was clearly reflected in the interlocking provisions of the Paris Agreements.

*   *   *

The goal of unifying West and East Germany was of an entirely different order because it could be achieved only with the consent of both Cold War camps. Consequently, Adenauer's long-range unification policy was based on two central assumptions that (1) Washington and Moscow held the key to the German question and (2) with the passage of time the balance of power between the Cold War blocs would shift in favor of the West, thus allowing negotiations "on the basis of strength," which would induce the Soviet Union to settle the German question on Western terms.

The first of these assumptions was correct, the second, false. From the first assumption it followed that Bonn would need political leverage within the Western alliance in order to gain for reunification the support of the Western powers, especially the United States, and to ensure that the West would not trade off the German issue in an overall settlement of the Cold War. Adenauer realized that the Western powers viewed the prospect of a unified Germany with apprehension. Thus, Bonn's unification policy required increasing German influence within the Western alliance in order to solidify on the political plane the legal and moral commitment of the Western powers to support reunification and acknowledge the Bonn government as the only legitimate spokesman for all of Germany. Yet the only way that Bonn could increase its leverage within the Western alliance was by becoming an indispensable partner in it. This partnership would be directed against the Soviet Union and thus would be ill-suited for inducing the Kremlin to settle the German question on terms acceptable to the West.

As a consequence, Adenauer's Moscow-oriented reunification policy was much more passive and negative, merely an appendage of Bonn's Washington-oriented policy. This was unavoidable. At the height of the Cold War, the Western powers most likely would have obstructed German overtures to the Soviet Union — a point that is almost always ignored by those who speak of the missed opportunities of the 1950s — and a more active Eastern policy would have jeopardized the entire treaty structure that was to restore sovereignty to the Federal Republic. This would have undermined the power base in the West from which Adenauer expected to deal with the Soviet Union at some future date. Inevitably, Bonn's Eastern policy appeared flaccid and unimaginative, especially in contrast to the political acumen and tenacity displayed by Adenauer in his dealings with the Western powers. It consisted almost entirely of a policy of denial through which Bonn refused to recognize East Germany and the Oder-Neisse line — in short, the existing state of affairs in Central and Eastern Europe.

But even though the Western powers backed Bonn's rigidly legalistic stand vis-à-vis the Soviet bloc, they showed no great enthusiasm for the cause of German unity. Both Cold War camps considered it politic to give at least verbal support to German aspirations for reunification. But neither the United States nor the Soviet Union wanted a unified Germany that would be genuinely free to conduct its external affairs because that would upset the balance of power in Europe, with adverse effects on the cohesion of either Cold War alliance. Securing the allegiance and power potential of the part of Germany that each Cold War camp already controlled promised a substantial increase of strength for each side.

At crucial junctures in the shaping of Bonn's rearmament policy, Moscow held out the prospect of unification if West Germany would abstain from military, economic, and political ties with the Western powers. But the Soviet Union demanded in effect (as in the note of March 1952) that the West accept a power vacuum in the heart of Europe at a time when clearly drawn spheres of influence seemed most promising for Washington's policy of containment. The line through Germany that divided the two power blocs in Europe was clear-cut and manned on both sides by the armed forces of the major Cold War antagonists. This "trip-wire" setting, and its symbolic representation of forward containment, was precisely what the United States sought to establish on all Cold War fronts. It is easy to see why the United States was unwilling to replace this relatively tolerable and stable status quo with the uncertainties that would have followed if Moscow's proposals had been implemented. For Adenauer, acceptance of

Soviet plans for a neutralized united Germany would have meant the end of his most fundamental political aim — to include Germany in a West European union and to tie the future course of German society to the cultural, religious, and political values of Western Europe. The West, and Adenauer, had to weigh the uncertain and risky prospect of a neutralized Germany against the certainty of increasing Western power at a crucial stage in the Cold War.

By 1955, when West Germany joined NATO and East Germany became a member of the Warsaw Pact, the Western-oriented dimension of Bonn's policy had proven fairly successful. Germany had achieved a remarkable economic revival, Bonn's political leverage within the Western alliance had increased enormously since 1949, and the Western powers were at least paying lip service to the cause of German reunification. But the very success of this policy, through which Germany became the bulwark of Washington's containment policy, had further accentuated the Cold War division of Europe and sealed the division of Germany. Joining West Germany to the Western alliance thus aggravated the conditions that made unification difficult in the first place. Unless circumstances changed, Bonn could not have hoped to improve the chances for reunification by pursuing a policy of integration with the West.

Chancellor Adenauer was fully aware of this. His long-range calculations anticipated a time when circumstances would not be the same and when the balance of power would have shifted in favor of the West — the second central assumption of his reunification strategy. The single most important development that scotched these expectations was the Soviet Union's acquisition of nuclear capabilities. A Western policy of "roll back" and liberation now became inconceivable in light of the retaliatory power the Soviet Union was developing.

Even the possibility of exerting strong diplomatic pressures on the Soviet Union became increasingly unlikely. The political consolidation of the Eastern bloc and of Nikita Khruschev's position in the Kremlin, coupled with the Soviet Union's improved military position, was soon reflected in Moscow's Germany policy. The opposite of Adenauer's premise for a policy of strength in fact occurred: instead of becoming more conciliatory on the German question with the passage of time, the Russians' attitudes stiffened. After failing to prevent West Germany's membership in NATO, the Soviet Union shifted to a "two Germanies" policy, symbolized in the Kremlin's readiness to establish diplomatic relations with Bonn. By 1955, the Soviet Union had come to accept the status quo in Central Europe, and from then on its central aim was to solidify the existing state of affairs politically and contractually — a process that culminated almost two decades later in Bonn's Eastern treaties and the Helsinki accords.

This shift in Moscow's Germany policy had important consequences for the Western base of Bonn's reunification policy—a base that Adenauer feared was eroding as the Western powers became eager to move away from Cold War confrontation toward a more relaxed period of coexistence. As the Soviet Union began to support the territorial status quo in Europe rather than threaten it, fear of direct Soviet military aggression waned in the West, with a corresponding readiness to turn to arms control arrangements as an actual as well as symbolic step toward a relaxation of East-West tensions.

This placed Bonn in an awkward political and psychological position. After 1955, Bonn's major unification efforts necessarily became limited to denying the Soviet Union and East Germany a de jure recognition of the existing state of affairs—there was little hope of bringing about unification itself—and Bonn expected its allies to support this policy of denial diplomatically. On the verbal level this support was forthcoming, especially from the United States. But Adenauer remained suspicious. The arms control and disengagement proposals put forth by official as well as unofficial sources in both East and West invariably provided that the status quo—the division of Germany and Europe—would serve as the basis for agreements; and they explicitly or implicitly called for the participation of East Germany as an equal partner. Implementing such proposals—Adam Rapacki's and George Kennan's were the most publicized—would have solidified the *political* lines of division in Central Europe (reflecting the Soviet interest in legitimizing the territorial status quo) and blurred at the same time the East-West *military* boundary running through Germany (reflecting the Soviet interest in denying the West the Federal Republic's military and industrial power). Such arrangements would have ended plans for a Western European community and undermined NATO's forward strategy, which both Washington and Bonn wanted maintained for its reassuring psychological effect on Germany and because it seemed to make nuclear deterrence more credible.

Bonn now found itself in an uncomfortable diplomatic spot. Not only had Bonn become the only European power to question the territorial status quo in Europe—opening itself to charges of revanchism from the East—but it invariably felt compelled to reject arms control proposals because of their political and juridical implications for the German question. Most serious perhaps, on both counts—resistance to accepting the status quo and resistance to arms control—the Federal Republic not only complicated its relations with the East, but gradually began to lose support in the West as well. In 1959 Charles de Gaulle recognized the Oder-Neisse line; and in the 1960s Bonn's foot-dragging on the nonproliferation treaty became a serious problem for the Federal Republic's Western policy.

By the late 1950s, Bonn's Germany policy, weak in substance and brittle in its formalism, had not succeeded in either its Eastern or Western dimension. This failure reflected the fundamental paradox of the German question. Bipolarities of tensions, interests, and power were not conducive to German reunification: that was the lesson to be drawn from the international circumstances of the pre-1955 period. But the developing nuclear balance of terror, the gradually changing perceptions of the Soviet threat, the Gaullist pressures on the Western alliance, and the general reconfiguration of power and interest from a bipolar into a multipolar pattern were equally unfavorable to prospects of unification. Without an easing of East-West tensions, neither side could afford to allow German unification on the opponent's terms — yet an East-West détente contained the likelihood that the division of Germany would get not only a tacit political but also an explicit legal blessing.

II

In the second stage of the Federal Republic's foreign policy development — in the decade from the late 1950s to the late 1960s — the central dilemma of West German foreign policy was the necessity of making painful choices between Washington and Paris, or to put it in equally stark terms, the dilemma of choosing between its perceived security interests and its desire to participate in a viable European community.

Even prior to 1955, there had of course been disagreements between Washington and Paris that posed problems for Adenauer's diplomacy. Whereas Washington wanted to expedite the Federal Republic's membership in the Western military alliance and an integrated Western Europe, France understandably was reserved and sought to curtail West German influence in these international bodies. At the same time, Adenauer's long-range political goals — a European union and reconciliation with France — required France's sympathetic cooperation. Although this situation was at times awkward for Bonn, it was still manageable as long as the Western alliance was fairly cohesive, as long as the United States could pressure France with "agonizing reappraisals," and as long as Bonn could advance its interests in the name of an integrated Western alliance. But the pre-1955 problems foreshadowed the much more serious dilemma that German decision makers had to face in later years, after Charles de Gaulle returned to power in 1958, when taking sides with either the United States or France sharpened the developing tensions within the Atlantic alliance.

Konrad Adenauer and Charles de Gaulle quickly established a remarkable rapport. But even though the general was prepared to implement the economic provisions of the Treaty of Rome, he was vehemently opposed to the political aspirations embodied in it. Both Adenauer and de Gaulle preferred a "little Europe" integrative structure; but de Gaulle opposed genuine political integration because that would curtail the national independence of France, and he expected Germany to help the French regain their position in world politics by providing economic and political support. De Gaulle wanted the economic benefits of the Common Market without paying a political price, whereas Adenauer was ready to pay an economic price for political benefits. De Gaulle sought a European base for his global political ambitions; Adenauer sought an Atlantic base for his European ambitions.

The conflicts that developed between the Anglo-American powers and France during the late fifties and early sixties immensely complicated Adenauer's aim of integrating the Federal Republic in a cohesive West European community. While the United States remained the indispensable partner of Germany's security policy, de Gaulle, the indispensable partner for Germany's Europe policy, was determined to shut out Anglo-American influence on the continent after his proposal for French participation in a NATO three-power "directorate" had been rejected by President Eisenhower. This meant that during the 1960s Germany's security policy no longer meshed with its Europe policy — in contrast to the 1950s when the complementarity of Bonn's Atlantic and European policy was the cornerstone of Adenauer's foreign policy program. Moreover, Adenauer felt obliged to turn to Paris for support of Bonn's Eastern policy since the United States (during the Kennedy administration) had revamped NATO strategy despite German misgivings and appeared ready to reach an accommodation with the Soviet Union — and yet the chancellor must have known that de Gaulle could only support a solution to the German question that would fall short of actual reunification.[1] The difficult choices between Washington and Paris imposed upon Bonn thus were not choices between policy alternatives that Adenauer favored: Bonn's interests were not fully supported either in Paris or in Washington. Personality clashes further complicated Bonn's diplomacy. Although Kennedy enjoyed an almost avuncular relationship with Harold Macmillan and admired the histrionic grandeur of de Gaulle's diplomacy, he tended to view Adenauer as an inflexible remnant of the Cold War days who could not be expected to appreciate the management-oriented rationality of the New Frontier.

By that time there were, in effect, two German foreign policies, not one. The first was Adenauer's, which resulted in the Franco-German Friendship Treaty and allowed de Gaulle to blackball Britain's membership in the EEC with Germany's implicit acquiescence. The second policy direction was preferred by Economics Minister Ludwig Erhard and Foreign Minister Gerhard Schröder, who advocated a more flexible course and tended to support the Anglo-American position not only on the Common Market and the Atlantic alliance, but also on a more imaginative Eastern policy.

When Ludwig Erhard succeeded Konrad Adenauer in the fall of 1963, the policy differences between France and Germany were leading to a major confrontation, if not a crisis. Almost every item on de Gaulle's agenda opposed German foreign policy at a time when the new chancellor in Bonn was much less sympathetic to French projects than Adenauer had been. The EEC crisis of 1965 over the political future and membership of the Common Market pitted Bonn against Paris (although it ultimately strengthened Germany's position in the EEC), and Franco-German disagreement over political fundamentals was further aggravated by clashes over economic and monetary specifics. The NATO crisis of 1966, resulting from France's withdrawal from NATO's command structure, not only affected German security interests, but also raised the touchy political and legal question of how French troops could remain in Germany (as Bonn hoped they would, for reasons of deterrence) once they were transferred from NATO control to French national control. Most importantly perhaps, Bonn was deeply disturbed by the fundamental shift of French policy toward the Soviet Union. This shift toward a Franco-Soviet accommodation had a profound impact on Franco-German relations. De Gaulle's new course not only called into question a long-standing premise of Bonn's reunification policy[2] — that Bonn would, as much as possible, support France's Atlantic and European policy if France would support Bonn's Eastern policy — but also served notice to Bonn that de Gaulle intended to fully exploit the new international circumstances, at Germany's expense if necessary.

Undoubtedly, Ludwig Erhard was remiss in failing to nurture the special Franco-German relationship with more devotion and circumspection. But the larger reasons why de Gaulle allowed the understanding to lapse were beyond Bonn's control because they stemmed from fundamental international shifts of power and alignment. After World War II, the polarization of power and tensions between the Soviet Union and the United States obstructed French interests because France was forced to join the Western alliance to avoid diplomatic isolation, and thus could not play the flexible and mediatory role she would have preferred. Washington's containment policy favored a renascent Germany because of its location and power potential and put France, compared with Germany, at a distinct disadvantage within the Western alliance.

This began to change in the late 1950s and early 1960s when the two Cold War blocs loosened up and American and Soviet leaders began to explore the possibilities of peaceful coexistence. Germany, which had played a crucial role during the Cold War phase of the postwar international system, not only lost some influence in Western councils during the co-existence phase, but also was at times viewed (especially during the Kennedy administration) as an irritating obstacle to a more flexible American global policy. France, on the other hand, gained considerable leverage from the fragmentation of bipolarity because the new international system provided Paris with a wide range of opportunities to restore flexibility and dynamism to French foreign policy. Franco-German relations suffered as a result.

Erhard's relations with Washington were troubled as well—as was exemplified most prominently in the handling of the hapless multilateral force scheme. The MLF idea had no military-strategic value (President Kennedy called it "something of a fake") and was designed primarily to give European NATO members the appearance of nuclear ownership without providing it in reality. Although Germany was presumably the beneficiary of this symbolic project, German-American relations suffered as a result of it. After Bonn had committed itself fully to an MLF scheme—which was strongly opposed by de Gaulle, who wanted a European defense structure—President Johnson's scrapping of the proposal in 1965 and his subsequent refusal to accept a reduction of German offset purchases seriously damaged Erhard's prestige.

In the face of strong objections, Erhard had consistently supported American policy (on NATO, Vietnam, higher conventional troop levels for Central Europe) and he had relied on Johnson's readiness to reciprocate by supporting the MLF. But tensions developed between fundamental American interests and the major political purposes that Bonn sought to advance through nuclear control sharing. Throughout, an important reason for Bonn's interest in the MLF was the hope that it could be traded for Soviet concessions on the German question—a point very explicitly made by Foreign Minister Gerhard Schröder in the summer of 1965. This anticipated leverage, which was probably illusory to begin with, obviously required continued American support for the MLF—especially since de Gaulle had indicated that German participation in the MLF would stand in the way of a "European solution" to the German question (the only kind of solution he would support), because it would tie Bonn too closely to Washington. In pushing for the MLF the Federal Republic risked diplomatic isolation on its unification policy without gaining more than a token of joint nuclear control.

This kind of support President Johnson was unwilling to provide because the implied anti-Soviet dimension of Bonn's MLF policy jeopardized two of Washington's most cherished foreign policy goals—a détente with the Soviet Union and an arms control agreement. Negotiations for a nuclear nonproliferation treaty were already well under way, and the Soviet Union

had repeatedly made it clear that Washington would have to choose between the treaty and the MLF. Sacrificing the MLF was relatively easy for
Johnson since most NATO members had shown no real interest in it. The
Germans, however, felt that their suspicions about a possible Soviet-U.S.
deal at the expense of German interests were confirmed by Washington's
about-face on the MLF.

Against this background, it is not surprising that the nonproliferation
pact met with a cold reception in Bonn from the very beginning. Bonn's
reservations stemmed not so much from a desire to own nuclear weapons,
but from the reluctance to be deprived of the threat of acquiring them. In
addition to technical-economic reasons, the Erhard government opposed
the pact because it wanted to keep open four major options for German
policy: total renunciation of nuclear weapons as a bargaining lever against
Moscow; participation in an allied force on the basis of coownership; participation in nuclear planning and crisis management; and the creation of a
European nuclear force. It was becoming increasingly clear, however, that
many Western leaders began to view German attempts to gain a nuclear
voice with a good deal of impatience — the nonproliferation treaty seemed
to be in jeopardy, and there was little enthusiasm to begin with about a
German finger on the nuclear trigger. But the Germans were reluctant to
relinquish an opportunity to extract concessions on the reunification issue,
since they had had so little bargaining leverage on this question in the past
and since it was clear all along that the Russians' main purpose in
negotiating the treaty was to deny West Germany nuclear arms. The
Grand Coalition government that replaced the Erhard government in 1966
also had deep misgivings about the treaty although it played down the first
two options Erhard had clung to so insistently: the linkage between nuclear
self-denial and progress on the German question, and the hope of obtaining
nuclear coownership in the context of an allied nuclear force.

*   *   *

In sum, the choices between Washington and Paris imposed on three
German governments in the 1960s were not really choices between policy
alternatives the Germans themselves favored. In contrast to the 1950s,
when the Adenauer government could obtain only one of two mutually exclusive but inherently desirable alternatives — a viable *Westpolitik* and a
viable *Ostpolitik* — the alternatives of the 1960s amounted to a choice between an eviscerated European option and an equally tattered Atlantic option. There were two large ironies in this development. The first was that
with the waning of the integrated Atlantic option and the integrated Europe
option, Germany's power position ultimately increased in both. The second
irony was that the German domestic debate over foreign policy in the

1960s, especially within the Christian Democratic Union (CDU) and the Christian Social Union (CSU), took place over policy options that had no real counterpart in the international system. As Fritz René Allemann pointed out at the time,

> The "Gaullists," while eager to move closer to Paris, did not at all see eye to eye with President de Gaulle's Eastern European policies and were rather frightened by his visions of a Greater Europe embracing the Communist East. The "Atlanticists" were lured by the dream of German participation in nuclear defense and of a kind of "special relationship" between the United States and the Federal Republic, even long after it had become clear that Washington had dropped the MLF concept and was as interested as de Gaulle himself in furthering an understanding with the Soviet Union and with Moscow's Eastern European allies. To a large extent, the controversy between these schools of opinion was something like a tragi-comedy of errors: the German clients of France and America still fought out battles which their foreign friends had already abandoned.[3]

III

During the last three decades the elements of international power, as well as its overall configuration, have changed considerably. The virtual disappearance of territorial disputes in the industrialized world, the limitations imposed by the nuclear balance, the loosening of the Cold War alliances, the day-to-day realities of economic interdependence, the confluence of domestic and foreign policy, the precarious economic and political development of the Third World, the political clout of countries with essential energy and raw materials supplies, and many other factors have created new restraints and opportunities for the conduct of foreign policy. New purposes have suggested new techniques. Access rather than acquisition, presence rather than rule, penetration rather than possession, control rather than coercion have become the ligaments of power.

One of the consequences of economic and monetary interdependence is that such measures of power as military capacity are becoming less relevant. Given appropriate circumstances, economic power is a much more supple instrument of diplomacy than military power. This is not to say that military might is unimportant, or that the absolute and relative increase of Soviet military capabilities is not worrisome. But many states today see their security interests protected more effectively through the political rather than the military balance of power; and negotiations over such technical questions as arms control, trade agreements, monetary reform, and technology transfers are not only attempts at problem solving, but also reexaminations of the meaning and sources of power in the last third of this century. Many military-strategic and economic issues are at bottom political issues couched in technical terms.

At the same time, the power of the modern nation-state, although predominant in its domestic context because of its responsibilities for mass social and economic welfare, appears compromised in rather novel ways in its international context — in part because of the restraints imposed by the nuclear balance of power, and in part because the domestic power of the state can be sustained only through international economic cooperation and political accommodation. In order to meet domestic demands for social welfare, the modern state is compelled to interact with other states in ways that, although not lacking in conflict and competition, demand cooperation, the acceptance of the logic of interdependence, and a willingness to condone restraints on state behavior and sovereign prerogatives. Internal state power is sustained by external cooperation.

We are too close to these developments to speak with assurance of their effect on the new balance of power. But they have had a profound effect on the foreign policy options of many states, including the Federal Republic. As the sources and locations of power shifted, making for a much more complicated international system, grand foreign policy options disappeared in Europe, and German foreign policymakers were faced with less clear-cut choices.

This development was aided by the fact that German foreign policy goals themselves became more muted, in part because of the dynamics of German domestic politics and in part because Willy Brandt's *Ostpolitik* settled the last classical foreign policy issue of the Federal Republic, at least for the time being. The Brandt government realized that a general rapprochement with the East required Bonn's formal acceptance of the status quo. The Soviet Union in turn considered the treaty package resulting from *Ostpolitik* an essential step toward a European Security Conference, for which the Kremlin was pushing hard in order to legitimize the European territorial and political status quo, reduce American influence in Europe in an atmosphere of détente, intensify economic and technological contacts with Western Europe, and concentrate on domestic issues and the China problem. Dynamic as Brandt's *Ostpolitik* was in many ways, it was nonetheless fundamentally a policy of resignation, designed not so much to bring about changes for a foreseeable future as not to foreclose possibilities for an unforeseeable future. Even so, by attuning West German foreign policy to the dynamics of détente — the outstanding foreign policy aim of most members of the Warsaw Pact as well as of the Atlantic alliance — Bonn kept pace with developments and retained German leverage in an East-West setting in which various kinds of political, strategic, and economic issues were coupled in multilayered connections.

Ostpolitik also affected the triangular relationship among the Federal Republic, France, and the Soviet Union. In the 1960s, de Gaulle's vision of a Europe from the Atlantic to the Urals required reaching an accommodation with Moscow as well as curtailing the influence of Washington and Brussels. It was rooted in the assumption that the Kremlin leadership would see sufficient advantages in a gradual loosening of the two military blocs in Europe, even if this required a relaxation of Soviet power in Eastern Europe. But it is difficult to see how the Soviet Union could have perceived the situation in the same way since Moscow was interested in solidifying the status quo, not in changing it — as was demonstrated with the invasion of Czechoslovakia in August 1968. Germany's *Ostpolitik* of the early seventies, on the other hand, was intrinsically more effective because it offered what the Soviets wanted the most: recognition of East Germany, the Oder-Neisse line, and the territorial and political status quo in Eastern and Central Europe. German *Ostpolitik* solidified the status quo, whereas French *Ostpolitik* had threatened it.

In addition to its intrinsic importance, *Ostpolitik* was connected with Germany's security policy — not because it lessened the Federal Republic's strategic dependence on the United States or its allegiance to NATO, but because Bonn's readiness to accept the territorial status quo removed any rationally conceivable Soviet incentives to apply military pressures outside of the Warsaw Pact region, especially in NATO's central sector. *Ostpolitik* tackled German security problems at their political roots and thus became a complementary political part of Germany's military policy. In contrast to the fifties and sixties, when Bonn's security policy conflicted sharply with its Eastern policy, *Ostpolitik* overcame these stark contradictions. By recognizing the territorial and political realities stemming from World War II, the Germans meshed their security policy and their Eastern policy, developed a more constructive attitude toward arms control, and fully attuned West German foreign policy to the dynamics of East-West détente.

This came at a time when the evident vulnerability of the United States to Soviet attack had forced Washington to qualify the automaticity of its nuclear guarantee to Europe, impaired the credibility of that guarantee, institutionalized U.S.-Soviet nuclear parity in SALT agreements, and ultimately brought the strategically distinct positions of America and Europe into clear focus. Owing to geography and history, the Federal Republic was from the beginning a NATO member with special inhibitions, obligations, anxieties, and opportunities. Whatever problems plagued NATO in the 1960s because of the waning American nuclear superiority were always felt more keenly in Bonn than in other West European capitals. Although doctrinal debates within NATO were less strident in the 1970s than in the 1960s, the willingness of the United States to sustain a forward strategy on NATO's central front became even more questionable. The issue was swept under the rug, and when it reappeared—which happened whenever the Europeans saw or imagined reasons to question American resolve—the rug was simply moved to cover it up again. But tensions persisted. Whereas the European NATO members, above all the Federal Republic, saw their security interests best maintained by the early use of nuclear weapons, the United States wanted their use postponed as long as possible. This issue of the "conventional pause," which goes back to the flexible response doctrine of the early 1960s, was further aggravated by the related question of forward defense. Although NATO planners had all along questioned the military feasibility of defending Western Europe along the West German border with the East, it was politically imperative to assure the Germans with the principle of forward defense that their geographical position would not condemn them to being the first (and perhaps only) victims of a conventional war.[4]

The Carter administration reiterated U.S. support of forward defense and also did not exclude the use of tactical nuclear weapons as a question of principle. The central question, however, as to the timing of a tactical nuclear response, remained as ambiguous as ever. Since many Europeans viewed tactical nuclear weapons as an essential link in the chain of escalation from conventional response to a strategic nuclear exchange between the Soviet Union and the United States, American ambivalence as to when (or even if) tactical nuclear weapons would be used was seen as undermining the totality of NATO's deterrence structure. These anxieties were deepened by the conviction, shared on both sides of the Atlantic by political as well as military experts, that NATO's conventional capabilities were insufficient either for purposes of deterrence or for purposes of defense once deterrence should fail. A NATO strategy based on a time-buying conventional flexible response implied the sacrifice of West German territory for the overall benefit of the alliance.

In sum, the central dilemma of NATO during the last ten years or so could not be resolved: the United States, in seeking to limit the arms race and arrive at a stable nuclear balance, was compelled to deal with the Soviet Union on the basis of *parity*, as was reflected in the arrangements of the Strategic Arms Limitation Talks. At the same time, Washington could not convincingly guarantee the security of Western Europe except on the basis of an implied American nuclear *superiority*. This was a dilemma for which neither the United States nor the Europeans could be blamed, nor was it likely that they could escape from it. Developments in weapons technology, and the Soviet determination to catch up with the United States, brought about nuclear parity between the two superpowers. This led to conflicts be-

tween the United States (which needed to take into account the potential
nuclear devastation of the United States and therefore sought to delay the
use of nuclear weapons) and NATO partners at the forward line of defense
who could not accept a strategy that implied sustained conventional warfare
at the expense of their territory and population.

*   *   *

In addition to the fact that the security interests of the United States and
the Federal Republic had become much less coterminous, the 1970s led to a
series of U.S.-German conflicts on economic and monetary matters. The
world monetary crisis of the summer of 1971 was the culmination of
economic-monetary controversies between the United States and the Common Market countries that had developed in the 1960s. At issue were a
wide range of political and economic questions—the enlargement of the
Common Market, the European Community's plan to establish a common
currency area, and the overall political-strategic and economic relationships between the United States and Europe. The crisis heralded a long
overdue reorganization of the world monetary system and revolved around
the economic, strategic, and political role of the United States in world affairs and what part of this role her allies were willing to continue financing.
Although the essence of the conflict was over the privileged position of the
United States in the Bretton Woods monetary regime, a position that in
European eyes Washington had irresponsibly abused in the late sixties, the
United States sought to sidestep the issue by sharp attacks on the exclu-
sionary trade practices of the Common Market—a somewhat fatuous argument since the United States consistently enjoyed a favorable balance of
trade with the EEC. The Europeans argued money, the Americans argued
trade. The basic shift in American policy toward the Common Market had
far-reaching implications for West German foreign policy because it signaled the abrogation of a tacit transatlantic agreement between the United
States and Western Europe that had been forged in the postwar era. The
essence of that bargain was that the United States, based on its hegemonic
economic and monetary position in the postwar period, would be willing to
make marginal economic sacrifices in return for political privileges and in
order to advance the cause of European integration. During the sixties, as
American hegemony declined relative to Europe and Japan, Europe
became increasingly restive about American privileges and pushed for an
alteration of the framework within which these political, economic, and
monetary arrangements had been made.

The need to alter this framework was made more pressing by the emerging primacy of economic-monetary matters relative to military-strategic
matters, growing economic interdependence, and the special political dif-

ficulties posed by the confluence of domestic and foreign policy. There is no question that the Federal Republic was one of the main political beneficiaries of these developments. Aside from the fact that Germany's political and diplomatic leverage increased along with its growing economic and monetary strength, economic and monetary "language" provided the Germans with an excellent opportunity to translate political demands—which might still have been suspect because of Germany's past—into respectable economic demands. The transformation of economic power into political power, and the translation of political demands into economic demands, compensated the Germans for their handicap of not being able to translate political demands into military-strategic language—which is what de Gaulle had managed to do so dramatically. Because of Germany's past, the West Germans could hardly have followed de Gaulle's example of couching political aspirations in terms of arms. Had they done so, they would have been accused of being unreconstructed militarists.

But as the transatlantic and European alliances were fading, Bonn's opportunities to advance national interests in multilateral integrative settings were becoming less ample. Bonn had always been highly effective in multilateral settings—in contrast to France whose foreign policy derived its vitality from a separatist line—and the Federal Republic had frequently succeeded in turning international cooperation to national advantage, with the added benefit that Bonn could express German aspirations in the language of Europe and the Atlantic alliance.

The Germans therefore faced a paradox. On the one hand, as the importance of economic and monetary issues increased relative to military-strategic matters, German political leverage also increased. But on the other hand, this leverage could be best applied in integrative and co-ordinating structures—and those structures were either weakening (in the transatlantic context) or stagnating (in the European context).

The problems arising from this paradox became especially troublesome after Helmut Schmidt took over the chancellorship from Willy Brandt in 1974—not because of the change in German leadership, but because Germany's dynamic Eastern policy had essentially run its course and German domestic issues and the worldwide recession brought economic matters to the foreground. Compared to the economic malaise of many West European countries and the United States, West Germany stood out as a pillar of economic and monetary strength. Although real GNP growth was modest, the German economy was basically healthy, exports were booming, and the unemployment and inflation rates were among the lowest in the Organization for Economic Cooperation and Development (OECD) area.

This impressive performance complicated West Germany's relations with both the EEC and the United States. The Schmidt government took a much tougher stand than any previous German government on the issues of fiscal responsibility and reform of the Community's entrenched bureaucracies. Bonn made it clear that it would agree to monetary demands by EEC members only if they would seek to solve the larger structural problems of the Community. This was clearly a reflection of the personal convictions of the new chancellor. Although Schmidt was willing to be a "good European"—and in particular to support measures that could lead to a monetary union—he also demanded that fellow EEC members make reforms in return for Germany's heavy financial contributions to the Common Market. But France's decision to leave the European single-currency area (although Germany would have been willing to underwrite with substantial loans the costs to France), Italy's imposition of import controls (in spite of massive German financial assistance), the uncoordinated Community response to the energy crises, Britain's waffling over some aspects of its commitment to EEC, plus several other smaller issues all persuaded Bonn that criticism of the Community was justified. Correctly or not, the Germans felt that the economic and monetary plight of some EEC countries was in large part due to fiscal and political irresponsibility, and that the sense of drift in the Community could be overcome only by political leadership that faced up to the challenges of the future and was more resistant to the day-by-day pressures of political expediency.

With respect to France, these issues were not resolved until the summer of 1978 when Germany and France launched a major new initiative toward a European monetary union, making a new attempt to coordinate more closely the currencies and economies of the EEC members. At the time, the idea of the currency snake had lost much of its meaning because the overwhelming predominance of the mark had forced weaker currencies out of the snake. In addition to furthering a greater harmonization of national economic and fiscal policies in the European Community, the Germans hoped that locking other EEC currencies to the mark in a European monetary unit would ease excessive upward pressure on the mark by reducing speculative dollar investments in German currency and spreading such investments among other EEC currencies. This would Europeanize the protective measures against the dollar that Bonn thought were called for and also make less glaring (through the creation of a European Monetary Fund) the political influence Germany had gained by having taken on a good portion of the dollar's reserve currency role.

The last point is particularly telling since it reflected Chancellor Schmidt's sensitivity to the risks of having Germany appear to be pursuing national power and international leverage too assertively. Schmidt did not want to see the mark play too large a role as a clearly identifiable reserve currency because of the possible negative implications — politically, psychologically, and monetarily. Again, as in many other instances, the Germans preferred a European institutional context for implementing their policies, shying away from purely national policies and thus avoiding the implication that they were striving for national independence of action or heavy-handed political influence.

These considerations were especially delicate with respect to German relations with the United States, which were uneasy during the Schmidt chancellorship for several reasons. Schmidt opposed Henry Kissinger's tough attitude on Eurocommunism, viewing it as nervous and short-sighted; the Middle East war in 1973 and the energy crisis caused irritations between Washington and Bonn; and the offset arrangements through which Germany had purchased American weaponry and U.S. bonds to finance American troop-stationing costs were for all practical purposes scrapped. During the Carter administration the issues of human rights, export of nuclear technology by Germany, American waffling over the neutron bomb, Washington's initial failure to support the dollar in international markets, and the American demand that Germany help the world economy through a more dynamic spending program aggravated problems between Washington and Bonn.

It would be inaccurate to describe these policy differences as a crisis in U.S.-German relations. Nonetheless, Bonn's policies and attitudes were signals that the Germans believed their economic and monetary power carried with it a sense of responsibility. This was reflected in an intensive German diplomatic effort, sustained by development aid, in the Third World; and generally in a more assertive foreign policy. By and large, this was not done in a heavy-handed way. From Bonn's point of view, the Germans were propping up the United States as well as the European Community — they were asked to support the French farmers as well as the American dollar; they were expected to underwrite Italy's attempt to overcome economic and political disarray; they were supposed to pay the lion's share of the cost of the EEC nuclear research program as well as American defense costs in Europe; they were to continue to subsidize the Community's regional development programs and absorb a major portion of the cost of petrodollar recycling. At the same time, the Germans saw themselves being asked to undermine the very basis of their economic well-being through what they considered ill-advised economic and monetary policies. In short, they felt that the equalizing measures suggested to them were a leveling down to a lower common denominator, when they believed that the process should be the reverse—that Germany's partners should make stronger efforts to match the Federal Republic's economic and monetary performance.

*   *   *

Because of their inherent complexity, and perhaps also because we are still too close to them, the international circumstances of the 1970s appear to have yielded no stark alternatives to which German foreign policy was required to respond. The absence of drastic options could also signal a coming of age—for both the postwar international system and the Federal Republic. As W. H. Auden has said, "Between the ages of twenty and forty we are engaged in the process of discovering who we are, which involves learning the difference between accidental limitations which it is our duty to outgrow and the necessary limitations of our nature beyond which we cannot trespass with impunity. Few of us can learn this without making mistakes, without trying to become a little more than we are permitted to be."

Notes

1. In 1962, Walter Lippmann wrote, "The hard line France takes about Berlin and the Soviet Union is founded . . . on a basic French national determination not to have to live with a large united Germany. At bottom the hard policy is directed not against the Russians but against those Germans who want to make an opening to the East." *Western Unity and the Common Market* (Boston: Little, Brown, 1962), p.32.

2. Alfred Grosser says that his theory about the "gentlemen's agreement" between Adenauer and de Gaulle on this reciprocal arrangement "was confirmed on December 31, 1963, at 8:30 p.m. in a single phrase spoken by General de Gaulle during his New Year's address. Indeed, in naming Pankow among the capitals of totalitarian states—totalitarian, but states—he was serving notice to Chancellor Erhard: 'If you don't respect your promise of support in Atlantic policy, I can change my terms concerning the German problem.' In my view, these simple words provided a sort of confirmation of the Adenauer–de Gaulle 'deal' dating back to 1958." Alfred Grosser, *French Foreign Policy under De Gaulle* (Boston: Little, Brown, 1965), pp. 60-61.

3. Fritz René Allemann, "The Changing Scene in Germany," *The World Today*, February 1967, p. 54.

4. This issue was revived in the summer of 1977, when Rowland Evans and Robert Novak wrote in the *Washington Post* that they had gained access to the so-called Presidential Review Memorandum 10 in which, among other options, it was suggested to President Carter that Western Europe should not be defended along

the West-East German border but along the rivers Weser and Lech in West Germany. This meant that about one-third of West Germany would be sacrificed in the early phase of an attack from the East. In addition, there was the implication that even after the Weser-Lech perimeter had been breached, the use of tactical nuclear weapons was by no means assured. (Of course, the battlefield use of tactical nuclear weapons at that stage would in any case involve the West German population and for that reason alone would be problematic.)

3

West Germany and the New Dimensions of Security

Manfred Wörner

In recent years all of us have had to learn that the traditional understanding of our security and, hence, the conventional instruments for safeguarding it are no longer adequate. Oil crises and terrorism have made us realize this with painful clarity. The second half of the twentieth century has brought us a threat of new dimensions that we must meet with the proper concepts and resources unless we want to live permanently with a significant security deficit, possibly with grave consequences. Each era has its own characteristics and challenges. This means that we shall be judged on the grounds of whether we succeeded in developing a new security concept to match a sudden expansion and sophistication of the threat spectrum. Some years ago former U.S. Secretary of Defense (and present World Bank president) Robert S. McNamara wrote that mankind had reached a point where in order to survive, it would have to struggle its way toward new, clearer insights into the inherent constraints of the concept of security. There is nothing we can add to this statement except, perhaps, that the process of acquiring new insights into the security problem has not proceeded very rapidly.

For centuries the word "security" has characterized the situation of a nation that was protected against destruction or aggression by external enemies. Security used to be defined in military terms and measured by the number of men at arms and guns available. To overcome military deficiencies, a nation would "borrow" from other nations via mutual assistance pacts limited in time, binding both sides but not affecting their sovereign rights.

Security in the traditional sense of the word was not only perceived on a predominantly national and one-dimensional military level—it was also a nation's most precious asset. External security depended in no way on internal policy; and other types of security, such as internal security, economic security, or social security appeared to have no relationship whatever to external security. The assumption that the meaning of security is purely that of external security has gradually been disproved by the events of the past ten years.

1. In the first place, we can no longer regard the military power of our potential adversary, the Soviet Union, merely as an instrument of warfare. While the military armament of the Soviet Union and the other Warsaw Pact nations still allows the option of aggressive warfare against Western Europe, there has come about a new interrelationship among power, influence, and sheer force. The actual use of force is not necessary in order to achieve political objectives. It is sufficient to demonstrate power in the form of potential force. The sword of Damocles, Nikita Khrushchev told us, won more victories than Caesar's sword. Consequently, we can no longer judge the military capabilities of the Warsaw Pact purely in terms of military strategy aimed at the conquest of foreign territory. The armies of the East, in a logical continuation of Karl von Clausewitz's principle, are political instruments aimed at constraining the political freedom of action of the Western nations, at their "Finlandization." This means that external security for the West is no longer assured merely by preventing the occupation of territory, but requires a defense against external pressure applied to national domestic and social policy. As a result, our military efforts must secure not only our territorial integrity, but also the "continued internal self-determination" of our nation. Those who have tried for years to convince us that the Warsaw Pact has not yet achieved the capability for attack with conventional weapons and that we therefore have no cause for concern should update their understanding of security. To apply pressure and blackmail, to cause an insidious erosion of Western confidence in our own military power, requires a significantly lesser military capability than actual aggression. Therefore, the purpose of the military balance of power is not only that of deterring aggression, but also that of countering political pressure and establishing a psychological equilibrium. It is important that those who advocate unilateral measures by the West or numerically balanced reductions of force levels at the mutual balanced force reduction (MBFR) talks in Vienna acquire an understanding of these relationships. Unilateral, if only symbolic, force reductions by the stronger power may be a goodwill gesture, but unilateral reductions by the weaker power and agreement to numerically balanced force reductions are sheer folly. They merely indicate that the weaker power urgently needs negotiating success, that it is even weaker than it appears to be, and that it has no confidence in its own future. But the West is very far from that point. We still have the power of shaping our own destiny. We still have the time to stop and to reverse any disastrous trend. However, this requires that our peoples are told the full truth again and that governments have the courage to demand unpopular and costly sacrifices. The use of Soviet military power as a

political instrument is a fact that the emancipated citizen can understand.

2. The second aspect of the new meaning of security concerns the geographical dimension. Until far into the sixties the threat to the West was characterized by the direct military confrontation in the heart of Europe. The threat was regionally confined. But those times are past. The Soviet Union has learned that, on a short-term basis, the West can be neither militarily overrun nor forced to its knees by massive military-political pressure. It has drawn the necessary conclusions and has modified its strategy. What was formerly a regional, direct strategy has become a global, indirect strategy. At a time of verbal détente, when direct confrontation is reduced, this strategy consists of establishing other fronts against the Western nations—not just military fronts but also economic and ideological fronts, not always noisy and visible but often silent and unnoticed. The Soviet Union rarely takes direct action but uses others as substitutes and tools. The Soviet reach for Africa is a striking example of this type of strategy.

The West cannot afford to watch this idly. The times when nobody cared whether people fought each other "far away in Turkey" are long past. They have passed because the West can no longer ignore the activities of the Communist nations and can no longer control the raw materials imports from the Third World. They have passed because the West is no longer master of its economic security. The NATO alliance can provide a nuclear shield, but not an oil shield and certainly not a raw materials shield for the entire territory of the alliance. In the future, no country or regional alliance will be self-sufficient. Global interdependence is the characteristic feature of our era. As the American historian Fritz Stern recently put it, we live in a "global minefield." We can meet this global challenge only by a global response, a response that no individual country, not even the United States, can establish by itself but that all Western countries must establish together. This response must consist, first and foremost, of economic and political assistance to the nations in the regions exposed to the threat. However, where the USSR attempts to extend its sphere of influence through military force, the West must not be content with verbal protest but must decide on an adequate reaction.

3. Not only has the formerly regional military threat become a global, multidimensional threat, but it has also become apparent that national security is greatly dependent on economic security. The early years of the Federal Republic, which were years of striking economic growth, removed all doubt about our ability to finance military forces of adequate size. This held true all the more because then the only threat to the Federal Republic, an expansive Soviet Union, was there for everybody to see. In the meantime, however, history has caught up with us. The reduced intensity of the

direct military confrontation in Central Europe and especially the
economic recession since the early seventies have had the result that defense
expenditures are primarily measured by what is considered economically
affordable and socially justifiable. This development is understandable but
disastrous. It is true that nobody in our country could and would demand
that we arm ourselves at the expense of our basic economic needs. But we
are far from that point. In terms of the gross national product, the Soviet
Union spends at least twice as much for military purposes as we do.
Therefore, much as we appreciate the explosive problems of economic and
social security, we must make it clear again to our people that there is a
connection between external security and economic security. Territorial integrity and political freedom of action are prerequisites even for a well-
functioning economic system of the Western type.

There is also an indirect relationship between external security and
economic security. Economic success not only provides the financial
resources to acquire the means of external security; economic and social
security are also indispensable for the internal peace of a country. Only a
state in which social justice prevails will be considered worthy of defense by
its citizens. History has taught us that inflation, recession, and rising
unemployment can lead to crisis situations that open the door to political
extremism and endanger the existence of democratic nations. What is the
use of well-functioning military forces if the state disintegrates from within?
It is against this background that successful economic and social policy
becomes practical security policy.

4. There is, finally, the new dimension of security that arises from the
dangers of terrorism. The events of 1977 have shown us how a small group
of hate-blinded fanatical terrorists can almost paralyze a well-functioning
lawful government. It is true that there have always been active enemies of
our state in the Federal Republic's short history. But it has now become
clear to us all that it is not sufficient to protect the Federal Republic of Germany against her external enemies by means of her armed forces. Today
the internal enemy, too, is heavily armed, unscrupulous, and plots his
atrocities with the precision of military staff planning. We should not
underestimate this threat, even though we have achieved initial success and
all is quiet at the moment. Ideological fanaticism, Henri de Montherlant
once said, is a kind of rabies of the human mind. The terrorists are
ideological fanatics, unpredictable in their actions and no longer capable of
being politically resocialized. The only thing that will impress them is the
demonstrated resolution on the part of a democratic lawful state not to yield
them an inch.

Moreover, we cannot maintain a credible external policy of deterrence if
we show weakness in deterring our internal enemies. Preparedness for

defense is indivisible. Negligence in fighting the terrorists will have its full effect on our military security. Internal security is also a piece of external security.

Under the leadership of Konrad Adenauer, the Federal Republic of Germany made three historical, irrevocable decisions. First, it made the decision to seek freedom on the side of the West. We must not waver in this principle. Any German seesaw policy between West and East would have disastrous consequences. The North Atlantic alliance remains the indisputable and unshakable basis of our foreign and security policies. To us the Atlantic alliance is far more than a conventional defensive pact. It is based not only on the community of interests, but also — and this is much more important — on the community of values. Our alliance has value and substance as long as the freedom of the West is endangered. And that will be for a long time to come — certainly for the foreseeable historical time span. All the concepts for pulling apart the power blocs in Europe, for a European security zone, or even for dissolving NATO and the Warsaw Pact — no matter how well meaning — in the last analysis must lead to a preponderance and, hence, hegemony of the Soviet Union in Western Europe.

Second, the Federal Republic of Germany made the decision to seek a United Europe. This decision too, is irreversible. Germany will go where Europe goes. There can be no security for the Federal Republic in isolation from the rest of Europe. Therefore, it is also impossible for the Federal Republic to have any type of special relationship with non-European nations. Concepts of a self-contained and independent defense of Western Europe are illusionary and dangerous. In order to safeguard its freedoms, Europe must continue to depend on the alliance with North America, even if it is eventually politically united and has joint military forces at its disposal, which remains one of our firm objectives.

Third, it was decided under Adenauer's leadership that freedom is more important than unification. National unity at the price of freedom is not an option for German policy. Neutralization of whatever type, involving the Federal Republic or all of Germany, would place Germany in the middle between the power blocs and lead to the loss of freedom for all of Germany. Yet the unity of the German nation remains a priority policy objective of the Federal Republic of Germany. Although the chances for its realization may be small at present and in the foreseeable future, this is not a policy of lip service only. Like any other people the Germans have a deeply ingrained desire for national unity, although it may not always be visible on the surface. If West Germany were to abandon this objective, then the Communist part of Germany would be able to exploit this desire for its policy. The first indications of this exist already. Moreover, permanent peace can exist only where it is founded in justice and freedom. A stable and durable peaceful order cannot be built on suppression. Therefore, the Federal Republic will continue to do everything in her power at least to keep the German question an open question. But we know that reunification of the two Germanies can and will take place only within a larger European context.

The new dimensions of the security threat involve a great variety of new uncertainties and difficult tasks for us and for our allies. The challenges of the future will not be easy to meet. Yet there is no cause for pessimism. Oswald Spengler's *The Decline of the West* is not a realistic scenario for the destiny of the West in the last quarter of the twentieth century. We still have freedom and strength—economically, technologically, and socially. What we have lost and what we must restore is confidence in our future. Not fear but hope, not resignation but reasonable optimism, not fatalistic indifference but creative commitment is the mental attitude that our challenges demand.

4

Germany and NATO: The Enduring Bargain

Catherine McArdle Kelleher

Introduction

"No NATO without Germany; no Germany without NATO." This in essence was one of fundamental transatlantic bargains painfully hammered out within the West during the first postwar debates on Atlantic security.[1] Rearmament and entry into the Western alliance were the essential preconditions for the restoration of German sovereignty. NATO, unique among peacetime security organizations in its force requirements and integration, was predicated on the availability of German manpower and territory, and on the control of the German role in the development of a new European military balance. The base conditions were, of course, Germany's defeat and division and its role as a central prize in East-West confrontation, military and ideological. Of at least equal importance was the remarkable convergence of German and American interests and strategies, of the dictates of Konrad Adenauer's "politics of necessity" and the Truman-Eisenhower concept of European security.

The intervening decades have witnessed numerous major changes in power and definitions of security. The ebb and flow of détente have replaced the statics of the Cold War; direct Soviet attack, conventional and nuclear, against Central Europe is expected by very few. The Federal Republic stands in the last phases of the German miracle—increasingly self-confident, assertive. It is now the unquestioned second power in NATO, leader and banker to Europe, and confident, independent interlocutor of the East. The Atlantic alliance itself appears to have lost much of its earlier significance and vitality. The launching of the Carter initiatives has led to limited resurgence and capability improvements, but these are merely phases in what is seen as the continuing decline, if not the effective end, of NATO in an era of détente, low politics, and strategic parity.

It is easy to overestimate the impact of these changes. Indeed, the basic German-alliance bargain still holds and will continue for the foreseeable future. A NATO without a major German role would be inconceivable (if

43

not irrelevant) for the other Western powers and particularly for the United States. Neither present form nor alliance substance could be maintained, with major consequences for Western and global security.

Equally unacceptable to the allies (and to the East and seemingly the majority of the German population) would be a Federal Republic, still a major military power but outside NATO or some transatlantic security grouping. This presumably would hold even if German capability was limited and its future security and conflict behavior bound by traditional international legal restraints.

The German-alliance bargain therefore appears now and for the near term as a basic parameter of Western, and particularly German and American policy. Its centrality makes short-run perturbation and irritation more intense and dramatic. But, without major transformationns in the current international system or in the German domestic context, it represents a durable bargain of continuing value. And there are developments in the strategic and economic environments that portend even greater strength and durability.

I plan, therefore, to explore the developments in this bargain over time, to assess its present dimensions, and to sketch out possible conditions and directions of future evolution. Since considerable effort here and elsewhere has been directed toward "NATO as a German precondition," I will focus primarily on the other half of the bargain: the centrality of a major German involvement to maintenance of the alliance in particular and Western security in general. Accordingly I will turn first to the major alliance roles assumed by or imposed on Germany in the past and then to present and future German role definitions. A final section will attempt to tie these themes together in terms of the opportunities and costs, the risks and constraints these pose for West German foreign policy.

Which NATO?

We must begin by clarifying which aspect of NATO is involved in the German-alliance bargain. For security purposes, NATO is only secondarily the treaty community of fifteen; its core is the political bonding and more-or-less integrated military-political organization of the seven "Central Front" states (the United States, Britain, Canada, the Benelux states and the Federal Republic) plus France. It is this group (with perhaps the addition of peripheral Italy and Denmark) that constitutes the bulk of effective Western military capability for both deterrence and defense, and the operational link, if there is one, to American strategic nuclear power.

Within this framework, the Federal Republic is clearly now the second alliance power in every area except independent nuclear forces. It provides essentially one-half of total Central Front manpower, at least an equivalent percentage of all military equipment (with major naval exceptions), and a level of defense expenditures, direct and indirect, surpassed only by that for total U.S. forces. Its potential is equally significant. The Federal Republic holds the second largest effective reserve force pool, the second largest force of nuclear capable launchers and platforms, and the greatest European capacity for rapid defense expansion and general economic mobilization. The German share in the formal alliance organization and in military-political decision making is roughly proportionate to its military contribution.

The German definition of the purposes of this participation has changed little since the first rearmament discussions and the development of the "Adenauer concept."[2] The primary goal is to ensure the inextricable involvement of the United States in the security of the German state against political threat and military attack. A corollary is the involvement of other Western states, allowing for the maintenance, at acceptable costs, of a multilateral military presence on German soil. This provides, first, an equalizing framework and a legitimizing cover for German national capabilities and, second, multiple reinsurance for the operation of the American guarantee.

Translated into operational terms, basic German security goals have been seen by successive German governments as requiring:

1. The maintenance of sufficient alliance forces, both conventional and nuclear, to ensure the operation of deterrence and the American guarantee and to assure full German (if not all European) participation in crisis management.
2. The maintenance of sufficient alliance war-fighting capability to allow for forward defense—the security of German territory as far forward and as soon as possible—until the activation of the American guarantee.

The precise definition of sufficiency levels is formally an alliance responsibility but largely, from Bonn's perspective, a matter for American decision. Deterrence in essence is the preferred strategy, even given the grave doubts about American nuclear intervention under conditions of strategic parity. Despite Germany's forward defense concerns, the principal purpose of European military forces is political, the securing of the American guarantee. The aim, broadly sketched, has been to maintain as few forces as necessary to convince successive American leaderships that a Europeanization of defense would fail and to outflank domestic oppositions. But the European allies, and particularly the Federal Republic, have had to maintain a sufficient level of alliance effort to ensure a continuing American presence, to preserve an assured Washington channel, and to maintain or improve their status vis-à-vis the other allies in the NATO hierarchy.

It is in the pursuit of these goals that the Federal Republic has assumed two major alliance security roles, each involving four or five critical functions, within the Central Front alliance. Not all these functions are exlusively military; the lines of functional separation, particularly over the last decade, have become increasingly blurred. Moreover, not all have been functions willingly accepted; at least two have been imposed or dictated by the increasing defaults of others. But however grudgingly, German leaders have defined these as burdens that must or can be borne.

Germany as NATO Resource Pool

Perhaps the principal German role is that classically assigned to alliance partners: the role of resource pool. From the first NATO discussion, the Federal Republic was seen as the Western "makeweight." It was to be the source of men, money, and matériel (and indeed territory) needed to (1) close the gap vis-à-vis a superior opponent, (2) remedy allied deficiencies, and (3) meet the terms posited by the alliance leader(s) as preconditions for participation. Adenauer's demands for equality and equity would be met at least in the formal sense. German forces would not simply be "foot soldiers" and the economic burdens of defense would be allocated in roughly equivalent proportions among the major states and with appropriate regard for Germany's domestic political constraints. But Germany would serve as the new power source, both for the staging of day-to-day capability and for the increases required in crisis or in a changing international environment.

Over the life of the alliance, this German role has involved four principal functions. The initial demands on the German resource pool were to allow *replacements* for major Western conventional retrenchment — indeed before there were more than limited German forces in existence. For the United States, well into the 1950s, the goal was replacement of the American forces that must inevitably be reduced and withdrawn (e.g., the Radford Plan of 1956). British calculations were more complex — the juggling of the competing requirements of domestic economic recovery, nuclear ambitions, and the last phases of decolonization (e.g., the British Defence White Paper of 1957). France had similar long-term aims, but these were secondary to the immediate demands for forces in Indochina and Algeria, and in support of France's "global mission." The arguments heard in governments and especially in legislatures all stressed that the Federal Republic should, after all, shoulder the greatest burden given the conditions of German rehabilitation and the inevitable centrality of the defense of German territory in NATO's security planning.

Direct demands for replacement remained key, however, only in German-American relations. The most overt pressure throughout the 1960s and early 1970s came from the Congress and the set of continuing initiatives (broadly categorized as the Mansfield amendment) that foresaw a direct drawdown to two or perhaps fewer American divisions deployed on the Central Front.[3] Official demands for greater German burden sharing were only somewhat less frequent, and the threat of force reductions and the congressional card were used in Bonn-Washington disputes over strategic doctrine, tactical nuclear weapons distribution, and multilateral force (MLF) participation—to cite only several prominent instances.

An increasingly frequent claim was the use of German resources to allow *redistribution* of alliance burdens. By the mid-1960s, all Central Front states treated the ceilings on German forces set in 1954 as both maxima and minima; 500,000 men were to be *the* German contribution. On the other hand, they were to be allowed force reductions, formal or informal, over the short or the longer term. The most significant in absolute terms was clearly the American stripping of men and matériel for Vietnam, which began in 1966 and has only recently been fully reversed. But proportionately, the impacts of the cuts by the other states were similar: (1) the British practices of rotation and then Northern Ireland reassignments, (2) the French reorganization efforts, and (3) the Canadian and Benelux redeployments in the face of domestic budgetary pressures.

A parallel, more specific admixture of alliance economic and military requirements were the resource claims for German *economic offset*.[4] The broad argument, pressed most forcefully from 1960 on, was that overseas stationing placed an additional, inequitable burden on the major Central Front states, clearly reflected in adverse balance of payments effects. A burgeoning German economy could well afford additional indirect support first as equalizing compensation and then as a prerequisite for allied maintenance of existing force levels. The result was a series of negotiated arrangements, lasting vis-à-vis the United States into the mid-1970s, taking various forms: direct local support of facilities and personnel, military procurement packages, purchase of long- and short-term securities, and the extension of short-term loans outside the alliance itself.

A final category of claims consisted of those that treated the Federal Republic's resources as a type of *alliance crisis reserve*. The range of the precipitating crises was considerable. Those most salient to this analysis are the post-Sputnik buildup requiring greater tactical nuclear capability (MC 70); the Berlin call-up of more troops for longer terms of service (1961-1962); the shift of strategic concept (flexible response); the post-

Czechoslovakia demonstrations of readiness and rapid reinforcements (1968); the pressing need for infrastructure improvements (the European Defense Improvement Program [EDIP]) or reserve reorganization (the Carter 1977 initiative). The pattern of claims was similar throughout: Germany as the residual category, the alliance partner able to assume the major share of any new burden or military or economic challenge. The responsibility was almost never to be exclusive in the interests of both alliance solidarity and intraalliance political influence. But in contrast to the weaknesses, defaults, or extraalliance responsibilities of the other seven, Germany had both the resources and the direct reserves to intervene rapidly and effectively.

Germany as NATO Anchor

The second critical role assumed by the Federal Republic in the Central Front NATO is far harder to specify. Particularly over the first fifteen years, Germany has come to be seen by others, if not always by itself, as the European anchor of the alliance.[5] Increasingly, Bonn was expected to be the source of alliance cement, the *animateur* of integration, the senior partner of the United States both for and in Europe. In many respects, this role is the political analogue of the resource pool. Germany has been defined as the residual bulwark of the political West, anxious and willing to sacrifice for broader integration and unity in the face of challenges within the alliance as well as from the East.

As with the resource role, this German role assignment has not always implied positive orientation or support from other alliance members. Most of the European states — as the Federal Republic itself — prefer to treat NATO matters primarily as issues for negotiation within their bilateral relationship with the United States. Discussions come only secondarily with others or the alliance as a whole. Moreover, the German role has always been viewed as virtue in necessity, a forced option flowing from German security dependence and political vulnerability. Without a viable European alternative or a realistic prospect of reunification, what other avenues for influence, status, and legitimacy did the Federal Republic have?

The broadest functions prescribed by this role are unquestionably those assumed as the *European partner of the United States* from the mid-sixties onward.[6] This status represented the belated triumph of Adenauer's earlier concept (and at times that of Franz Josef Strauss) concerning the best means of ensuring and directing American involvement. Yet the circumstances were hardly propitious. On the one hand, there was a Gaullist France obviously estranged from the alliance and perceived by many to be pressing Germany for a choice between Europe and the American alliance.

On the other was a weakened Britain (1) unable to maintain but unwilling to cede the "special relationship" it had had with Washington throughout the first fifteen years of NATO and (2) ever suspicious of German capabilities and intentions.

American expectations were at least as risk laden. Most simply described, the American preference in the early 1960s was for a junior partner, with a military organization and doctrine as close to a made-in-America posture as possible, a partner able and willing to provide a direct follow-through for American conceptions. Policy disagreements—as on the appropriate threshold for tactical nuclear use—were topics for discussion and German education, not joint decision making among equals. Too, some in Washington saw Germany as the European discussion partner in two senses: first, as the sounding board for American concerns and, second, as the medium for indirect influence (as persuader, example, or threat) over other Europeans, most hopefully the French.

Events and increasing evidence of German power and of independence in the last decade have led to U.S. acceptance of a far more equal and differentiated German partnership. A number, especially in the Nixon administration, indeed expressed occasional interest in an even greater direct sharing of alliance power and responsibility.[7] One view saw Bonn as the explicit European pole, the synthesizer, coordinator, and, if necessary, the director of European alliance contributions and organization. The United States would continue its force presence at least for the short run and would remain alliance leader and strategic reserve in the overall sense. Bonn, however, would be assured equal decision-making power in all alliance questions (including nuclear use and arms control negotiations with the East) and fundamental American support for its foreign policy and economic initiatives outside the alliance. Eventual German nuclear ownership would not be precluded, although preferably through the creation of a European force. The final organizational outcome indeed would be left to time, the progress of German-Franco-British negotiation, and Bonn's reservoir of skill and opportunity. But it might well approach the original Kennedy "two pillar" concept or the Strauss vision of essential European-American "bigemony."[8]

Others under Nixon (and clearly the powerful within the Carter administration) favored a more restricted division of labor. Within the military alliance, Germany was to be treated as an almost equal—except, in accordance with Bonn's own preference, in areas involving the direct control of nuclear weapons. Equality, though, involved a requirement for both positive and negative inputs to alliance decision making. Germany had the right to criticize and reject American initiatives but also the responsibility to suggest alternatives and to work for their acceptance by other European

states as well as by the United States (e.g., on tactical nuclear modernization, reserve readiness, airborne warning and control system [AWACS]).
After almost ten years of military stagnation and in an era of declining
American military predominance, German initiatives for reform and
renewal were not only to be welcomed but imperative.

Rather different expectations about Germany's partner role have been
intermittently voiced by the other Central Front states. Their emphasis is
on Germany as the most influential European representative, the source of
criticism and correction for a too-often preoccupied United States.[9] The
specific focus of concerns has varied, largely as a result of European perceptions of either too much American leadership and control in the early
seventies or the diffuse capricious style of more recent years. The catalog of
general criticism is at least as long:[10] (1) the continuing American obsession
with war-fighting requirements rather than supports for the deterrence
system; (2) recurring American predilections toward implicit nuclear
decoupling and a limited parochial conception of the Eurostrategic balance;
and (3) unpredictable American negotiating behavior vis-à-vis the Soviet
Union toward SALT II and III.

Rarely explicit and often inchoate, these European expectations foresaw
an eventual German assumption of the alliance role once played by France.
Given increasing two-way military dependency, it is both in German interest and in German power to advance the interests of the Europe that
might be as well as of the Europe that is. American irritation might be considerable, and the imposition of real costs, particularly by the Congress, a
more probable (though not certain) risk. Nonetheless, there is a substantial
possibility for major improvements—both in American leadership and in
alliance decision making—and eventual American alienation and withdrawal are probably inevitable in any case.

In marked contrast is a second set of functions ascribed to Germany
within this role: that of *alliance holder* or ramrod for *multilateral organization*.
The continuing German stakes are again clear. An integrated alliance
would produce (1) more effective capabilities for deterrence and defense,
(2) more assurance of multiple state involvement in German political and
military security, and (3) more opportunities for growing German control
over crucial points of alliance decision making. On any major alliance
issue, therefore, the Federal Republic could be expected to oppose decisions
that promoted special bilateral relationships (e.g., United States and
United Kingdom, or United States, United Kingdom, and France) or that
enhanced the alliance's inherent centrifugal tendencies (e.g., separation of
the northern or southern flank, condemnation of an errant alliance member).

Perhaps the first function of this type pressed on the Federal Republic was that of *standardization advocate*.[11] Beyond the obvious standardization stimuli inherent in a multilateral layer-cake defense of German territory, German rearmament represented a substantial opportunity for joint procurement and development. This held not only for those wishing to sell arms (the United States, Britain, and France), but also for those who wanted to harness German purchasing power to expand their own involvement in nuclear and conventional weapons modernization (e.g., Italy and the Netherlands). The primary and perhaps predictable result by the mid-1960s was Germany's emergence as the "most standardized NATO state," involved in more than twenty sales or production consortia, within an alliance that increasingly looked "like an army museum."[12]

Over the past decade, successive German governments had pushed harder on standardization, albeit with tougher bargaining strategies. In part under American pressure, but largely on independent initiative, Germany has demanded broader coproduction schemes on preferential financial and technological transfer arrangements. German policies have led to more far-reaching early agreements on design and mission requirements, evaluation standards, and more equitable national trade-offs in the framework first of the NATO Eurogroup and then in the European Programme Group involving direct French participation. The number of new cooperation projects undertaken has, however, fallen considerably.

A related decline can be noted in another anchor function: Germany's role, often voluntary, as the proponent of *new collective alliance organizations*. In the early phases, the Federal Republic supported virtually every common initiative — successive plans for a European medium-range ballistic missile (MRBM) force (1958-1961), a multilateral force (MLF) or an Atlantic nuclear force (ANF) (1963-1966), a Nuclear Planning Group (1966 to present), and an Alliance Strike Force (for flank contingencies, 1968 onward), and even intermittent talk of a revived European defense community concept (1973, 1975, 1976). The range of enthusiasm did vary, as did the degree of new financial support Bonn was prepared to pledge. The basic pattern remained fairly constant: given American acceptance or tolerance, early expression of German commitment to integration, early negotiation over the appropriate German share, and some direct pressure for the participation of others.[13]

A final function assumed intermittently by Germany was that of *integration advocate*, especially vis-à-vis the French.[14] In the late 1950s Adenauer saw this as a clear German responsibility and by his own report argued for alliance programs at several of his historic meetings with de Gaulle from 1958 to 1962. Successive governments continued this strategy, although after effective French withdrawal seemingly with more conflict (Ludwig

Erhard in 1965-1966), or lessened enthusiasm (Kurt Georg Kiesinger in 1967-1968), or limited hopes for success (Willy Brandt vis-à-vis Georges Pompidou).

The early 1970s and particularly the accession of Valéry Giscard d'Estaing and Helmut Schmidt brought new opportunities for and new significance to German efforts at persuasion. Although European, rather than alliance, cooperation was clearly the primary concern, German pressures toward informal coordination of French military efforts with German (and consequently alliance) policies achieved considerable success in both Paris and in Washington. At several key points, German officials and military commanders reportedly acted as honest brokers or perhaps harmonizers of past irritations and present disagreements.

Present German Role Choices

Present German policies regarding the continued assumption of these alliance roles obviously flow from the more general Atlantic policies of the Schmidt government. Broadly sketched, the emphasis is on the full realization and recognition of Germany's new political status within the continuing alliance framework. The NATO military structure is in need of major reorganization and reform; the credibility of the American nuclear guarantee can only be expected to decline further. Bonn is willing to assume its proportionate share in these alliance rebuilding tasks so long as it is consistent with its domestic priorities and with its conception of its own security requirements.[15]

A proportionate German share, however, is that of the second alliance power. In essence, therefore, present policies involve acceptance—limited, grudging, and toughly bargained—of the basic structures involved in both the resource and anchor roles. Some specific functions are rejected outright; others are heavily weighted by preconditions and legal formulas to ensure equity and proportionality. Still others are improbable subjects for allied debate or pressure given the basic buildup formulas agreed to at the NATO summits of 1977 and 1978. Yet within the limits set and the conditions granted, the Schmidt government continues to see these roles as broadly necessary to preservation of German security interests and the securing of the American connection, however changed.[16]

This new tone and emphasis in the German position are in large measure the culmination of past trends in the weighing of alliance claims against domestic needs and foreign policy priorities. With respect to resource claims in particular, Bonn from 1949 developed a fairly successful set of passive defenses—of stretch-outs, long lead-time programs, conditional agreements. Adenauer correctly foresaw that under a system predicated primarily on deterrence, promises of military buildup by a future date were virtually equivalent to actual force creation in political trading value. He (and, to a far less degree, Erhard) was quite skillful in garnering immediate political advantage and long-term good behavior credit for each increase in German activity or new allocation of German resources. Moreover, he steadfastly resisted any alliance decision or American pressure that formally increased only the German burden (e.g., Berlin, 1962) or that would directly substantiate Eastern charges of independent German initiatives or military adventurism (e.g., the American Gates plan for mobile MRBMs in 1959).

More positive defenses were made possible by the completion of the re-armament program and the German financial crisis of the mid-1960s. The imposition of the Medium Term Financing Program set clear budgetary limits on all future expenditures for guns as well as making explicit the relationship between general resource allocation and rates of economic growth. Increases in manpower even up to ceiling levels, for example, could only come through trade-offs with military procurement programs—with obvious implications for both offset arrangements and military efficiency. Further, Germany's simultaneous emergence as the principal European discussion partner of the United States allowed for a far more forceful role in alliance planning and increasing leverage against a weakening Britain, a withdrawing France, and ultimately a United States preoccupied in Vietnam.

German responses to integrative pressures have followed a similar pattern, although with far fewer clear breakpoints. Both the claims for and the payoffs in integrative efforts declined sharply during the 1960s when, for a long period, the United States benignly neglected the Atlantic alliance because of U.S. involvement in Vietnam and the need to nurture super-power détente. Inflation, declining European growth rates, and increasing military personnel costs meant more equipment–stretch-out programs and fewer new standardization programs. Active German resistance to alliance claims was therefore less necessary and fairly easily submerged in general alliance debate.

What functions are now specifically rejected or designated highly unlikely by an assertive, increasingly self-confident Schmidt government? As before, the most limited force replacement functions have been completely rejected as both inappropriate and in some sense unnecessary. Alliance force levels are still considered critical and increasingly necessary in light of Soviet expansion and modernization efforts. Government policies stress rather the fallacies of past insistence on "magic numbers," on the retention of every allied (especially American) soldier almost at prohibitive cost. Privately, officials suggest there are many acceptable ways to mount the necessary defensive capability—as the German plan to raise cadre units supplemented by ready reserves. They further suggest that a "safe" negotiated force reduction (should MBFR revive) might involve as much as a 20 percent reduction in standing force levels.

Economic support functions within a military context are also clearly rejected. In 1976, Chancellor Schmidt pronounced offset officially dead and gained the explicit concurrence of the United States, the last claimant. Cost sharing on a case-by-case basis is possible, as for the construction of facilities for new American deployments in northern Germany. Broad-based economic support, both short and longer term, is available to all allied governments. It is, though, to be on an instance-by-instance basis, clearly separate from the costs of military maintenance, and in the context of broader Western efforts at fiscal and monetary coordination.

Similar considerations characterize the official stance on the future use of German resources for purposes of burden redistribution and crisis reserve but with a further MBFR dimension. German insistence on pragmatic decision making and the imperatives of domestic constraints must be weighed against the probabilities of intraalliance trade-offs and the overall East-West political-military balance. The Schmidt government, for example, has rejected recent Soviet MBFR proposals, which essentially would freeze preagreement national military levels, as discriminatory and as an attempt to interfere with internal Western decision making.

Perhaps the clearest point of new emphasis in this respect is the Schmidt government's insistence on the broad equivalence of political and military security in the West vis-à-vis the East. The concern is not new, but the continuous, explicit treatment of this theme is—in the MBFR negotiating group, in bilateral conversations, and at the NATO summits of 1977 and 1978. A characteristic tone was set by former Defense Minister Georg Leber in a 1975 response to reports of American pressure for a 600,000 man *Bundeswehr:*

> There are many arguments against that. It is not as if the Federal Republic of Germany led a charmed life—not from an economic perspective either—and could afford everything. But more importantly if the Germans were to increase their army while others were to reduce theirs, inner-European problems would arise with certainty, because of the excessive weight that such a German army would then have in a circle of the Western European military powers. And I must preserve Europe from that.[17]

Bonn's position on a future anchor role reflects a similar pattern of pragmatism and political caution. The key issue, Schmidt has asserted in various forums, is the development of a new alliance political balance between the United States and all its European allies, not just the Federal Republic. The final resolution will turn on American answers to a number of continuing dilemmas. How much of its independent decision making is the United States willing to surrender and under what conditions? What impact will this have on popular and congressional interpretations of the alliance guarantee? What consequences is the United States prepared to draw from the accomplishment of strategic parity in terms of its strategy and deployments in Europe? And what new means are available to prevent decoupling or the bypassing of legitimate European concerns about forward-based nuclear weapons (FBS) and "gray area" technologies sure to be the subject of superpower bargaining in SALT III?

Schmidt, however, has been quick to reject pressures for greater German predominance in either the military or political aspects of the Central Front alliance or elsewhere. He has repeatedly underscored the possibility of West Germany's economic difficulties, its continuing political vulnerability, and its unwillingness (and incapacity) to attempt activism where others will not follow. The development of a different German role must be a slow process involving quiet diplomacy, bilateral negotiations, and German preferences for broad cooperative efforts in both her Atlantic and European activities.

Moreover, Germany's emergence as a more independent actor does not change the basic need for a fully unfolded American nuclear umbrella. Major new doctrinal debates may soon emerge; the level of mutual irritation and disagreement over tactical nuclear modernization for the 1980s is sufficient indication already. Germany also has the clear responsibility to seek some reinsurance, presumably in Europe, against eventual decoupling or physical withdrawal. But the evolution of any new system—Atlantic, Euro-American, European—has not yet begun; it will still depend on American decisions and the terms the United States sets for future deployments and decision making. Greater German leadership in issues of developing military strategy or military planning is therefore neither politically astute nor a low-risk option in terms of present and future security. The time for Germany to step up in this as in many other areas is not yet here.[18]

Toward Future Change

Under what conditions would there be a major reversal in basic German willingness to serve as both resource pool and alliance anchor? The list of possible scenarios is a long one; that of rather probable precipitating changes in the international system, the alliance, or German domestic context, is significantly shorter. We are struck, too, by the durability of the change variables first identified in the 1950s—American withdrawal, a possible and capable set of European partners (including Britain or France or both), a radical shift in German politics toward either a new Right or Left, or the opening of a new, effective reunification option.

Since the early 1950s, most analysts have begun with the probable consequences for German behavior of a phased American withdrawal from the Central Front, involving either conventional or tactical nuclear forces or both. Many believe this would lead to the collapse of Western security and to the steady expansion of the Soviet sphere of influence through the Finlandization of West Germany, if not of all of Europe. Without a major physical presence (the "buckets of blood" guarantee), the credibility of a continued American nuclear umbrella would diminish — in Washington, if not in Moscow. The German military effort, indeed most European national defense systems, would survive only at low levels for the performance of relatively untraditional security tasks (as peacekeeping or national emergency forces) as well as frontier defense. Or, as several studies in the 1970s have suggested, there would be basic reconstruction of national security systems in the direction either of the "total defense" discussed in Sweden or of the unitary, limited Canadian model.

Those more optimistic about German and perhaps French determination, if not the resolve of all Europeans, have predicted a quite different chain of circumstances. American withdrawal might well make possible the European organization of defense. A familiar French blueprint that has had intermittent support within the CDU-CSU would foresee the core as a Franco-British nuclear force, with assigned (no longer integrated) conventional troops and negotiated rules among equals, particularly the Germans, regarding consultation and shared decision making. The precise conditions of American decoupling might even allow an attenuated dumbbell partnership, perhaps along the lines of the nineteenth century's treaties of reinsurance or secondary guarantee.

The experience of the last thirty years indicates that both alternatives represent relatively extreme changes. The Finlandization model reverts to the bleak forced choice model of national security policymaking hardly consonant with Germany's new found political and economic stature. It also ignores the still considerable pull of the various European nationalisms and the very substantial political, economic, and social stakes these states would be most reluctant to sacrifice for Soviet favor. The European scenario, on the other hand, assumes far greater German agreement with the major European powers on priorities and finances, not to mention role sharing, than has ever existed. The functionalists' dreams of spillover from the EEC to a new defense community, a looser European Defense Community (EDC), would seem dashed once again without a major revitalization to overcome the political stalemate in the Community, in its present or expanded form.

If at all, it would seem that only a very hostile American withdrawal would serve as a proximate, if no longer sufficient, cause for Europeanization. Anything more cooperative would again raise the questions, dormant since the Johnson years, of the logical compatibility of proclaimed American preeminence and full European partnership in decision making, nuclear and conventional. A hostile America, in itself, would raise a myriad of other problems probably antecedent to Europeanization—the breakdown of superpower agreement or the losing of economic interdependence, to cite only two.

Of greater probability would seem a third alternative—the search by some European states, Germany probably in the lead, for affordable, relatively autonomous forces that would sustain national form, yet be loosely coordinated with each other and not radically decrease capacity further. Domestic constraints, financial and social, would undoubtedly continue; domestic enthusiasm might regain at least some nationalistic fervor (as the present symbolism of the *force* across the French political spectrum). There would certainly be differences in national goals and achievements, once again exacerbating the differences in national economic health, political and cultural stability, and tradition. It might also fracture the elite consensus between the Federal Republic and its allies. Yet Germany and at least France and Britain would probably attempt to maintain forces at interwar levels, involving all arms and nuclear-capable elements, if not full-fledged strategic forces by American definition. Each country's ties to the United States might provide whatever additional guarantees were required during extended détente.

A major reversal of détente would almost certainly spark an additional set of alternatives. Among the most obvious would be reintegration of the alliance, increased American pressure for higher war-fighting capabilities, and retention of nuclear redundancies at the tactical and strategic levels. But, again, much would depend on the specific circumstances and timing of this reversal, the specific set of Soviet moves that would indicate present cost-benefit calculations were overturned. Soviet buildups in conventional forces at present rates would not seem a sufficient indicator, nor would a short-term failure to conclude or extend SALT agreements. Conceivable, higher-level scenarios all share overtones of the 1950s: (1) a Soviet invasion of post-Tito Yugoslavia that would not stop at the Adriatic; (2) a new, active Soviet beachhead in or near the NATO area; (3) a limited probe perhaps at the Baltic straits; or (4) a return to the harassment of Berlin or feints toward Hamburg.

Moreover, the precise implications of such developments on German policy and that of the alliance as a whole would seem somewhat unclear. Soviet hard-line actions from Berlin to Czechoslovakia in 1968 have always seemed to bring a Western stiffening, although the principal impact has usually been on American attitudes and leadership. But in recent years, domestic factors have markedly limited the duration, and often the intensity, of reaction in all the European states, though to a lesser extent in Germany. Money has been pledged, but not spent; induction rates raised, but hardly ever sustained. It seemingly would take quite direct, unmistakable threats to reverse this trend, and the options of retreat and diplomatic submission would still remain.

A final set of alternatives involves a more gradual revaluation of the utility of military force by all of the European states, but especially the Federal Republic. Prolonged strategic parity and sytem stability will almost certainly enhance the military significance of conventional force balances in Europe, extend the existence of limited national nuclear capabilities, and raise new incentives for force expansion. There are also the new opportunities presented by the numerous gray area technologies, many within easy reach of Germany and most other middle powers. The availability of greater accuracy, improved propulsion, and cheaper production technologies, for example, may well overcome some of the earlier superpower advantages based on economic preponderance and the direction of successive technological revolutions.

Most speculative of all, might not superpower stalemate and neutralization essentially end the hold of nuclear-induced deterrence? Middle powers, among them the Federal Republic, would then enjoy new opportunities for the autonomous use of low-level force, without the risk of escalation or effective superpower reprisal. The political sensitivity, if not the density, of the Central Front balance will surely exclude most limited land force use. But the advantages to be gained from limited naval engagements, for example, could be considerable (e.g., the demarcation of spheres of influence, the drawing of political limits) and might demonstrate the threshold of deterrence and political will.

Conclusions

The specification of alternative future scenarios, however, always risks the obscuring of basic present realities. The traditional rules regarding the formation and the maintenance of military alliances still hold, even in the nuclear age. For the alliance member as for the alliance leader, the basic calculation is one of cost and risk. Does the alliance partnership provide new sources of needed resources—political or military, human or material—that are not available elsewhere or that are so important that they must be denied to an opponent?

For the Federal Republic, the basic security goals that have been pursued since 1949 dictate continued support of and major participation in the German-alliance bargain. The key factor is still the American connection, however much its political and strategic value has declined in comparison with the past. So long as the United States maintains a substantial Central Front presence, so long as the United States favors a transatlantic security grouping, the Federal Republic will remain committed to the alliance, most probably as its key European partner.

German criticism, frustration, and irritation within the alliance will almost certainly continue to grow. There are still a few residues within the alliance of past impositions and discriminatory restrictions. As German power has grown, traditional European fears and anti-German campaigns have gained new political potency, particularly among leftist parties. More important, there are real reasons, as well as good reasons, for continuing disagreements between the United States and the Federal Republic—doctrinal, organizational, strategic, and political. And increasingly, more in Bonn will question the value of ultimate reliance on an alliance leader whose domestic political system virtually assures unpredictability and ambivalence.

Notes

1. In its treatment of past events, this essay draws heavily on my own previously published work, especially Catherine M. Kelleher, *Germany and the Politics of Nuclear Weapons* (New York: Columbia University Press, 1975), and on the accounts of Wolfram Hanrieder's *West German Foreign Policy 1949-1963: International Pressure and Domestic Response* (Stanford: Stanford University Press, 1967) and of Robert McGeehan's *The German Rearmament Question* (Urbana: University of Illinois Press, 1971).

2. Recent commentaries on continuity and change in German security definitions include Walter F. Hahn, *Between Westpolitik and Ostpolitik*, Foreign Policy Papers, vol. 1, no. 1 (Beverly Hills and London: Sage, 1975); Gerald Livingston, "Germany Steps Up," *Foreign Policy*, no. 22 (1975); Gebhard Schweigler, "A New Political Giant? West German Foreign Policy in the 1970's," *The World Today*, April 1975; and the various essays included in Johan J. Holst and Uwe Nerlich, eds., *Beyond Nuclear Deterrence* (New York: Crane, Russak, 1977).

3. The origins and fate of these congressional initiatives are discussed in Philip Williams, "Whatever Happened to the Mansfield Amendment," *The World Today*, July-August 1976.

4. These issues are comprehensively and insightfully treated in Gregory F. Treverton, *The "Dollar Drain" and American Forces in Germany* (Athens, Ohio: Ohio University Press, 1978).

5. For a somewhat contrasting view of this anchor function, see Peter J. Katzenstein's "Die Stellung der Bundesrepublik in der amerikanischen Aussenpolitik, Drehscheibe, Anker, oder Makler," *Europa-Archiv,* no. 11 (June 10, 1976), from his longer chapter of the same title in Richard Rosecrance, ed., *America as an Ordinary Country* (Ithaca: Cornell University Press, 1976).

6. See here the broadly parallel development in Roger Morgan, *The United States and West Germany, 1945-1973* (London: Oxford University Press, 1974).

7. Compare here the treatments by Livingston and Schweigler cited in note 2 above and the discussion of the relevant American decision-making frameworks in Wilfred Kohl, "The Nixon-Kissinger Foreign Policy System and U.S.-European Relations," *World Politics* 18, no. 1 (October 1975).

8. Perhaps the best statement of the latter concept can be found in Franz Josef Strauss, "An Alliance of Continents," *International Affairs* 41, no. 2 (April 1965).

9. Compare here Uwe Nerlich, "NATO, EEC, and the Politics of Détente," in Nils Andren and Karl Birnbaum, eds., *Beyond Détente: Prospects for East-West Cooperation and Security in Europe* (Leyden: Nijhoff, 1966) and Michael D. Mosettig, "Nuclear Defense Debate," *European Community,* no. 209 (September-October 1978).

10. Compare Andrew J. Pierre, "Can European Security Be Decoupled from America?" *Foreign Affairs,* July 1973.

11. See here the limited but incisive overview of past and present standardization debates in Gardiner Tucker, *Towards Rationalizing Allied Weapons Production* (Paris: Atlantic Institute, 1976).

12. General a. D. Johannes Steinhoff quoted in Tucker, ibid., p. 3.

13. Compare here Theo Sommer's brief, pointed statement about the "integration ideal" of the Germans in his "Germany's Strategic Position in the European Power Balance," in E. J. Feuchtwanger, ed., *Upheaval and Continuity* (London: Oswald Wolff, 1973).

14. A similar, though far briefer function was undertaken by the Schmidt government vis-à-vis the revolutionary government of Portugal. See the limited treatment in Tad Szulc, "Lisbon and Washington: Behind Portugal's Revolution," *Foreign Policy,* Winter 1975.

15. One of the clearest statements of German alliance policy is still that contained in Schmidt's *Bundestag* foreign policy address of December 1976.

16. See final Ford-Schmidt communiqué, *New York Times,* July 18, 1976.

17. Quoted in Hahn, *Between Westpolitik and Ostpolitik,* p. 70.

18. Compare Livingston, "Germany Steps Up."

5

Germany and the Atlantic Community

Jan Reifenberg

Germany's relation to the Atlantic Community has been shaped by the changes that have occurred in the last thirty years. Three decades mean very little in human history. To the European continent, however, they meant the absence of armed conflict and the maintenance of peace for a remarkable timespan, if compared to the history of the last hundred years.

Thirty years after the creation of NATO and of the two German states seems a good time to take stock, without undue illusions, yet with firm convictions as to the necessity of safeguarding a common Western heritage. There are facts, foremost in the realm of security, that ought to remain constant. There are other facts that reflect the change and movement that came about in Europe. There is an uneven relationship between hopes for a brighter future and apprehensions about increased Soviet military capacity in Europe.

Like it or not, Germany remains at the center, and not just the geographical one. What the French used to call *les incertitudes allemandes* have been successfully restrained by the system of alliances that came about after World War II. The most important remain the Atlantic alliance on the Western side and its answer on the Eastern side, the Warsaw Pact. The vital relationship between Western Europe and the United States is the basis, the umbilical cord, of the Atlantic Community. To weaken, or worse, to sever it would shatter the very balance of power that has preserved peace since 1949. It is safe to assume that neither the United States nor the Soviet Union wishes this to happen. As a matter of fact, the West German *Ostpolitik* of the early seventies and the principles of the final act of the Helsinki Conference on European Security and Cooperation acknowledge that borders are inviolable and cannot be changed by force. In the eyes of Germany's neighbors both to the West and the East, any upsetting of the balance in Europe would give to the German problem a new and threatening dimension. The Atlantic Community would be dealt a severe, if not a fatal, blow.

That does not mean the total subservience of the European members of the alliance to American policy. Increasingly, Europeans have reasserted their national identities as Western Europe has emerged as a strong economic power. But it does mean that the basic principle — the political and military presence of the United States in Western Europe — should not be overturned for the sake of tempting but dangerous schemes that would ultimately result in a Finlandization of the old continent. In the absence of the United States, the Soviet Union would be strongly tempted to fill such a power vacuum; and at that moment the German or Western European part of the Atlantic Community would no longer exist.

Chancellor Adenauer was a sober, realistic, and shrewd statesman. Acting on deep convictions, he decided to anchor the Federal Republic firmly in the Atlantic alliance and in a Western community. For him this Western orientation had absolute priority over any dreams of a future reunification of Germany. To this Rhinelander, this Westerner, the sources of democracy, of culture, were located in the West. Reconcilation with France became a primary task; and the American nuclear umbrella became the indispensable protector of the fledgling West German state.

Adenauer was sworn to the Basic Law or constitution of the Federal Republic, which stipulates that the people of Western Germany, in giving themselves the first democratic institutions since the short days of the Weimar Republic, had spoken their free will also for those who lived in East Germany. But the codified obligation to seek reunification was, as Adenauer knew, more a profession of faith than a viable possibility for the foreseeable future. Securely confident of the black-and-white tenets of the Cold War, morally and materially supported first by Dean Acheson, then by his close friend John Foster Dulles, the first chancellor of the Federal Republic saw himself as a paragon of Western defense. On this he had no doubts.

Adenauer set a course that his four successors did not basically change. History has to decide whether this policy was the right one and the only feasible one: it could be said that it solidified the partition of Europe, or that it was the only way to reintegrate the Western part of Germany into the society of Western and Atlantic nations. It meant nothing less than a total readjustment to the hard facts that Hitler's folly had brought to Europe and upon which the Soviet Union built its sphere of domination over a part of Europe that, with the exception of Bulgaria, had always been Western oriented. But Adenauer, whose clear (and, to his detractors, over-simplified) views determined West German policy in its formative stage, never wavered. He feared a trait in the German character that seemed to him dangerously adventurous and that had, ever since Bismarck's days, led to the illusion that German dominance over Europe was necessary. Hence

Adenauer pledged total allegiance to the Atlantic and Western European idea, to the stark and clear perceptions that for him were embodied in the policies of Acheson and Dulles.

The old chancellor had consented to — and planned for — the re-creation of a German army. Yet he saw the new *Bundeswehr* exclusively as a part, and instrument, of NATO. It thus became the first German army of modern times that functioned within the Atlantic alliance, rather than under national command. This was another turning point in German history. It was another response to the situation that was created by the partition of the old continent. It allowed for a rather simplified foreign policy, because it temporarily delayed — or projected into a faraway future — the solution to all the problems that Germany had with its Eastern neighbors. It also made Adenauer's party, the Christian Democratic Union (CDU), and its Bavarian affiliate, the Christian Social Union (CSU), the prime repositories of an Atlantic and Western European orientation.

Many an illusion flourished in this context: a "policy of strength" vis-à-vis the USSR and Eastern Europe would — somehow miraculously — solve the German problem; one day — and Dulles clearly encouraged such thoughts — a "rollback" of the iron curtain would happen, and Western-inspired freedom would again come to those who yearned to express their own free will but were forbidden to do so by the presence of Soviet forces. However, the facts of the thermonuclear age were stronger. They dominated — and still dominate — the whole scene. If the United States and the Soviet Union recognized, like "the two scorpions in the bottle," that any forceful territorial change in Europe would unleash their strategic nuclear arsenal and thus bring unimaginable destruction to their countries, then their primary responsibility was, in spite of verbal declarations to the contrary, to maintain the status quo in Europe. That meant to keep the West Germans in the Atlantic alliance, the East Germans as part of the Warsaw Pact. The capital difference, however, remained that the West Germans did this by free choice, while the East Germans had no alternative but to submit to the command of the Soviet Union. The front lines of the Cold War and of a vigilant, often weary coexistence had been drawn.

It is fundamental to recognize that neither the workers' revolt in East Berlin in June 1953 nor the Hungarian rebellion of 1956, the building of the wall in Berlin in 1961 nor the occupation of Czechoslovakia in 1968, has altered this. In East Berlin, in Budapest, during the crushing of the "spring of Prague," the nuclear facts of life prevailed. They precluded any American action beyond the iron curtain and destroyed illusions to which those who knew quite well, even then, that Washington would not risk the lives of millions of its citizens for a rollback, had paid constant lip service.

The present relationship of Germany to the Atlantic Community grew out of the realization of the fact that, ever since the nuclear realities of life became dominant, a European policy must be cognizant of those "shades of gray" that mark our world and about which President Kennedy spoke. If there was to be any political, economic, or cultural movement at all, if an effort to reconcile with the East had to be undertaken, then it could only happen on the basis of the Federal Republic's firm commitment to the Atlantic alliance and in recognition of the realities after World War II.

It is not surprising that the first ideas toward a more active Eastern policy were conceived in West Berlin after that city was cut into two by the wall. Something had to be done to make the Federal Republic a partner in the diplomatic sense to the USSR and the Eastern European neighbors instead of the prime target for their frustrated propaganda against "the hotbed of imperialism." This was, in many ways, anathema to Chancellor Adenauer. But it became inevitable, especially after the consequences of the Cuban missile crisis of 1962, when the United States lost its undisputed nuclear and strategic superiority over the USSR and when "rough strategic parity" was achieved.

At the time when Adenauer left the political scene, the first efforts toward arms control between the two superpowers had already been made. The Federal Republic was well on its way to become the foremost economic power in Western Europe. The visible outer scars of World War II had disappeared. But one of their most positive consequences—the efforts to integrate West Germany into a political union such as the Treaty of Rome, which created what the European Economic Community had envisaged as the ultimate, political goal—had been undermined and almost destroyed by General de Gaulle's concept of a "Europe of the fatherlands." It thus threw the Western part of the continent back into the times before visionaries like Jean Monnet and Robert Schuman conceived their ideas of a supranational Europe as the only way to reassert the old continent's place in a world increasingly dominated by the fiat of the two superpowers.

Franco-German reconciliation had been formalized by the Franco-German Friendship Treaty of January 1963, which the general, shortly afterwards, compared to "roses and young maidens that wither soon," because it was overshadowed by Bonn's primary allegiance to NATO and to its link to the United States. As Washington, during Kennedy's presidency and Robert McNamara's aegis over the Pentagon, began to reconsider and adapt its strategy to the changing scene, as the White House began to think aloud about viable alternatives to the immediate escalation of any conflict into all-out nuclear war, as Washington became increasingly irritated by constant West German demands to confirm its undying love and fidelity to its partner in Bonn, and as the United States became more and more bogged down in the Vietnam war, it became imperative for the responsible people in Bonn to adapt their thinking and their policies to the new situation.

This was not easy for Chancellors Ludwig Erhard and Kurt Georg Kiesinger. The Gaullist doubt about the willingness of any American president to risk domestic nuclear devastation for the sake of Western Europe found many a follower. Bonn was torn between Washington and Paris. As de Gaulle, in 1966, left the military integration in NATO (although French forces remained in the Federal Republic by virture of a bilateral agreement) and began his own "Eastern policy," the West Germans felt increasingly alone. Could France become the spokesman of Western Europe for Moscow, Warsaw, and the rest? Was she to be the sole guarantor of "good German behavior" for Eastern Europe as well? Did de Gaulle really think that France's national nuclear force could replace the nuclear shield of the United States? Was he not, by stubbornly refusing Great Britain's entry into the Common Market, closing another important door to Atlantic policies? Did not this all prove how little political maneuverability West Germany had, that it was merely functioning as the political instrument of others? And where would it be left if, as de Gaulle gloomily foresaw, the United States were one day to leave the continent, particularly since the ideas of Senator Mansfield, the then majrotiy leader, of cutting down American forces in Europe sounded realistic in his country, which was torn by the war in Vietnam, the internal disorders, the racial tensions, and the assassinations of the sixties?

These fears, these apprehensions, had certainly some justification. They were often grossly exaggerated. The West Germans, economically powerful as they were, tended to superimpose their deep-rooted complexes of guilt and inferiority, which resulted from Hitler's days, upon the cool facts of postwar U.S. national interest in Europe. As close as the relationship between Bonn and Washington had become, somehow, for some reasons, many a West German politician seemed to be unable to come to grips with the ways in which the foreign and defense policies of the United States were planned and carried out. Adenauer's black-and-white thinking had led to the phenomenon that Bonn shuddered every time Washington developed new ideas or, worse, asked for them. The slow evolution from the freeze of the Cold War to a period of endeavors toward some sort of rules of conduct between the superpowers and its political consequences appeared to those Germans as a dangerous deviation from well-practiced ways. The complex machinery of decision making in Washington eluded them, notwithstanding the fact of a steady, often tiresome flow of official, semiofficial, and private visitors to Washington. They were the close, if not the closest allies of the United States. And yet, each time the president, the secretary of state, or some senator or congressman made a declaration, it was invariably scrutinized in Bonn under the heading: "Do they still love us?"

Small wonder that Washington, while officially proclaiming the strength of the alliance, was often irritated. This led to strange ways to woo European confidence in the American commitment, the strangest of which, in Johnson's days was the ill-fated "multilateral fleet," with "many fingers on the trigger," that was sunk before it ever floated, for it was not even possible to agree about the cooks who would cook the meals aboard these ships. It led to complicated, ramified systems of "double-key" activation of tactical nuclear weapons in case of war in Europe. It led to repeated American professions of faith in a European economic and political union in the face of de Gaulle's challenge and in spite of the fact that, quite early, strong forces on Capitol Hill perceived such a Europe as a potentially dangerous competitor to American exports.

If Konrad Adenauer had been "the good German toward the West," Willy Brandt, the first chancellor of a socialist-liberal coalition, should be called "the good German toward the East." The effort to normalize Bonn's relationships with the USSR, with Poland, Czechoslovakia, Hungary, and, last but by no means least, with the other German state, had begun under Chancellor Kiesinger and then Foreign Minister Gerhard Schröder, a fact that is often overlooked. But it was too early then, and the ties the Federal Republic had established between Washington and Paris did not lend themselves to the successful realization of that effort. Brandt made it conscientiously and forthrightly. He went to Moscow, to Warsaw, and to Erfurt. He established a modicum of trust in the Federal Republic in those countries that, after all, had primarily suffered from the terrible ravages of Hitler's war and where that memory had become an almost sterile obsession as well as the means to hinder every flexibility, every small movement. This step was not easy, nor did it prove popular with those citizens in the Federal Republic who saw it as proof that the hope for eventual reunification of the country had indeed gone away. But it was courageous. It was applauded by Bonn's Western allies if, tacitly perhaps, with a small amount of apprehension, since the ghost of a Rapallo agreement appeared to those who did not understand the nuclear facts of life. It was endorsed by the United States. For it seemed the only way really to achieve some easing of tensions, further commerce, reestablish broken human relationships, and avoid the conflict that nobody wanted.

Quite obviously, it influenced the Atlantic Community. NATO was primarily created as a defense organization. Now it was also to become a means to secure détente. But this could not be if the alliance was weakened in its defensive capacity. If the disparity between the conventional forces of the Warsaw Pact, especially its armor, and NATO grew, then détente would be nothing but a dangerous interlude that might finally tempt the

Soviets to threaten, to blackmail, or even to attack Western Europe. By the same token, as the seventies began, the Atlantic alliance and West Germany as its European center became influenced by the Strategic Arms Limitation Talks (SALT) between the United States and the Soviet Union. If Brandt and his successor Schmidt tried to enlarge political cooperation between Eastern and Western Europe, then the establishment of rules of conduct between the two giants in the strategic fields was an even more important factor, the consequences of which touched European security to the highest degree.

There has never been any official German criticism of or doubt about the SALT negotiations between Washington and Moscow. But any direct negotiation between the two superpowers on strategic matters must have a direct impact upon the security of Western Europe. In an extreme view, any such undertaking could be another effort to solidify the partition of the continent; for any movement, even a purely political one, beyond the established spheres of respective strategic interest could be seen as unbalancing and thus as a threat to peace. This, of course, was not the idea of Secretary of State Henry Kissinger. To him, SALT was mainly the setting of rules of conduct, the beginning of a more rational approach to the terrifying facts of constant nuclear armament, a way to negotiate among equals by setting some numerical limits and thus curtail the arms race. In its setting—before the end of the Vietnam war, accompanied by the historical breakthrough in relations with the People's Republic of China—SALT I remains a diplomatic masterstroke. In Kissinger's view, it could only come about by applying the classical principles of secret diplomacy. And that meant at times that even those who, like the West Europeans, had a direct stake in the outcome, had to be excluded from the process of the superpower dialogue. Kissinger, with his pronounced sense of history, knew that if one negotiates with a secretive power like the USSR, only the avoidance of public diplomacy can lead to results and real achievements.

Nixon and Kissinger practiced, for good reasons, a type of diplomacy that was basically alien to American thinking, but that certainly was—or should have been—understandable to Europeans. There was a definite accent of Gaullism in this diplomacy: sobered by the tragedy of the Vietnam war and the extent of its overcommitment overseas, faced with a multitude of domestic problems from the big cities to racial tensions, to the alienation of a part of American youth, and beset by doubts about its future role and purpose, such as most European countries had already experienced in their long and often tragic history, the United States began to redefine its national interests. It was certainly not easy for Americans to realize that one simply cannot win friends and influence people everywhere. The Wilsonian dream of a better world had foundered upon the resistance of a Congress that wanted America to retreat into the splendid isloation of the Roaring Twenties. Franklin Roosevelt's One World never came about. Nixon knew that America could no more function as the exclusive "policeman of the free world." Its policy had to set priorities. The foremost one was to avoid nuclear war by maintaining a credible deterrent and by negotiating about arms control, by engaging its main adversary in a dialogue that, hopefully, would open the way to real arms reduction and, finally, to disarmament.

This was the basis for SALT. For the first time, Washington and Moscow engaged in a process of mutual evaluation of the balance of terror by comparing their arsenals. A new breed of specialists in arms control was created. They could quite soberly discuss details that, in the final analysis, had to be resolved by an act of political will by the chiefs of government — hence the relationship of SALT to summitry. At the same time, a race for modernization and perfection of long-range strategic weapons within the set limits of the treaty began.

For the Germans it was quite important, right from the beginning, to establish certain relationships between the superpower dialogue on strategic arms control and those areas of European security that affected their national interest. In German thinking, which has since been voiced and described in the Atlantic decision-making bodies, SALT can have positive effects if, as a consequence, it will reduce the threat along the central sector of NATO. To Bonn it was quite important that, at their meeting in Vladivostok in December 1974, President Gerald Ford and General Secretary Leonid Brezhnev had excluded the so-called forward-based systems — nuclear carriers assigned to NATO — from the SALT II negotiations. For these medium-range weapons are a strategic threat to Europe. This applies especially to the new, mobile intermediate-range Soviet SS 20 missile and to the Backfire bomber. Conversely, the Soviets feel threatened by American land-based cruise missiles and the tactical aircraft with nuclear capabilities stationed in Western Europe and Great Britain and by the French and British national nuclear forces.

Within the Atlantic framework and as a consequence of the efforts toward détente, both the Vienna negotiations on mutual force reductions in Central Europe and the implementation of the final act of the Conference on European Security and Cooperation (CSCE) have had considerable influence upon Bonn's policy. The asymmetry or numerical inequality of the conventional forces of NATO and the Warsaw Pact are well known. The USSR and its allies have more tanks and men, and they constantly modernize and enlarge these forces, although this is disproportional to their real security needs. If, therefore, MBFR — in the German view — were to solidify this disparity without allowing for NATO to counter the threat by having weapons to deter it, if the Soviet goal of reducing the *Bun-*

deswehr below its present level were achieved, a dangerous upset of the balance of power would result. Also, these negotiations should not reduce the existing American commitment to the nuclear defense of Western Europe in case of war. Stabilization on the basis of unilateral reductions is to be avoided. This has been embodied in several resolutions that have been adopted among the Atlantic allies. Certainly, MBFR does not bear directly upon SALT. But if and when negotiations about a third SALT treaty begin, not only will they have to address the problem of gray zone weapons and thus of the immediate security of Central Europe, but also, in an indirect way, they will have to be related to the respective balance of conventional forces that is the subject of MBFR. Again, Germany will be a central topic, for it is there that the main dividing line exists and there, in case of conflict, the very first battles would be fought.

Chancellor Helmut Schmidt has quite definite views about these problems. To him, the gray zone weapons and their control are the basis for future arms control in Europe. He is an Atlanticist of the second generation: for him, there cannot be a substitute for the U.S. alliance in the area of security. As an inveterate pragmatist, Schmidt sees the changes that came about during the past three decades. He knows and embodies the economic and political power of today's Federal Republic in Europe. He does not hesitate to refer to either, even in talking to President Carter. Quite different from the Adenauer days, Schmidt voices his approval or rejection of American policies without hesitation. He does not shy away from lecturing the senior partner on such matters as economic or monetary policy and, at the same time, has no illusions about the real scope of a common Western European policy. Deep in his heart, he is skeptical about integrationism, he has profound doubts whether supranationalism is ever possible, and he wants Europe to evolve step by step by concrete measures, such as the new monetary unit.

Within the Atlantic councils, this chancellor has never shied away from outspokenness. Thus, he shocked the Carter administration when, with stubbornness and purpose, he refused to upgrade inflation in West Germany in order to help the United States out of the depression after 1974, voiced skepticism about the viability of the new president's human rights policy, or acted indignant when faced with a basic decision about production or deployment of the enhanced radiation or neutron weapon in NATO. There cannot, however, be the slightest doubt about Helmut Schmidt's allegiance to the Atlantic Community, especially to the Anglo-Saxon pragmatism that has characterized it for a long time. This does not exclude his personal relationship to French President Giscard d'Estaing, his former colleague as minister of finances and economy, whose cool, Cartesian pragmatism — and command of English — appeals to the chancellor. By the same token, Schmidt is a pragmatist toward détente: for a long time he has realized that the optimum of the efforts by his idealistic predecessor Brandt toward normalization and reconciliation with the East had soon been reached. Therefore, while it remains important to maintain these efforts especially in the human and economic areas, it is imperative to see their limits as realistically as possible.

It took the Germans—and many other Europeans—a good while to understand the person and the phenomenon of Jimmy Carter. It remains a fact of Atlantic life and especially of the German relationship to Washington that, in spite of the jet age's ever-shrinking distances, of the relative benefits of strong European currencies toward the dollar, and thus of tens of thousands of visitors to America every year, the bases and mechanisms of policy in the United States or, simply stated, "what makes them tick" are still rarely understood in Europe. The eminently American phenomenon of Carter, the setting of this president within his Southern Baptist origins and their mixture of idealism and fiscal conservatism, the appeal of the anti-Washington syndrome in today's America, the feelings and wishes of Middle America—all this eludes most Europeans. Thus, a proclamation of ideals is often seen as naive, the effort to come to grips with the energy problem as weak, the belief in fundamental good as antiquated. This created misunderstandings, most of which are quite un-necessary when projected against the real and pressing problems of our times.

Some German tourists are not assets to the Atlantic Community. Well-supplied with deutsche marks, they swarm through U.S. department stores, hunting for bargains. They point to so-called weaknesses, social ineptitudes, a "lack of culture" (as exemplified by chain-food stores and television commercials). Ultimately, they carry home intact the burden of their prejudices. They would probably be quite indignant if told that, basically, their attitude is not far apart from that of professional, young extreme leftists among German students and others, who make it a fashion to be anti-American for lack of knowledge about the United States and who, willy-nilly, are thus instruments of an Eastern propaganda that has not been silenced by the benefits of détente. But it would be naive to over-look this factor in an analysis of the past thirty years. It is, ironically, a consequence of the very prosperity of a consumer society that postwar American aid made possible. It is also a negative aspect of that reasser-tion of national identities in Europe that well-meaning Americans had demanded as early as the sixties.

President Carter has left no doubt that, to him, the Atlantic alliance and the basic American relationship to Western Europe are the cornerstone of the foreign and security policies of the United States. In fact, he has considerably enlarged the process of mutual and permanent consultation with the allies and sought, by frequent summit meetings with his partners, to deepen personal relationships that were quite unknown when the Atlantic Community and the Federal Republic began. The chiefs of government phone each other frequently; they try to solve upcoming and existing problems by talking directly. On this level, the physical and mental distances have shrunk from year to year.

And yet, compared to the 1950s and 1960s, there are certain trends of drifting apart. America and West Germany do not talk to each other as if Bonn were a part of a Western European political union. Bilateralism is by and large predominant, except in NATO meetings. The national legacy of de Gaulle is alive in spite of the fact there there is interdependency in such vital fields as security and energy. Europe has come of age. But it looks quite different from those hopes of the early 1950s. It is unable to speak with one voice, for there are considerable regional and economic differences between north and south. The reawakening of national interests manifests itself. Britain, although a member of the EEC, stands aloof from it. The great social questions in France and Italy are unresolved. Euro-communism is a fact, although it remains to be seen whether it really represents another form of an effort to master economic and social problems or whether it is the harbinger of a total change by revolution and the end of democracy. Terrorism, the most violent form of protest of the "children of the rich," is still a factor. Inflation is as well. And the modern weapons of war are costing such astronomical sums that, in order to maintain NATO's efficiency, a common effort must be made to maintain defense at the necessary level. Détente has lulled the senses of many a European, perhaps least those of the Germans. It could undermine the willpower requisite for the maintenance of a viable Atlantic Community.

The United States and the Soviet Union remain strategic competitors while trying to contain the arms race. Soviet expansionism, the symbol of which has become, among other things, a large, ocean-spanning modern fleet, continues unabated in areas around Europe, that is, in Africa, in Asia. The dawn of a new age may have broken when President Carter announced the full normalization of relations between the United States and the People's Republic of China. This development, in itself, is bound to destroy the remaining vestiges of the bipolarity between Washington and Moscow that has dominated the scene for well over a quarter century. The events in the Middle East bear directly upon Europe, the constant rise of the price of crude oil affects the Atlantic community in the most direct way. The diversification of the challenges is ever growing.

But it is necessary to distinguish between the shades of gray. For if there were any blurring of the real dividing line between individual freedom and the existence within a state-dominated order, then the Atlantic Community could fall apart at its spiritual base while its military mechanisms were still intact.

Nowhere but in Germany would this have the gravest consequences. There are very few people in West Germany who would go it alone, who think that by sheer economic power, the country could survive if the Atlantic link disappeared. They are in dire error. There is simply no substitute for freedom. And those who attack our society by denouncing its fat consumerism, by vowing to destroy it, while insisting upon reaping every guaranteed social benefit that is given to them, would then find themselves bitterly disappointed. However, it would be too late.

What is needed, at the outset of the fourth decade of Atlantic relationships, is a visible, renewed dedication to the principles of common heritage, of common defense, of common moral strength as the basis for the maintenance of peace. Neither the Americans nor the Germans can afford to drift apart. Solid national interests and economic investments determine the presence of the United States in Western Europe. Isolationism is, in our world, a total illusion. There is literally no room for it. But it will not be easy to combine the necessary resolve with the efforts to relax tensions. The Atlantic Community would have no raison d'être if it only functioned in times of those crises that it was created to avoid.

And lastly, it cannot be overlooked that we are living in what Sir Winston Churchill once described as "an age of outstanding mediocrity." The great men, the stirring words seem to have gone. But, as in life itself, the real proof of character comes more often in seemingly humdrum times than during the peak of a crisis. The Germans have had their share of crises. They have tried to normalize in a changing world. From their vantage point, there remain only two alternatives: to live in a society of free and diverse nations, as represented by the Atlantic Community and the Western European efforts, or to turn to the East. Most West Germans reject the latter. And if they continue to do so, they will remain partners of the United States within the Atlantic Community, in a more pragmatic, more mature way.

6

The United States and Germany

Martin J. Hillenbrand

The Formative Years

If a modern-day Rip van Winkle who had been associated with the early American occupation period in conquered Germany were now to awaken in the Taunus hills after more than thirty years of slumber, he would have a difficult time adjusting to the realities of the contemporary Federal Republic of Germany in all of its economic power and prosperity. The one familiar sight would perhaps be the visible presence of numerous American soldiers — no longer dispensing chocolate bars and cigarettes as symbols of victorious wealth and largesse, but still indispensably linked by their physical proximity to that minimal security that most adult Germans feel necessary for a reasonably normal life.

Certainly none of the Allied officials charged in those difficult formative years with responsibility for getting the elemental mechanisms of daily life functioning again would have dreamed that, within three decades, the larger part of a still-truncated Germany would become the strongest economic force in a non-Communist Europe — a force whose total volume of foreign trade would in 1978 exceed in value that of the United States. Economists often make poor prophets. The pessimistic predictions of those who staffed the economic sections of the U.S. military government and High Commission, or who were brought in as expert consultants, now lie mercifully buried under tons of files, never to be resurrected, in some federal storage center in the Middle West.

The success story of the Federal Republic is, of course, not one of purely economic achievement. Along with economic growth came the establishment and development of a stable and democratic political order that has proved its workability over thirty years. Successive German governments were able to overcome the heavy heritage of the Nazi regime and win gradual acceptance as members of the Western defense alliance and the general community of nations. But it was not all an easy process, destined to work out as it did. There were crises and decisive turning points along the way, when a different combination of men and circumstances might have changed the course of history. Similarly, it would be a mistake to assume that the German-American relationship, as it developed during the early postwar years and in the formative period of the Federal Republic, was in any way predestined.

The Federal Republic of Germany came into being in 1949 because the United States and its British and French Allies had, during the period of military government, made decisions about their zones of occupation in Germany, reflecting a radical change from the position they had held in 1945. Their purpose then was essentially punitive; and while their longer-term aims for Central Europe were confused, the idea of an extended military occupation was not one of them. Least of all did the United States have any imperialistic goals, if that definition would entail the permanent control of German territory or of the German economy.

The debate between revisionists and antirevisionists, which has been proceeding at various levels of politeness for more than a decade, mainly among American historians, is of more than academic interest in assessing the postwar German-American relationship.[1] For if the revisionists' theses were true — that the Western Allies, dominated by the United States, were primarily responsible for the breakdown of quadripartite military government in Germany and that the Cold War and the construction of the Western alliance was not a reaction to Soviet conduct, but an expression of Western imperialism or paranoia — then the entire moral basis for the initiatives of the late 1940s and early 1950s would be undermined. It is true that the judgments of historians on what happened more than thirty years ago cannot change the political, economic, and military realities of today. But great causes require that there be broad and continuing acceptance of the underlying truth they purport to represent. The establishment of the Federal Republic of Germany was part of a chain of events connected to what was seen as a worthy and great cause.

I have been associated with the postwar history of Germany as an American official, in one capacity or another, since early 1946; and I have made an extensive study of revisionist writings. It is my view that the Western response to Soviet conduct, or to reasonable deductions of motives from that conduct, was neither overblown nor insincere. Allied leaders may have made mistakes of judgment, but those mistakes were made in the peculiar psychological climate of those early postwar years, understanding of which seems to be almost totally lacking in revisionist literature. This is obviously not the place for an extended discussion of the subject, but it is not perverse to maintain that the basis for the postwar system as it emerged and developed was historically strong and morally valid.

Be that as it may, the original, essentially punitive, objectives of the

United States and its French and British allies quickly became obsolete in the face of the human realities of a country in total political and economic collapse. Moreover, Soviet aspirations came across as aggressive, obstructive, and ultimately absorptive with respect to Berlin and Germany as a whole. But Allied action to move toward the gradual economic union of their zones of occupation was not purely a response to Soviet obstruction of all-German economic cooperation. A rapidly decaying economic situation in the Western zones, where the black market reigned supreme and thrift and diligence had lost their normal value, required urgent action. Bizonia, then Trizonia, came into existence, and a harsh but successful currency reform in June 1948 (largely under American pressure and devising) prepared the way for the convening of the Parliamentary Assembly (*Parlamentarischer Rat*), the task of which was to draft a constitution for a new West German state. The Soviet blockade of Berlin and the spectacular airlift that it inspired confirmed that Allied policy was moving in the right direction and removed any lingering doubts the French might have had about the speed with which all of this was happening.

It would be idle to pretend that Americans did not try to influence the proceedings of the Parliamentary Assembly, but it was not done with a heavy hand—partly because the political scientists in military government and the special consultants enlisted for the purpose were not unanimous in their objectives. The document that finally emerged was essentially the product of its German drafters, infused with a strong dose of federalist theory. By any test of performance, the Basic Law has worked reasonably well. It has provided the Federal Republic with a functioning and stable constitutional order; and if certain inadequacies make it fall short of perfection, that is a distinction it shares with all other operating constitutions today. None of the hypercritical observations about the Basic Law came even close to appreciating the potential strength and flexibility of the new federal state.

It is a subject of continuing fascination to imagine what direction the Federal Republic of Germany might have taken if the dominating figure of Konrad Adenauer had not become chancellor in 1949 for what turned out to be a period of more than fourteen years. At seventy-three he was neither as imperturbable nor as conservative and Rhenish-minded as the superficial descriptions of journalists would have him, but a leader of strong will dedicated to several simple and overriding themes. In the implementation of those themes, which were of primarily formative influence in the foreign policy of the new Germany, the United States played an important role—even when it could not become a direct member, as in the case of the developing European institutions.

Once the Federal Republic had come into being, it was not always easy during the early years to separate foreign policy from internal policy. The

U.S. High Commission was very much there. High Commissioner John McCloy exercised great personal influence, and the inevitable insecurities and uncertainties of the new German state did not stop at any easily seen line of demarcation. The problem of German unity and the closely related problem of Berlin provided such a unique mélange of internal and external policy, with the three Western Allies alone competent under the residual occupation powers that they had retained to deal with the Soviets on these subjects, that this whole segment of German policy has necessarily had an unbalanced, complicated, and contrapuntal quality that it retains at least in part up to the present.

The Long Quest for Unity

To a whole generation of German specialists in the State Department (along with their counterparts in the French and British foreign ministries), the seemingly endless series of conferences, preparations for conferences, and related crises over Berlin and all that went with them provided many years of exhausting and frustrating effort. There was never much conviction that all of these negotiations with obdurate Soviet diplomats, sometimes under ultimative or quasi-ultimative threat directed at Berlin, had much chance of arriving at mutually acceptable agreements either on Berlin, on a method of arriving at the reunification of Germany in freedom, or on the kind of security arrangement for Central Europe that, it was assumed, must accompany any staged plan for the achievement of reunification. The effort, however, had to be made. Responsible American and Allied officials understood that unwillingness to engage in what might seem like purely ritualistic exercises would profoundly and negatively affect their whole relationship with the Federal Republic. The Eden Plan of 1955 and the Western Peace Plan of 1959 were both efforts to provide a comprehensive approach to the related problems of unification and European security. They were meticulously prepared and their component parts carefully articulated, but few on the Western side really entertained much hope that they would lead to productive negotiations with the Soviets.

A peculiar obsessive concern of Konrad Adenauer that plagued German-American relations during the period of his chancellorship was his fear that somehow, at some time, the United States and the Soviet Union would get together and work out a deal at German expense that would presumably sacrifice German interests in national unity and perhaps even security. The periodic crises of confidence between the two countries that occurred during the Adenauer era in one way or another involved this deep-seated suspicion of the chancellor. The means of relieving such "crises" became almost a matter of routine, involving either a visit by Adenauer to

Washington or a visit by the American secretary of state (and occasionally even the president) to Bonn. What these visits achieved was a reduction of suspicion, not its elimination.

This was coupled with the need for frequent public and private reassurance from the United States: reiteration of American devotion to the cause of unification, adherence to U.S. military commitments, and repetition by every visitng senior official of standard language guaranteeing the security of Berlin. By and large, Americans were understanding of these psychological needs, and if high officials sometimes grumbled and were minded to rebel, State Department briefing officers and the American ambassador in Bonn were, in the end, always able to persuade them that the likely price of refusal would far exceed any effort involved in overcoming personal distaste for repeating once again what had been said many times before.

The related issues of German reunification, European security, and Berlin were the great themes for East-West discussion during the Adenauer years; and most of the tensions between the United States and the Federal Republic arose within that general context. Even when there was little prospect for real negotiations, the chancellor feared that the three powers, and especially the United States and the United Kingdom, were prepared to go too fast and too far, making concessions that could threaten the ultimate existence of the Federal Republic. The problems that arose in the spring of 1959, when Adenauer in effect countermanded his Foreign Minister, von Brentano, in the preparation of the Western Peace Plan, provided a classic example. Needless to say, this evaluation was not shared by the Allied governments which were much more skeptical regarding Soviet tactical flexibility and willingness to negotiate seriously. They did not share the chancellor's lack of confidence in the strength of Western political institutions, which would have been tested with those of the Communist world had the Soviets accepted Western proposals.

We have now moved on to new concerns, or at least to new ways of formulating the old concerns. Yet the basic issues of a divided Germany remain unresolved and will continue in one form or another to burden the future of the Federal Republic and its Western Allies. If Chancellor Adenauer was overly suspicious of some senior American officials whose awareness of their own country's security interests in Europe would never have permitted them to accept the sort of arrangement that he feared, their expressed attitude toward the old chancellor and their understanding of German psychology sometimes fell considerably short of the desirable. It is fortunate that what seemed like damaging storms then now appear more like brief squalls. The Kennedy administration's attempt to avoid use of the term "reunification" and to substitute that of "self-determination" was not only psychologically inept, but totally unnecessary. It served no practical purpose and faded away with the administration that had given it birth.

The Federal Republic Joins
the Western Alliance System

Just as Soviet policies toward Germany hastened the creation of the Federal Republic of Germany, so Soviet actions during the Cold War speeded up the process by which, only a decade after the end of World War II, the new German state became a full member of the Western alliance. There were serious setbacks and disappointments along the way. Once the basic decision had been reached to proceed with the creation of the North Atlantic Treaty Organization, the question of German membership arose inevitably. Not only was the Federal Republic the forward line of defense, but Western conventional defensive strength would always fall short without German manpower. It was relatively easy for Americans to accept this, but for the leaders of European countries, which only a few years before had suffered the ravages of Nazi invasion and occupation, the dosage was too bitter to swallow in a single gulp. With the invasion of South Korea, the United States moved quickly in Europe to complete the organization of the NATO framework; and by the summer of 1951 had decided that some form of German defense contribution was essential. To make the idea more palatable, French Prime Minister René Pleven came forward with a proposal for an integrated, supranational European defense force in which the equivalent of twelve German divisions (the maximum to be allowed) would be incorporated. Thus there would be no possibility of a German general staff, and even at lower levels of command the responsibility would be multinational.

The sad story of the European Defense Community (EDC) is well known. Weak French governments were afraid to present the treaty for ratification to the National Assembly, and frequent requests for one last *condition préalable,* which the U.S. government uniformly met, never quite seemed to suffice. Even the threat of a possible "agonizing reappraisal" by Secretary of State Dulles had little effect. When the new French prime minister Pierre Mendès-France finally submitted the treaty to a vote in the National Assembly in August 1954, there was no longer a majority for it.

Both the German and American governments were glad to latch on to the improvization of Sir Anthony Eden, who proposed reviving the moribund Western European Union and converting it into an organization with certain control functions aimed at the Federal Republic. This arrangement was able to obtain French and general European acceptance of direct German membership in NATO. By the summer of 1955, with all the required ratification obtained, the Federal Republic entered the North Atlantic Treaty Organization as a full-fledged member. The end result was to enable a rapid buildup of the *Bundeswehr* in the 1950s and early 1960s until it became an impressive part of the conventional forces available to NATO. The role of the United States in providing equipment, guidance, and training during those early years was of great importance and created bonds between the armies and air forces of the two countries that continue up to the present. A special factor, of course, was the system of dual control over those tactical nuclear weapons deployed by the *Bundeswehr:* while the Germans possessed the delivery systems, the custody of the nuclear warheads remained in American hands — an arrangement still in effect.

The Federal Republic, Europe, and the United States

Konrad Adenauer was dedicated to the ideal of a united Europe based upon common Western ideals in an era when the old enmities (particularly those between France and Germany) would finally be laid aside. In Robert Schuman, Jean Monnet, Alcide de Gasperi, Paul Henri Spaak, and other contemporary statesmen and parliamentarians, he found a group of national leaders who thought in similar terms and were prepared to accept the diminution of national sovereignty as a necessary part of the movement toward a supranational integrated Europe. They were not always agreed as how to begin, or having begun with the European Coal and Steel Community, where next to move. But there was no question about their genuine idealism, or the attraction that the European movement had in those years for a generation of young Europeans looking for a cause amid the ruins left by World War II.

The same sort of sympathetic and generous appreciation of European needs that went into the Marshall Plan also characterized the basic American approach to European integration. There were some in Washington, of course, who saw an emerging Europe as a divisive force within NATO, but the policy that emerged strongly supported European efforts to unite — in fact so enthusiastically that American corridor activities at European conferences at times bordered on the importunate. In any event, the Europeans who drafted the treaty creating the European Coal and Steel Community, and later the European Defense Community, always knew what the United States thought about specific proposed language, and the detailed instructions from the State Department sometimes verged on the ridiculous. It was all well meant, however. The Americans had become enthusiastic Europeans, and since the Germans were generally in the forefront of drafting efforts toward integration, close German-American cooperation at the working level developed naturally.

The standard American doctrine, adhered to through successive administrations, with varying degrees of conviction, was that the United States was prepared to accept the short-run economic disadvantages that European integration might bring in order to achieve the long-run political gains of a united Europe able to speak with a single voice.

This close confluence of German and American policy on European integration did not derive only from the desirability of the main objective itself, but also from the realization that the moral rehabilitation of the Federal Republic would be greatly facilitated in a larger framework. Just as the European Defense Community seemed to provide such a framework for a German military contribution to Western defense, so the broader movement toward European integration served the larger psychological purpose.

As the emphasis shifted to economic integration with the Treaty of Rome (supported strongly by the United States), the coming to power in France of President Charles de Gaulle in 1958 created a new dilemma in German-American relations. The French leader, who thought in terms of a *Europe des patries,* resisted derogations of sovereignty by a supranational authority in Brussels (except the Common Agricultural Policy), and the close relationship that developed between Chancellor Adenauer and the French president made the former reluctant to push any policy in Europe that he knew would run into French opposition. The result was minimal movement toward political integration, and a frustrating struggle over British membership in the European Economic Community. This strained American patience and strengthened the position of those officials in Washington, particularly in the Department of Agriculture, who were primarily interested in American economic concerns in the community. Thus the great hopes and lofty idealism of the early 1950s were dissipated in the relative stagnation and transatlantic bickering of the 1960s. Even though the European Economic Community aided the economic growth of its members and the flow of trade among them, the European movement was never able to regain the momentum it had lost. A new generation of young Europeans found other interests, and the American enthusiasts for Europe (particularly in the Department of State) were forced to accept a reality considerably short of their earlier aspirations.

The American Military Presence

Certainly one of the most remarkable features of German-American relations during the existence of the Federal Republic has been the presence of a large American army and air force. What started out as a short-term, essentially punitive occupation has become a welcome, continuing fact of life, largely in the former American zone and Berlin (but recently also to the north). There is no historical precedent for the distinctive symbiotic relationship that has developed over the years between local German communities, governing authorities, and American forces in the areas concerned. Good working relations between American officers and German officials have become the rule, and when in the past they did not exist it was not automatically assumed on the American side that the U.S. command was blameless.

The most unusual arrangement spawned by the presence of so many American soldiers and airmen in the Federal Republic was the series of offset agreements negotiated between the German and American governments from the early 1960s until 1975 (emulated on a smaller scale by the United Kingdom and the Federal Republic). Although the American balance of payments problem dates back to the Eisenhower administration, it was President Kennedy's Secretary of Defense Robert McNamara who pushed through the first offset agreement. The idea caught hold and renewal of expiring agreements became more or less an automatic assumption on both sides, as unpleasant as the actual process of negotiating the agreements might be. Any American or German diplomat who became involved in the negotiations will not easily forget how protracted a haggle they were, often requiring intervention of the highest levels of government to settle unresolved issues.

There was always an element of gimmickry about the final offset package. The major component was U.S. arms sales to the Federal Republic, and skeptics might question whether a good portion of those sales would not have taken place anyway, with or without an offset agreement. Some sales, however, might have gone elsewhere, and the grand totals were in any case always impressive. Then there were the items of U.S. Treasury interest: low-interest loans, *Bundesbank* deposits in the United States, and other financial arrangements that could be counted as a German contribution to our balance of payments situation. Most helpful perhaps were direct German disbursements in the Federal Republic to help with the burden of local expenditures, such as the costs of a major barracks rehabilitation program. Each negotiation also regularly involved a dispute over what could and could not be counted as part of the German total. The United States was never willing to accept, for example, that the considerable annual German contribution to the American portion of Berlin occupation costs be included as part of the offset.

When Helmut Schmidt became chancellor, he brought with him the negative prejudice against the offset of a former finance minister and looked forward to the early demise of the whole arrangement. In 1975, the U.S. balance of payments situation temporarily improved; and during a visit to Washington in the summer of that year, he and President Ford reached the agreement that, since the reasons for the offset arrangements no longer existed, they should be terminated. Considering future American international economic performance, they could hardly have been more wrong. Not only did the U.S. balance of trade and current account position deteriorate drastically, but the sharp depreciation of the dollar in the past few years has greatly increased the annual foreign exchange cost of the U.S. forces in the Federal Republic, reducing as well the living standard of the individual soldier. It may seem somewhat surprising under these circumstances that neither in the U.S. Congress nor in the executive has there been any call for a revival of the offset agreements.

Détente, *Ostpolitik*, and Their Aftermath

The origins and interrelationship of détente policy and the *Ostpolitik* of the Federal Republic in the late 1960s and early 1970s make an interesting study in historical causation as well as in the creation of historical myths. Certainly Foreign Minister Gerhard Schröder showed considerably more flexibility than his predecessor in contemplating openings to the East, but the rigidities of the Hallstein Doctrine continued to prevail and the typical Foreign Office exercise was to mobilize its allies to engage in another worldwide campaign to prevent some country from recognizing the German Democratic Republic (GDR). The United States was neither enthusiastic about this policy nor believed it to be viable in the long run, although the State Department did its best to support it loyally in third countries.

Willy Brandt's period as foreign minister during the Grand Coalition under Chancellor Kurt Georg Kiesinger was essentially preparatory. When he himself became chancellor in the fall of 1969, he was ready to set his new policy in motion. It rested upon a few simple assumptions: (1) there was nothing to be gained by a refusal to recognize irrecoverable German territorial losses in the East due to the war; (2) the Hallstein Doctrine was about to collapse; (3) a policy of conciliation expressed through treaties with the Soviet Union and other Eastern European countries, and particularly willingness to move toward acceptance of the GDR, could win concessions in return, including improvements in the situation of the Western sectors of Berlin; and (4) all of this would, in effect, create the conditions for longer-term extension of German influence in Eastern Europe and for competition between Social Democracy and orthodox Marxism-Leninism, in which the superiority of the former would eventually be manifest and lead to a process of gradual change in the entire area.

It was, of course, legitimate to ask whether these assumptions were realistic. The initial White House reaction was much more simplistic, however, implying that a kind of Rapallo-type mentality had suddenly taken over in Bonn. National Security Council staff members voiced their suspicions and displeasure to all who would listen, including members of the press. The German effort to deal with this campaign was equally inept. Special emissaries were sent to the United States to plead the German case, some of whom attempted to use the Washington press corps to attack American officials held to be unsympathetic. Since such so-called backgrounding invariably came to the attention of the persons concerned, the net result was heightening of mutual bitterness and lessening of mutual understanding. In fact, some of the State Department officials believed by the coterie around Brandt to be unsympathetic were actually qualifiedly positive in their attitude toward the *Ostpolitik* and tried their best to achieve an open-minded approach to what they saw as an important new development in German policy. The Washington line that finally emerged was that the United States welcomed efforts by the government of the Federal Republic to improve its relations with its Eastern neighbors, including the Soviet Union, but that the precise modalities were, of course, a matter for decision by that government. The sniping from the White House continued sporadically, however, and even after the United States, France, and Britain had engaged with the Soviets in quadripartite negotiations over Berlin, the degree of enthusiasm displayed by Henry Kissinger and his staff was strictly limited.

There is no need to recount here the long and complicated story of the negotiations that led finally (on September 3, 1971) to the signing of the Quadripartite Agreement on Berlin. (The actual document signed by the four ambassadors was headed simply "Quadripartite Agreement," since the area to which it applied was one of the basic unresolved points.[2]) Their success had become the necessary condition for ratification by the *Bundestag* of the Moscow Treaty signed on August 12, 1970, between the Federal Republic and the Soviet Union, as well as for the whole process by which the German Democratic Republic would achieve the status and recognition that it so much wanted. Moreover, NATO members made their willingness to participate in the Conference on European Security and Cooperation (CSCE), much desired by the Soviet Union, dependent on the satisfactory outcome of the Berlin negotiations.

Initially, the Bureau of European Affairs in the State Department had developed the basic conceptual scheme for the negotiations, and for more than a year issued the basic instructions to the American negotiators. But as the stakes increased, the linkages assumed increasing political importance; and as the possible advantages to be gained from détente policy within this developing framework became apparent, the White House showed increasing interest. It was at this point that the inevitable so-called back-channel messages started flowing between Washington and Moscow — to the frustration of the British and the French and to the lesser bewilderment of Bonn, which was kept at least partially informed. Because of the confusing final stages of the quadripartite negotiations, of which the full record is not yet available, it is still impossible to write a definitive version of what really happened. The efforts made so far fall considerably short of telling the whole story.[3]

On the whole, the Quadripartite Agreement has worked to the advantage of the Western sectors of Berlin. As I have noted elsewhere,

> Whether a better agreement might have been obtained — through a little more patience, and under different negotiating conditions — is a controversial question, one which historians can dispute but can never answer with certitude. In any event, the primary Western objective — namely to obtain important improvements in the procedures for overland travel to and from Berlin by German civilians — was achieved in about as full measure as anyone could have expected.
>
> Other parts of the agreement, however, particularly those having to do with the ties between the Federal Republic and West Berlin and with the representation of the city's interests abroad by the Federal Republic, have been a source of difficulty and controversy with the Soviet Union and, undoubtedly, will continue to be so. Problems also have arisen in other areas, such as the movement of Berliners into East Berlin and the GDR; and the whole question of the applicability of the agreement to greater Berlin remains unresolved, the Soviets maintaining that the agreement pertains only to the three Western sectors of the city over which they now claim to have a certain *droit de regard*.[4]

Apart from the Quadripartite Agreement, the post-1972 period has been disillusioning for both the Federal Republic and the United States as far as relations with the Soviet Union are concerned. To the Soviets, détente was just another expression for the old concept of peaceful coexistence (a term that the United States carelessly allowed to creep into the Moscow Statement of Basic Principles of U.S.-Soviet Relations of May 29, 1972). This simply meant, as the Soviets have amply demonstrated in other areas of the world, particularly Africa, that they feel free to intervene on behalf of so-called antiimperialist liberation movements without regard to the effect that such intervention might have on the advanced industrialized countries of the Western world. Aside from a change in tactics, there is no real indication that their ultimate objectives with respect even to the Western sectors of Berlin have changed. They no longer see any advantage in dramatic attempts to force the Allies out of Berlin, but are prepared to wait until the city atrophies to the point that it becomes more of a liability than an asset to the West and hence ready for absorption by the GDR. The United States,

France, and the United Kingdom, together with the Federal Republic, have of course a continuing interest in maintaining the viability of the Western sectors of the city and in ensuring that this process of wasting away does not take place.

Nuclear Policy: A Thorny and Emotional Issue

Anyone who has witnessed the discussion between the United States and the Federal Republic of nuclear policy at any point along the way is likely to conclude that he has witnessed a classic case of a *dialogue des sourds.* The American approach, based upon intimate knowledge of nuclear weapons technology and the horrible destructiveness that it involves, has always been infused with a strong sense of moral fervor and a feeling of impatience with other countries that do not appear to understand the real issues at stake, or that raise essentially secondary issues as excuses for not doing what to the United States seems clearly right and proper.

The trouble started with the Non-Proliferation Treaty of 1968 (NPT), the purpose of which was to prevent the spread of nuclear weapons to all states that had not manufactured or exploded such a weapon or other device prior to January 1, 1967. Although disclaiming any intention of acquiring nuclear weapons, the manufacture of which had already been renounced at the time of Germany's entry into NATO, Bonn underwent great soul-searching about what was considered to be the asymmetrical nature of the NPT's provisions, which imposed obligations on the nonweapons states but not on the nuclear weapons powers. The Germans were particularly sensitive about possible commercial advantages that the nuclear weapons states might have and that the safeguards system under the International Atomic Energy Agency might give those states not being inspected as against those states being inspected. After much hesitation, the Federal Republic did sign and ratify the Non-Proliferation Treaty, and most of the fears that it would work to the commercial disadvantage of the nonweapons states have proved relatively groundless.

A whole series of other issues have since arisen, however, that have further strained the European-American relationship, and especially the American-German relationship. There was, first of all, the erratic performance of the United States in supplying enriched nuclear fuel, which led the Europeans to believe that the United States wished to preserve a monopoly of enrichment technology and facilities rather than permit the European Community to develop a Euratom enrichment plant. Without going into the details of a still tangled situation, the U.S. performance in this area has been neither a model of consistency nor diplomacy. The decision by the Nuclear Fuel Regulatory Commission in March 1975 to stop all exports of nuclear fuel and reactors pending a case-by-case examination of physical security measures came as yet another blow to the Europeans.[5]

The deal between Brazil and the Federal Republic to provide the former with uranium enrichment and reprocessing technology particularly led to years of talking at cross-purposes between the United States and the Federal Republic. Both sides failed to make a persuasive case with the other. The tone of moral superiority in the American position tended to infuriate the Germans, who regarded development of the fast breeder technology as both inevitable and desirable. The Carter administration took up the battle, begun under President Ford, with renewed vigor and managed to raise the level of mutual exacerbation without succeeding in changing German determination to proceed with the Brazilian transaction. Finally, at the London summit of May 1977, the agreement reached to sponsor the International Nuclear Fuel Cycle Evaluation Conference (INFEC), together with German commitments not to make any like arrangements in the future, removed the immediate heat from the issue, since the Germans understood that the Americans would now desist from attacking the Brazilian deal as such.

Since this whole area has become cluttered with misunderstood commitments and bungled diplomacy, some aspects of nuclear policy will most likely continue to trouble German-American relations in the future. One can only hope that intensity of moral fervor and righteous indignation on both sides will not again interfere with rational discourse. The American case is legitimate and important, but Washington needs to find more effective ways of presenting it.

The Quality of German-American Diplomacy

An important factor in the thirty-year relationship between the United States and the Federal Republic has been the quality of the diplomats on both sides. In the years after the war, no other single country now friendly has attracted the lasting interest and accumulated experience and knowledge of so many professional American Foreign Service officers as the Federal Republic. Experience in the military government period provided some, the generous staffing patterns of the United States High Commission others. And by the middle fifties a corps of highly competent American diplomats were prepared to dedicate the better part of their careers to service in Germany or, when in Washington, to dealing with Germany. The Office of German Affairs in the Bureau of European Affairs in the Department of State was consistently one of the strongest concentrations of specialized talent in that department under a succession of experienced directors. As the years went by, members of this group of German experts advanced to more senior positions both in Washington and abroad, and there was never a lack of talent to draw on during the various Berlin crises and the numerous high-level conferences on Germany and Berlin that characterized so much of the postwar period.

On the German side, there was on a somewhat smaller scale a similar focusing of talent on relations with the United States within the Foreign Office and the German embassy in Washington. During the late 1950s and early 1960s, the embassy was staffed with some of the most able German diplomats of that era. Gifted individuals like Osterheld, Schnippenkoetter, Balken, Straetling, von Staden, and many others were part of that group. Personal relationships between them and their American counterparts tended to become very close, closer than is normally the case in the itinerant and somewhat *déraciné* life of diplomats, and these friendships remained as professional and personal bonds in the years that followed.

The situation in the United States Foreign Service today is, regrettably, somewhat different than it was. The State Department has generally neglected the problem of professional succession in the Western and Central European area and has made no attempt, systematic or otherwise, to provide for the replacement of a whole generation of highly motivated Europeanists and, more specifically, the group dedicated to German affairs. The process of decomposition was accelerated by the premature departure from the department, because of organizational failures and bad personnel policies, of some of the most talented of the Germanists who might have been expected to rise to senior positions. Although there are, of course, some very able officers in the service who qualify as German experts, their number is small compared to the situation even a few years ago.

On the German side, a somewhat different process has taken place. Several able officers who had experience in American affairs died relatively young, whereas others were part of that fortunate generation that came to the fore in the last five years, advancing very rapidly to the top of their profession because of a missing generation within the hierarchy. With the retirement of most of the generation of German diplomats who served in senior positions throughout the postwar period, there was no generation to follow them because of the wartime gap. This has meant that officers in their forties have been able to advance very rapidly to senior positions, a development obviously good for personal careers but bad for continuity in dealing with American problems as a field of specialization at middle levels.

The Uneasy Present: Problems and Promise

There is a certain uneasy quality to German-American relations today. Few things seem to go quite right, and some things obviously go badly wrong. One hears in Bonn from old friends that relations between the two countries have never been worse, and while the sweep of such generalizations may perhaps be discounted as the hyperbole that stems from frustration, they do reflect a mood. Ironically enough, only a few years ago, during the Ford administration, one heard that German-American relations had never been better — likewise hyperbole reflecting little sense of history.

In European and German eyes the Carter administration brought with it a clear shift in emphasis. Not that the president did not say and do all the right things when he came to the NATO alliance. He has been reasonably effective (with the exception of his handling of the neutron bomb), although some crucial problems affecting the alliance and the German-American relationship obviously remain. In a deeper sense, however, Europeans have felt a real shift of primary interest in Washington, or at least that part of it that makes foreign policy, to other areas of the world. The alleged statement of a senior State Department official identified with the new administration to the effect that "Europe plays only a secondary role in the thinking of this administration; our priorities are elsewhere" has been widely quoted. One hears complaints in Bonn and other European capitals of the lack of an *interlocuteur valable* at senior levels in the State Department — someone with a deep and lasting interest in and knowledge of Europe, with the time to discuss intelligently problems of concern to Europeans (senior level being defined as above the level of assistant secretary, or, in other words, on the seventh floor of the State Department). The same generalization is made about the White House and the bureaucratic situation that prevails there. One of the established traditions, almost since the founding of the Federal Republic, has been the constant stream of visitors to Washington from the *Bundestag* — sometimes a nuisance for overworked State Department officials, but part of a highly important educative process. There was always a certain element of competiton (at times ludicrous) about who could see the most senior officials, and party leaders would rather cancel their trips (and sometimes did) if they could not be assured of seeing the president. It may have been a bother, but the fact that it was really important to the German visitors justified the time and effort spent. The president is generally still accessible to such dignitaries, I am informed, but contacts elsewhere in the senior Washington hierarchy do not seem to satisfy as they once did.

Whether these are immediately remediable problems is doubtful, given the individuals involved and their interests and prejudices. Nor is there much that can be done about the fact, well known in Bonn and Washington, that Chancellor Schmidt and President Carter do not find each other particularly congenial. Antipathies between leaders have existed before, and they have been able to work together when they must for the good of their countries.

What is of overriding importance is the increasing dominance of economic and monetary factors in recent years, and the erosion of American influence and prestige that our international performance in those areas has brought about. Some Europeans, including the chancellor, with his economic training and experience, have an easy explanation for the pressures and imbalances that have developed among the advanced industrial countries of the OECD world. They regard the United States as, in effect, having obtained for many years a free ride with its overvalued currency, a period during which American multinational firms were able to expand their direct investments in Europe on an extensive scale. At the same time, and continuing after the abandonment of the fixed exchange rate system, the United States was able to finance its balance of payments deficits, which were of course augmented by these heavy capital flows, by flooding Europe with dollars, thus creating and expanding more or less without inhibition the so-called Eurodollar market, the source, in this version of events, of much of the inflationary pressures in Europe during the past decade.

Many German economists and bankers would not accept such a simplistic line of argument without considerable qualification, but elements of it provide the intellectual background against which the performance of the United States in the past two years has been judged (notably in the Federal Republic and generally in Western Europe).

To Europeans and specifically Germans, the initial U.S. Treasury policy of announced indifference to the exchange rate of the dollar seemed totally incompatible with the leadership role of the United States and with the function of the dollar as a world reserve currency. Even the most pessimistic among them did not foresee the catastrophic fall of the dollar on the monetary exchanges (relative to the strong—and some not so strong—currencies of the world) that took place between the summer of 1977 and the end of October 1978.

As time went on and the dollar continued to decline, the U.S. government changed its alignment. The enemy was now "disorderly market conditions," and these could be rectified through timely central bank intervention. Reference was also made to the fundamental factors affecting the value of the dollar, presumably the balance of payments situation and particularly the oil import component, the greater U.S. economic growth rate as compared to the Federal Republic and Japan, and finally the increasing U.S. rate of inflation. What was difficult for Europeans—and not least the Germans—to understand was Washington's apparent failure to appreciate that American economic and monetary performance was not an isolated phenomenon; and that American political and military leadership would be impaired if its currency and the quality of its economic policymaking became an object of derision. Hence the Federal Republic strongly welcomed President Carter's program of November 1978 to stabilize the dollar, mobilizing some 30 billion dollars from various sources for support operations, plus other measures including Federal Reserve Board interest rate increases. It seemed, finally, to reflect the president's realization that more was at stake than purely dollar depreciation or the effects of such depreciation on the U.S. internal rate of inflation. The initial impact on the dollar exchange rate was favorable, but what will happen in 1979 and beyond is an open question.

As one looks at the issues between the Federal Republic and the United States—nuclear fuel supply policy, the sale of full fuel cycle reprocessing technology to Brazil, Germany as the locomotive of economic growth, the neutron bomb, the question of Eurostrategic systems and SALT II, U.S. human rights policy and its possible effect on German repatriation arrangements with the Soviet Union and Eastern Europe, differences of approach in the General Agreement on Tariffs and Trade (GATT) negotiations at Geneva—one can see both continuities with the past and the foreshadowing of new problems.

As so often before in the thirty-year relationship between the United States and the Federal Republic, the problems that will face the two countries will frequently arise within a multilateral rather than a bilateral framework. In other words, they cannot be solved simply between Bonn and Washington, although agreement between those two capitals can sometimes provide a helpful impetus toward solution. There have been voices suggesting that the United States should give up the whole effort of trying to deal with Europe and rely essentially on a bilateral relationship with the Federal Republic of Germany. Such an approach has never been practical, never acceptable to the Federal Republic, and today makes less sense than ever.

In the decade ahead—years of difficult structural change for the advanced industrial countries of the West and for Japan—economic problems are likely to play an ever more important role in determining the policies of governments and in placing strains upon the Atlantic world. In this context, the need for a sympathetic relationship at senior levels of government dealing with economic matters in Bonn and Washington is obvious. Required also is continuing recognition in Washington that economics may involve matters of highest political concern and consequence, and that in such cases political judgment must be brought to bear from the outset.

The alliance system centered in NATO remains as indispensable as ever to the security of the United States, the Federal Republic, and its other member states. The mainstream of thinking both in Bonn and Washington holds firmly to this conviction and is likely to continue to do so as long as there is no fundamental change in the circumstances that provide the basis for it. The strange idea that Europe, either in a military or economic sense, has become of secondary interest to the United States is demonstrable nonsense. Nothing must occur that would significantly weaken the credibility of the U.S. nuclear deterrent, the bedrock of NATO strategy and the basis of Western security. Although the suspicion aired occasionally in the United States that there exists a neo-Rapallo or neutralist tendency among a group of Social Democratic Party (SDP) politicians is, in my view, unfounded,[6] it could become a reality if the conviction were to spread in the Federal Republic that the U.S. strategic deterrent were effectively being decoupled from the defense of Europe.

In writing a review that encompasses thirty years of phenomenal growth and difficult problems, one inevitably emphasizes the problems. Historians and journalists both tend to do so, for the interest lies in the problems not in the panegyrics. But it would leave a sense of imbalance not to conclude on a note of qualified optimism. Certainly the problems in German-American relations are many and difficult, but they were so thirty years ago. If the same qualities of dedication, talent, and intelligence are devoted to the solution of the problems ahead, there is no reason to think that they cannot be mastered with the same success as were those of the past. Much depends on the orientation and the will of the successor generation in both the Federal Republic and the United States.

Notes

1. The most balanced presentation of a non-Marxist revisionist approach is Daniel Yergin's *Shattered Peace* (Boston: Houghton Mifflin, 1977); the best anti-revisionist treatment is John Lewis Gaddis's *The United States and the Origins of the Cold War 1941-1947* (New York: Columbia University Press, 1972).

2. See *Quadripartite Agreement on Berlin. Final Quadripartite Protocol*, Treaties and Other International Acts Series 7551 (Washington, D.C.: Department of State, 1972).

3. So far, the best published account of the negotiations is Honoré M. Catudal, Jr., *The Diplomacy of the Quadripartite Agreement on Berlin* (Berlin: Berlin Verlag, 1977).

4. Review of Catudal's book in *Orbis* 22 (Fall 1978):756-757.

5. For a succinct review of U.S. policy evolution in this entire area, see Charles K. Ebinger, *International Politics of Nuclear Energy* (Washington, D.C.: Center for Strategic and International Studies, 1978).

6. Egon Bahr, SPD party business manager, who is frequently identified with this group, has recently issued a statement describing as foolish any ideas about the neutralization of Germany, saying that the only security for Europe lies with the United States and that he envisaged no change in this situation in the foreseeable future. *Die Welt*, December 1, 1978.

7

Germany, France, and Europe

F. Roy Willis

Franco-German reconciliation has become one of the truisms of international politics. Commenting in 1976 on the possible consequences of the coming *Bundestag* elections for West German foreign policy, Alfred Frisch noted:

> Close Franco-German cooperation is no longer a dream but a daily reality. The mutual trust that unites the two heads of government [Helmut Schmidt and Valéry Giscard d'Estaing] is not its only foundation. Henceforth it has a wide base, thanks to the permanent contacts between all the ministries and the principal administrative offices. We are far from the preamble added, at the time of the ratification of the Franco-German treaty of 1963, by the *Bundestag* to assure the primacy of the Atlantic ties. No one today can fail to know that there will be no progress in Europe without perfect Franco-German understanding, which has thus become an indispensable factor in Western stability.[1]

The process by which this harmonious relationship was achieved, after centuries of "traditional enmity," was fraught with hazards.[2] At every new stage, crises of misunderstanding and conflicts of interest threatened what had already been achieved. The essential reason why no crisis ever culminated in the destruction of the bases of understanding was, however, that this understanding was founded upon "common bases of economic development"—as French Foreign Minister Robert Schuman proposed in his speech of May 9, 1950, calling for the integration of the French and German coal and steel industries. From that moment, the effort "to eliminate Franco-German hostility once and for all" became inextricably linked with the effort to integrate Western Europe, both politically and economically. In that way, the reconciliation of France and Germany, which might have raised the terrifying prospect of Franco-German hegemony, was made desirable to their smaller neighbors.

This chapter will examine the evolution of the role of France and of European integration in West German foreign policy. From 1945 to 1949, a basis for future understanding was laid in the French zone of occupation, in spite of the implementation by the French military government of a policy of economic exploitation. From 1949-1958, Chancellor Konrad Adenauer, working above all with fellow Christian Democrat Robert Schuman, sought to use the formation of the European Coal and Steel Community (ECSC) and the European Economic Community (EEC) or Common Market as the framework within which understanding with France could be given material bases. Between 1958 and 1969, French President Charles de Gaulle dominated a stormy, crisis-laden relationship with Chancellors Adenauer (until 1963), Ludwig Erhard (1963-1966), and Kurt Georg Kiesinger (1966-1969), in which the bilateral relationship culminated in the Friendship Treaty of 1963, but relations within EEC were disturbed by de Gaulle's determination to block any form of European political integration. Finally, since 1969, the two Social democratic Chancellors Willy Brandt (1969-1974) and Helmut Schmidt (1974-   ) have maintained a pragmatic, undramatic, but essentially unproductive working relationship with the French Presidents Georges Pompidou (1969-1974) and Valéry Giscard d'Estaing (1974-   ).

The Legacy of the Occupation, 1945-1949

West Germany was not entirely without a foreign policy during the four years of Allied military government. The reaction of the civilian population to the implementation of Allied directives in the three zones and in particular the degree of participation of German leaders in carrying out occupation policy were significant expressions of policy toward foreign powers. Moreover, with the restoration of a degree of autonomous *Land* government in 1947, the minister-presidents and the *Landtage* became spokesmen on foreign policy matters, until the formation of the federal government in Bonn in September 1949.

In addition to their sector of Berlin, the French controlled an hourglass-shaped zone cut from the original American and British zones, which they organized into three new *Länder*—Rheinland-Pfalz, Süd-Baden and Süd Württemberg. (The Saar was fused economically with France.) Until 1946, French policy toward Germany as a whole was based upon the so-called French thesis elaborated by General de Gaulle, which called for the dismemberment of Germany and the internationalization of the Ruhr.[3] The populations of the southern Rhineland, traditionally felt to be more influenced by France than the Prussianized Germans to the east of the Rhine,

were to be welcomed, in de Gaulle's words, into a "moral and economic
union" with France.[4] The 6-million German population of the French zone
welcomed every French initiative to seek a closer cultural and personal
understanding, but equally adamantly refused to support any French
moves to weaken their ties to the rest of Germany. As a result, the great
successes of French occupation lay in education and culture. The creation
of the University of Mainz was the crowning triumph of a policy that
brought about the exchange between the two countries of hundreds of
students, writers, artists, workers, and even politicians. It left an in-
estimable legacy of good will that was to be translated into political action
after 1949.[5] German willingness to reciprocate in the search for closer relations was proven with such actions as the foundation in 1948 of the *Deutsch-
Französisches Institut* of Ludwigsburg, the participation in Emmanuel
Mounier's Committee for Exchanges with New Germany, the rush to
enroll in French language classes at the four new French Institutes, and
especially the rapid growth of the movement of "twinning" of cities and
provinces in the two countries. The movement begun during the occupation became ever more widespread after 1949. By 1963, 115 German towns
had twins in France. Twenty-six towns had "Franco-German societies" for
the study of French culture. Private groups of almost every kind from ap-
prentices to mayors had links with corresponding groups in France.
Perhaps most important of all, from 1956 on French and German political,
business, and intellectual leaders met regularly in "Franco-German conferences," sponsored by the European Movement, to discuss topics of world
politics.[6] The multifarious personal contacts between individual French
and German people were the starting point of the new era of West German
foreign policy toward France, distinguishing it from the generations of
mutual incomprehension that contributed to the coming of the First and
Second World War.[7]

Germans in the French zone were less sympathetic to the political and
economic goals of the occupation. By 1948, Germans had virtually broken
off their participation in denazification. Workers had gone on strike and the
Land government of Süd-Württemberg had resigned in protest against the
dismantling of industrial equipment for reparations. The exploitation of
the Saar had been bitterly criticized both in the Saar itself and in the zone.
Above all, the *Landtage* and the *Land* cabinets had used their new authority
after the elections of 1947 to speak out against French efforts to delay the
fusion of the French zone with the British and American zones in a federal
republic.[8] The growing protests of the *Land* governments and *Landtage* undoubtedly hastened to some extent the French decision to permit the creation of the *Bundesrepublik*.[9]

Adenauer, Schuman, and the
Launching of Europe, 1949-1958

If the occupation period prepared the way for the closer personal relationships between Germans and French, the first four years of Adenauer's
chancellorship saw the construction of the organizational basis of European
integration, within which a new political relationship between the two states
could be developed. Credit for this achievement belongs to the three Christian democrats of the West European borderlands—Adenauer of the
Rhineland, Schuman of Lorraine, and Alcide de Gasperi of the Tren-
tino—as well as to Jean Monnet, the creative genius who first presented
them with the practical plans they might implement.[10]

In the early days of the Bonn republic, Adenauer tended to regard the
French as the main obstacle to the full restoration of German sovereignty.
His principal opponent in the Allied High Commission, which replaced the
military governments as supervisor of the new German democracy, was the
acerbically witty André François-Poncet whose tendency to lecture the
equally intransigent chancellor led Adenauer to think of his visits to the
commission's headquarters on the Petersberg as a "weekly Golgotha." Yet,
as Adenauer explained in an interview with *Die Zeit* on November 3,
1949: "I am resolved to make German-French relations a cardinal point of
my policy. . . . Friendship with France requires greater efforts [than friendship with Britain] because it has so far labored under inhibitions. It
becomes the cardinal point of our policy because it is its sore point."[11] In
German eyes, the most outstanding grievance was the economic fusion of
the Saar with France in 1948, as the chancellor pointed out in his in-
vestiture speech of September 20, 1949. German outrage increased in 1950
with the negotiation of conventions between the *Land* government of the
Saar and the French government without consultation with the federal German government; and the attempts to Europeanize the Saar by agreement
between the governments were rejected by the Saar population itself, when
it voted in October 1955 to return to Germany.[12] In Adenauer's view,
drastic measures were needed to reverse the attitude of mistrust that created
such conflicts as the Saar question. His first, rather ill-timed gesture was his
suggestion to an American journalist in March 1950 that France and Germany should be completely united, beginning with a customs union and
customs parliament like that of the German *Zollverein* in the early nineteenth century.[13] Although this startling proposal was ignored by the
French government, it was a sign that Adenauer was prepared for precisely
the form of integration that Schuman was to offer on May 9, in his proposal
for the formation of a European Coal and Steel Community. Although he
was only informed of Schuman's intention the very day of its public an-

nouncement, Adenauer welcomed it at once. As he wrote in his *Memoirs*, "Schuman's plan corresponded entirely with the ideas I had been advocating for a long time concerning the integration of the key industries of Europe. I informed Robert Schuman at once that I accepted his proposal wholeheartedly."[14]

The Schuman Plan, however, emphasized the vast gulf in Germany separating the foreign policy goals of the Christian Democratic party and the opposition Socialist party headed by Kurt Schumacher. To link the western portion of a divided Germany in an integrated, capitalist Europe would, in Schumacher's view, permanently prevent the reunification of Germany. Moreover, the new Europe, he said, would be dominated by the four Ks — *Kapitalismus, Klerikalismus, Konservatismus,* and *Kartels.*[15] Rather surprisingly, those very business leaders in Germany whom Schumacher saw as the gainers from the plan were equally opposed, although on very different grounds. Many saw it as another nefarious French scheme to break up German cartels, to get cheap access to Ruhr coal, and to dump French steel in an unprotected German market; and business groups finally acquiesced in the plan on the ground that economic sacrifices had to be made for the political benefit of strengthening Western Europe.[16] The Schuman Plan treaty was finally ratified in January 1952. By then however it had become embroiled in a far more explosive issue, that of German rearmament, which awakened all the mutual distrust between the two nations.

Adenauer was deeply concerned with the direct threat posed by the Soviet Union, and indeed by East Germany, to the security of the Federal Republic. At the same time, as Alfred Grosser has pointed out, as long as a state of Cold War existed, "the tension between the two camps tends to speed up the process by which federal Germany is integrated, on a footing of equality, into one of them, and becomes a free agent in the West instead of a mere object of international politics. The price is a deepening of the gulf between the two Germanies, but the Federal Republic gains greatly in prestige and influence."[17] German rearmament was thus both a necessary contribution to West Germany's own security and a gauge of its equality within the Western alliance. As late as 1949, however, the French were adamantly opposed to any form of German rearmament. The debate in the National Assembly on the North Atlantic Pact was marked by an outpouring, from all sides of the chamber, of expressions of distrust of Germany, with the result that Robert Schuman had to give assurance that the Germans would be given neither army nor weapons.[18] American pressure, following the early defeats in Korea in the summer of 1950, for the creation of West German defense forces precipitated the long crisis of the European Defense Community (EDC). To avoid the creation of a national German army, French Premier René Pleven proposed in October the creation of an integrated European army, within which the Germans could provide a number of small combat groups.[19] The appeal of the new proposal to the supporters of integration in both France and Germany was its impetus toward political integration, since a European government was seen to be necessary to command the European army.[20] Adenauer, whose goal was the restoration of full German equality by one means or another, first demanded a national army, but then followed the American swing to support of the French position, knowing that the essential gain for Germany was the abolition of the Occupation Statute.[21] The internal crisis in Germany far surpassed his expectations. The reviving veterans' groups enthusiasticaslly supported rearmament, which implied their own rehabilitation, but criticized the French desire to restrict the independence of the new German forces. Some Christian Democrats spoke out in favor because European integration would be advanced. But massive opposition was expressed by youths of draft age (especially in the universities), by the churches, by some of the trade unions, and above all by the Social Democrats.[22] During the second reading of the EDC Treaty, the police were compelled to battle with water cannons against the opponents of rearmament, who turned the *Bundestag* grounds into a battlefield. Thus for four years, from 1950 to 1954, Adenauer was compelled to stake his prestige, and the prospect for continuing Franco-German cooperation, upon implementation of a treaty whose existence was due to French distrust of Germany. The final blow appeared to have been struck by the French assembly when on August 30, 1954, it rejected the EDC Treaty in a vote that united both Right and Left in a common fear of German rearmament.[23] Paradoxically, the French vote strengthened the German claim to membership in NATO on a national basis, since, as Adenauer pointed out, the West Germans had fulfilled all their commitments to EDC.[24] The alternative solution, German membership in a broadened Western European Union, was far more popular in Germany than EDC had been; and its acceptance by the French assembly showed that the French Right had been more concerned about the denationalization of the French army than the re-creation of a German army.

With the resolution of the problem of German rearmament, Franco-German relations again became amicable. Between 1955 and 1958, the most concrete steps in cooperation of all the postwar years were taken. First, the Saar problem was settled, with the official reunion of the Saar to Germany in January 1957; and a physical gauge of future collaboration was created with the construction of the Moselle Canal. Second, a vigorous effort was made to expand Franco-German economic contacts, through the creation of the Offizielle Deutsch-Französische Handelskammer and the signing of a commercial treaty in 1955. Third, the French and German governments gave up the battling within the European Coal and Steel Community that had brought it to the point of collapse in 1954 and led its first president, Jean Monnet, to resign in disgust. Above all, however, in the long, involved negotiations in 1955-1957 of the treaties creating the European Economic Community and the European Atomic Energy Community, the French and German delegations never lost sight of the ultimate benefits to both from the creation of the new Community. Adenauer was no longer working with so trusted a collaborator as Schuman, who had ceased to be foreign minister in 1953, or even another Christian Democrat like Georges Bidault. But the government of Socialist Guy Mollet, formed in January 1956, proved itself almost equally European-minded, even if hardheaded in its demands for aid to the French colonies and for markets for French agriculture.[25] Moreover, inside Germany, the EEC Treaty was receiving wide support. The Social Democrats supported it from its inception, and the party chairman, Erich Ollenhauer, symbolized the SPD's change of attitude by becoming a founding member of Jean Monnet's Action Committee for the United States of Europe. Most business groups were in favor of participation in a wider economic union, although they shared the fears of Adenauer's Finance Minister Ludwig Erhard of the possible *dirigisme* of the future Community authorities. And public opinion was virtually united in favor of more rapid European unification.[26] When the EEC Treaty was presented in the *Bundestag,* it was ratified by a large majority with a show of hands.

Acceptance of the Treaties of Rome implied a major new orientation for West German foreign policy. With the completion of the three planned stages of customs reduction, which was achieved in 1968, industrial goods would circulate freely among the six members. At the same time, a more complicated method was to be created for ensuring the establishment of common agricultural prices in the Community, thus opening the highly protected German agricultural market to French production. Workers and capital were to circulate with much greater freedom. Even more important for the future, however, membership in the community was assumed, at least at the time of its foundation, to be a commitment to participate in the establishment of a genuine economic union, with common commercial and other policies and eventually with a common currency, and in the gradual renunciation of national sovereignty in favor of a supranational European government. Although an attempt was made to keep open the question of West Germany's relations with East Germany, such a union could only imply acceptance of the division of the country.[27]

The economic results for West Germany and France of participation in EEC were even better than hoped, especially in increasing their interdependence. Franco-German trade tripled during the first four years of EEC (1958-1962) and, by 1970, had quadrupled.[28] In 1960, France became Germany's most important customer. Eight years later, France became Germany's principal supplier. German sales in France rose from 4.9 billion francs in 1960 to 23.4 billion francs in 1970 to reach their highest point in 1974 at 48.9 billion francs. French sales to Germany rose from 4.7 billion francs in 1960 to 20.5 billion francs in 1970, also reaching a postwar height in 1974 at 37.9 billion francs. As might be expected, German exports to France were primarily finished and semifinished industrial goods. French agricultural products, however, accounted for only one-third of French exports. French exports never covered more than 92 percent of French imports from Germany; and this unfavorable trade balance helped explain much of the French determination to force Germany to accept their conditions on implementation of EEC's common agricultural policy.[29]

The freeing of capital flows within the European Economic Community brought about an acceleration of business investment. By 1973, French investments in Germany totaled 1,900 million DM, including both direct investments in German companies, especially in mining and metallurgy, and the opening of subsidiaries of French companies. The Saint-Gobin–Pont-à-Mousson chemical and metallurgical company was by far the most active in opening German subsidiaries. In the 1970s, it employed 30,000 German workers. German investments, which up to 1965 had been about level with the French investment in Germany, soared during the 1970s, to reach 3,207 million DM in 1973. The Common Market had thus helped bring about that tight interlocking of mutual interests that Schuman and Adenauer had envisaged in 1950. The more dramatic ventures included the building of the Airbus in 1969-1974 by French and German companies; and a nuclear reactor had been constructed for the Franco-German Institute of Grenoble. But the more significant progress was represented by the hundreds of banks, chemical and pharmaceutical companies, mining enterprises, automobile works, and sales agencies, which had covered the two countries with a network of cooperating groups.[30] In all the crises that pitted France against Germany within EEC during the 1960s and 1970s, the business community of both countries reminded their own governments that it was unthinkable that either country should permit the lasting paralysis of the community.

Franco-German Relations during the Presidency of de Gaulle, 1958-1969

From the first moment of his return to power in France in June 1958, Charles de Gaulle struck at two of the supporting pillars of Adenauer's foreign policy: the special relationship with the United States and to a lesser degree with Great Britain and the drive to create a supranational authority for Western Europe through the European Economic Community. In compensation, de Gaulle displayed a genuine determination to compel EEC to achieve its economic (though not its political) goals and a sincere desire to make Franco-German understanding the basis of his plan for a "Europe of the States."[31]

Adenauer had at first expressed disquiet about the circumstances of de Gaulle's appointment as premier, as a result of a military coup in Algeria; but during his first visit to de Gaulle at his country home at Colombey-les-Deux-Eglises, he was seduced. During the declining years of his chancellorship, he appeared (to German opinion) to be subordinating more and more his own long-term goals for Germany to the wishes of his persuasive French partner. François-Poncet explained the mutual attraction of the two men as due to their "profound humanity, natural elevation of thought, the ability to neglect details in order to grasp the main lines and the simple, basic structure of a situation, purity of motives, and obstinate energy in pursuit of a clearly perceived objective."[32] But there was little doubt that de Gaulle was willing to use Adenauer's almost desperate wish to crown his political career by making permanent the understanding between their two countries to force concessions on points to which the majority of German opinion was opposed.

De Gaulle's plans for the Common Market were most directly opposed by Finance Minister Ludwig Erhard, who wished to keep open all possible trading opportunities with Britain and the other members of the European Free Trade Association. Again and again, Erhard attempted to prevent the French from forcing EEC to adopt a high common external tariff that would inhibit trade with nonmembers. He opposed acceleration of the reduction of tariffs within the Community. And above all he fought against the French attempt to open the German market to French agricultural goods through the implementation of the common agricultural policy. The great EEC marathon negotiation of January 1962, from which the common agricultural policy finally emerged, was in reality a rearguard action fought by the Germans against French demands. Throughout these negotiations, Adenauer sided with de Gaulle against his own finance minister. He did not, however, support de Gaulle's efforts in 1960-1961 to persuade the six EEC members to form a political secretariat in Paris for coordination of their foreign policies, since that would only too clearly be an acknowledgment of French hegemony of the Community, yet most German observers felt that he failed to realize that the Franco-German Friendship Treaty negotiated in 1962 was de Gaulle's substitute for the unwanted political union.[33]

The Franco-German treaty was intended to be the culmination of the carefully staged state visits of Adenauer to France (July 2-8, 1962) and of de Gaulle to Germany (September 4-9, 1962). During those visits, symbolic gestures abounded — mass together in Rheims cathedral, a march-past of French and German troops, de Gaulle's surprise admission that one of his own ancestors was German. The treaty was to institutionalize these good relations, by providing for regular consultation at several levels of government, for prior consultation on important questions of foreign policy, and for vastly expanded cultural and youth exchanges. However, de Gaulle's veto on British membership in EEC, announced without prior notification to Adenauer, at his press conference of January 13, 1963, totally destroyed the élan that the state visits had provoked. In this context, the Franco-German treaty appeared to German politicians of all parties as an anti-American gesture, an acceptance of French dominance in a Little Europe of the six, and an abnegation of the future possibility of political integration. Only when a preamble had been added to the treaty restating Germany's goals of a close association with the United States, defense through NATO, and political integration and expansion of the EEC was the treaty finally ratified. The German attitude provoked one of de Gaulle's most famous asides: "Treaties are like maidens and roses. They each have their day. . . . 'Hélas, que j'en ai vu mourir de jeunes filles.'"[34] The treaty, however, has played its part in permitting a closer understanding between the governments, with the twice-yearly meetings of the heads of state and government permitting incipient disagreements to be identified. The well-financed Franco-German Youth Office, set up in Adenauer's home village of Rhöndorf, was probably the greatest success of the Franco-German treaty. During its first ten years of activity, the office organized the exchange visits — for language classes, professional training, and sports — of 3 million young people. Its work was supplemented by university exchanges carried out by the DAAD (German Office for University Exchanges) and by the Franco-German Conference of University Rectors that was founded in 1965.[35]

The *Bundestag's* ratification of the Franco-German treaty was almost in the nature of a farewell gift to Adenauer. The selection of Ludwig Erhard as chancellor strengthened the position within the Christian Democratic party of the Atlanticists, for whom Foreign Minister Gerhard Schröder had been speaking since 1961, against the Gaullists, led by Adenauer and Franz-Josef Strauss. For the next three years, de Gaulle found the new German leaders subtly unbending; and he responded by acting directly against their wishes, as in the recognition of Communist China in 1964 and in withdrawing from military participation in NATO in 1966, or by using diplomatic force, as in the Empty Chair Crisis in EEC in 1965-1966. This crisis was precipitated by the German president of the EEC Commission,

Walter Hallstein, who proposed giving the Community its own financial base through customs duties and giving the European Parliament greater legislative powers. De Gaulle infuriated the Germans by withdrawing all French representatives from Community negotiations, thus paralyzing the work of the Community for seven months; and the German government accepted with great bitterness the final compromise that brought the French back into the Community on the basis of renouncing the future political independence of the commission.[36]

Relations with de Gaulle were not improved with the formation in 1966 of the Grand Coalition of Christian Democrats and Socialists under the chancellorship of Kurt Georg Kiesinger, even though Kiesinger made great play of the good relations with the French he had enjoyed as minister-president of Baden-Württemberg.[37] The new German government feared that de Gaulle had abandoned any hope of making the Franco-German treaty the basis of a closer unity in Western Europe and, by deserting NATO and opening new relations with the Soviet Union, was in fact returning to the French thesis he had proposed in 1945.[38] The fifth anniversary of the signing of the Franco-German treaty was celebrated with notable coolness, the French Foreign Minister Couve de Murville remarking that it was a success that contacts should still be continuing in view of the numerous differences of opinion that had arisen.[39] The German press even took a certain pleasure in the decline of the general's prestige brought about by the rioting in Paris in May 1968 and by the subsequent need of France for German help in saving its currency. From 1968 on, the German government ceased to play the role of a complaisant minor partner in the Franco-German relationship and moved toward a position of equality and even toward a carefully masked position of superiority.[40]

Franco-German Relations since de Gaulle, 1969-1979

The year 1969 saw the formation of new governments in both France and Germany. De Gaulle, defeated in a referendum on regional reform, resigned in April; and Georges Pompidou was elected president in June. Following the September election in Germany, Willy Brandt became chancellor of a Socialist–Free Democrat coalition. Pompidou at once proved more flexible than de Gaulle on the admission of Britain to EEC, and he welcomed the *Ostpolitik* of Brandt as a major contribution to détente and — although he did not emphasize this point in public — as a hindrance to unwelcome pressure for further political integration of the European Community, since both the Conservative and Labour parties in Britain had repeatedly refused to delegate sovereignty to a European supranational authority.[41]

Most political observers felt that at first Pompidou was surprised, and perhaps irritated, by Brandt's forceful advocacy of an enlarged and strengthened Community. At the summit conference at The Hague in December 1969, Pompidou attempted to slow down negotiations on the entry of Great Britain, Ireland, Denmark, and Norway. When Brandt warned bluntly that "public opinion in Germany expects me not to return from this conference without concrete arrangements on the subject of the enlargement of the European Community," Pompidou agreed to go along with German wishes and received in return satisfaction on the nature of the financing of the common agricultural policy.[42] The following month, Brandt emphasized the continuing importance he assigned to good relations with France by paying his first state visit as chancellor to Paris, where he was welcomed with an unusually colorful display of Republican Guards and a festive series of banquets. But the regular meetings of Pompidou and Brandt over the next three years rarely achieved the same harmony. In 1971, the meetings in Paris in January and in Bonn in July were marked by sharp bickering on the nature of monetary coordination within the Community, an issue that was complicated by the continuing weakness of the franc in relation to the mark.[43] The German decision in May 1971 to float the mark had been strongly opposed by the French, who insisted on the necessity of a tightly controlled margin of fluctuation of the European currencies; but in 1972, at meetings in Paris in February and in Bonn in July, Pompidou and Brandt were able to agree on mechanisms for intervention by the Community central banks to prevent sharp oscillations of value. Pompidou reciprocated in this instance by agreeing to consider the establishment of a Community political secretariat and, above all, by giving what appeared to be unequivocal support of Brandt's *Ostpolitik*.[44] The summit conference of the Community, held in Paris on October 19-20, 1972, included not only the original six members but the three new members (Britain, Denmark, Ireland) due to be admitted in January 1973. The conference was in many ways a demonstration of a Franco-German compromise. Pompidou received guarantees of the establishment of a European Fund for Monetary Cooperation; German financing would be the primary support of a Regional Fund that would benefit the French West and Southwest as well as the Italian South and British North and West; and consideration of increasing the powers of the European Parliament would be further postponed. Germany was promised an easing of commercial links with nonmembers and the preparation of a report by the Community authorities on the measures necessary for the creation of a "European Union."[45]

This brief rapprochement soon dissolved. The French president showed increasing suspicion of the success of Bonn's *Ostpolitik,* which he felt might lead to the neutralization of Europe in return for the possible reunification of Germany. He opposed the MBFR negotiations and was deeply suspicious of the SALT negotiations between the Russians and the Americans that were favored by the German government. His increasingly unfavorable policy toward Israel was harshly criticized in Germany. And as tension with Germany mounted, Pompidou began to knot a new alliance with British Prime Minister Edward Heath that to the Germans appeared intended as a substitute for the weakening Franco-German alliance. Thus relations were poor when the energy crisis erupted at the end of 1973. The attempt of the French government to curry favor with the Arab oil suppliers and to maintain unilateral relations with the Arab powers in opposition to the policies of the other eight Community members drove the West Germans once again toward the United States. At the Washington energy conference in February 1974, the French were isolated, but returned reinforced in their determination to follow up their independent policy toward the Arab states.[46]

The death of Pompidou in April 1974 and the resignation of Brandt a month later again opened the way for a renewal of Franco-German cordiality. The new Chancellor Helmut Schmidt and the new President Valéry Giscard d'Estaing were personal friends and former finance ministers who prided themselves on their pragmatism. Their first meeting, in Bonn in July 1974, seemed to give substance to these hopes, since it ended with a declaration of support for the achievement of full monetary and economic union of the EEC by 1980. But Schmidt was more concerned with the inflationary dangers of the energy crisis to Germany than with compromising with France on the future of Europe. In September 1974, the German government refused to back a Community loan to the Arab oil producers and vetoed a rise in agricultural prices that would have benefited primarily France.[47] The following year, Giscard d'Estaing seemed to lose his pragmatic approach and to revert to attitudes that were dangerously Gaullist, notably the determination to seek a special relationship with the Soviet Union, to build up the French atomic force as the world's third largest, and to hinder where possible the military integration of Western Europe. "My fundamental idea," he declared on May 20, 1975, "is that the superiority of France is a superiority of the mind (*esprit*). . . . that is to say, that of the country that best understands the problems of its time and which brings the most imaginative, the most open-minded and the most generous solutions to them."[48] Schmidt replied somewhat undiplomatically in 1976 that there were important Communist parties in those countries of Europe where "social structures had been preserved for decades, in Portugal, Italy, and in a certain measure, in France where Gaullism has left its imprint."[49] While French political circles were enraged over Schmidt's remark, Giscard

d'Estaing roused again the traditional fears of German military predominance, by declaring, "I consider that it is important for the military
balance of our continent that the French army should be of the same order
of size as the other army of our continent, that is to say the German
army."[50] The bickering soon abated, as both sides moderated their stands;
but the underlying tension remained. In the late 1970s, Franco-German
relations were at a very low ebb.

Several factors help explain this tension. First and foremost, the movement to create a European supranational community within which France
and Germany could work together never recovered from de Gaulle's veto
on British entry in 1963 and his provocation of the Empty Chair Crisis in
1965-1966. Relations within the Community degenerated into a bargaining on mutual self-interest, and as a result public enthusiasm for, and even
interest in, integration flagged. Second, engaged in bilateral relationships
with little mediation from the Community or from the Atlantic alliance,
France and Germany continued to follow lines of foreign policy that were
basically opposed. France sought the dismantling of the military blocs of
the Cold War, the lessening of American influence in Europe, and the
maintenance of the structure of nation-states. Germany provided the major
European military contribution to NATO, pursued close Atlantic ties, and
attempted to speed up the political integration of Western Europe. Third,
the failure of the French economy to match the performance of the German
created increasing difficulties for the two countries in their bilateral trade,
in their approach to international economic planning, and in their goals for
EEC. Fourth, as the possibility of a Franco-German military confrontation
became ever more unthinkable, the necessity to place Franco-German rapprochement before other national interests appeared less and less urgent.
Thus, without fundamental changes in the economic standing and the
political goals of France and Germany, the relationship of the two countries
appeared doomed to remain in a condition of hardheaded but cool
cooperation.

Notes

1. Alfred Frisch, "Une année électorale," *Documents: Revue des Questions Allemandes*
March 1976, pp. 12-13. This review, published since 1945 by the Bureau Inter-
national de Liaison et de Documentation in Paris, and its companion review
Dokumente, published in Cologne, have been influential in keeping the French and
German public aware of the political, economic, and cultural evolution of each
other's country.

2. For balanced surveys of Franco-German relations, see Raymond Poidevin

and Jacques Bariéty, *Les relations franco-allemandes, 1815-1975* (Paris: Armand Colin, 1977) and Gilbert Ziebura, *Die deutsch-französischen Beziehungen seit 1945: Mythen und Realitäten* (Pfulligen: Neske, 1970). Excellent bibliographies are given in Deutsch-Französisches Institut, *Deutschland-Frankreich: Ludwigsburger Beiträge zum Problem der deutsch-französischen Beziehungen* (Ludwigsburg: Süddeutsche Verlagsanstalt, 1954-1969). This five-volume work is produced by one of the leading institutes in Germany for the furtherance of Franco-German understanding.

3. Eberhard Kostanzer, "Weisungen der französischen Militärregierung 1946-1949," *Vierteljahreshefte für Zeitgeschichte*, April 1970, pp. 204-37.

4. Speech in Baden-Baden on October 5, 1945, in *Revue de la Zone Française*, no. 1 (November 15, 1945), pp. 9-10.

5. On the educational achievements of the zone, see Percy W. Bidwell, "Reeducation in Germany: Emphasis on Culture in the French Zone," *Foreign Affairs* 27 (October 1948):78-85 and F. Roy Willis, *The French in Germany, 1945-1949* (Stanford: Stanford University Press, 1962), pp. 163-79.

6. Reports of the conferences were published in Deutscher Rat der Europäischen Bewegung, *Schriftenreihe*, 1956-

7. See, for example, Deutsch-Französisches Institut Ludwigsburg (Ludwigsburg: Süddeutsche Verlagsanstalt, 1968).

8. See the debate in Baden, Landtag, *Verhandlung*, November 23, 1948, pp. 34-36.

9. Rheinland-Pfalz, Landtag, *Verhandlung*, January 21, 1948, pp. 388-89.

10. Pierre Gerbet, "La genése du Plan Schuman: Des origines à la déclaration du 9 mai 1950," *Revue Française de Science Politique*, July-September 1956, pp. 525-53.

11. Konrad Adenauer, *Memoirs, 1945-1953*, trans. Beate Ruhm von Oppen (Chicago: Henry Regnery, 1966), p. 200.

12. On the Saar, see Jacques Freymond, *The Saar Conflict, 1945-1955* (New York: Praeger, 1960) and Walter R. Craddock, *The Saar Problem in Franco-German Relations* (Ann Arbor: University of Michigan Press, 1961).

13. *L'Aube*, March 10, 1950.

14. Adenauer, *Memoirs*, p. 257.

15. *Die Zeit*, May 18, 1950.

16. Ernst B. Haas, *The Uniting of Europe: Political, Social, and Economic Forces, 1950-1957* (Stanford: Stanford University Press, 1958), p. 163.

17. Alfred Grosser, *Germany in Our Time: A Political History of the Postwar Years*, trans. Paul Stephenson (New York: Praeger, 1971), p. 305.

18. France, Assemblée Nationale, *Débats*, July 25, 1949, pp. 5227-231.

19. On the history of the EDC, see Arnulf Baring, *Aussenpolitik in Adenauers Kanzlerdemokratie. Bonns Beitrag zur europäischen Verteidigungsgemeinschaft* (Munich: Oldenbourg, 1969).

20. On the European Political Community negotiations, see F. Roy Willis, *France, Germany, and the New Europe, 1945-1967*, rev. ed. (Stanford: Stanford University Press, 1968), pp. 159-61.

21. Ziebura, *Die deutsch-französischen Beziehungen*, pp. 70-73.

22. Lewis J. Edinger, *Kurt Schumacher. A Study in Personality and Political Behavior* (Stanford: Stanford University Press, 1965), pp. 229-34.

23. Daniel Lerner and Raymond Aron, eds., *France Defeats EDC* (New York: Praeger, 1951).

24. Karl W. Deutsch and Lewis J. Edinger, *Germany Rejoins the Powers. Mass Opinion, Interest Groups, and Elites in Contemporary German Foreign Policy* (Stanford: Stanford University Press, 1959), pp. 166-67.

25. François Bondy and Manfred Abelein, *Deutschland und Frankreich. Geschichte einer wechselvollen Beziehung* (Düsseldorf/Wien: Econ Verlag, 1973), pp. 169-83

26. Karl W. Deutsch et al., *France, Germany and the Western Alliance. A Study of Elite Attitudes on European Integration and World Politics* (New York: Scribner's, 1967), pp.160-69.

27. In Grosser's words, "The recognition of the D.D.R. as a state in the full sense of the term is not only a precondition of any agreement with it, but is essential to the structural and psychological stabilization of the European Community; and, until the stabilization is achieved, the Federal Republic cannot itself pursue a constructive Eastern policy." Grosser, *Germany in Our Time*, pp. 316-17.

28. European Communities, Statistical Office, *General Statistical Bulletin*, no. 3 (March 1963), pp. 29, 68.

29. Poidevin and Bariéty, *Relations franco-allemandes*, pp. 344-45.

30. Ibid., pp. 346-48; Carl J. Friedrich, *Europe: An Emergent Nation?* (New York: Harper and Row, 1969), pp. 56-68.

31. Alfred Grosser, "General de Gaulle and the Foreign Policy of the Fifth Republic," *International Affairs*, April 1963, pp. 298-313.

32. *Le Figaro*, September 13, 1958.

33. Willis, *France, Germany, and the New Europe*, pp. 282-305.

34. *Le Monde*, July 3, 1963; Ernst Friedlaender and Katharina Focke, *Europa über den Nationen* (Cologne: Bildungswerk Europäische Politik, 1963), pp. 85-88.

35. Poidevin and Bariéty, *Relations franco-allemandes*, pp. 351-52.

36. On the Schröder–de Gaulle conflict, see Ziebura, *Die deutsch-französischen Beziehungen*, pp. 119-31.

37. Theo Sommer, "Bonn Changes Course," *Foreign Affairs*, April 1967, pp. 477-91.

38. See Raymond Aron's comments, "Vingt ans après," *Le Figaro*, November 12, 1966. The French thesis proposed in 1945 included internationalization of the Ruhr, separation of the Rhineland from Germany, economic fusion of the Saar to France, the end of centralized government in Germany, and French military presence on the upper Rhine.

39. Bondy and Abelein, *Deutschland und Frankreich*, p. 237.

40. Ibid., pp. 238-39.

41. *Economist* (London), January 30, 1971.

42. *L'Année politique, 1969* (Paris: Presses Universitaires de France, 1970), pp. 317-23.

43. *L'Année politique, 1971*, pp. 244, 300-01.

44. *L'Année politique, 1972,* pp. 209-10, 261-62.

45. Ibid., pp. 289-92.

46. Gérard Valin, "La France et l'Allemagne de l'Ouest face à la crise de l'énergie," *Allemagnes d'Aujourd'hui,* September-October, 1974, pp. 31-43.

47. Poidevin and Bariéty, *Relations franco-allemandes,* p. 340.

48. *L'Année politique, 1975,* pp. 125-26.

49. *L'Année politique, 1976,* p. 197.

50. Ibid., pp. 198-99. On the underlying causes of dissension, see Alfred Frisch, "Les relations franco-allemandes: Une amitié solide et fragile à la fois," *Documents: Revue des Questions Allemandes,* September 1976, pp. 5-17.

8

The Soviet Union and Germany

William G. Hyland

If one were to make a list of the five most urgent international issues, the German question would almost certainly *not* be one of them. But if this same list had been composed twenty years ago, the German question would probably have been near the top, and thirty years ago it would have been *the* issue.

The passing of the German question symbolizes in a broad sense the withering away of the most virulent phases of the Cold War: the struggle over Germany was indeed the Cold War. The international and national acceptance of the division of Germany became a major Soviet objective while the restoration of German unity was a prime Western aim, even though the Western commitment to unification became increasingly doubtful. By 1970-1972 a German "settlement" finally emerged largely as a unilateral West German achievement. Together with the Helsinki Conference, the Eastern treaties marked the end of the postwar period in Central Europe. A new and uncertain phase in both Soviet and Western policy had begun.

Stalin and the Partition

One must credit Joseph Stalin with considerable nerve. In December 1941, German panzer divisions were within sight of Moscow, much of his country was overrun by an invading army, and his government had been evacuated to Kuibyshev. Stalin himself suffered some kind of a breakdown soon after the German attack. The issue between Germany and Russia was still in doubt.

At that particular moment the Soviet leader received Anthony Eden, the foreign minister of his new ally Great Britain. One might think that Stalin would have been preoccupied with obtaining military assistance or stimulating any desperate scheme to relieve the pressure on his front. Yet, the conversations primarily concerned Russia's postwar ambitions. Stalin presented draft treaties for a military alliance and for postwar political cooperation. In addition, he had a secret protocol, in which the British would agree to recognize new western boundaries for the USSR. As for Germany, Stalin's scheme was simple: Germany would be dismembered into rump states, including a separate Rhineland and Bavaria and a transfer of territory to Poland. The USSR would collect substantial reparations. When Eden balked, pleading that he would have to consult with Washington, Stalin became indignant. The matters were left for later negotiations.

Stalin never really varied from this original formula. At various levels and in various negotiations, Soviet representatives took the same view: Germany should emerge from the war a weak collection of small components, minus some territory in the East, owing the USSR a substantial sum of reparations. The Soviets stopped short of endorsing the Morgenthau plan only because they wanted some form of functioning German economy to provide reparations.

Stalin's position was understandable. He was subject to the same concerns of all wartime statesmen: to prevent a recurrence of the last war. His position was reminiscent of Marshal Foch's in 1919, who called for the dismemberment and occupation of Germany and mutual security guarantees plus physical barriers against Germany's revival. Whereas Stalin was fairly clear about his postwar aims, his Western counterparts were vague and uncertain. Franklin D. Roosevelt also was eager not only to prevent a recurrence of the last war, but also to avoid Woodrow Wilson's mistakes; so he avoided coming to grips with the German question. By late 1944 the absurd situation had developed that the European Advisory Commission had agreed to draw up the boundaries of German occupation zones without clear political guidance from Washington. Indeed, the American position at one point was reflected in a Joint Chiefs of Staff document that envisaged radically different zones, based on a rough sketch Roosevelt had drawn on a National Geographic map some time earlier.

As far as the USSR's aims were concerned, the division of Germany into four occupation zones and the eventual agreement on reparations met Stalin's essential demands. Indeed Stalin had reason to believe that all of the Allies agreed to his general approach to the problem of Germany; even in the increasingly bitter dispute over Poland, the Western Allies never disputed (at least not vigorously) that Germany was to remain a weak state. Since there was no attempt to establish a central German authority, Stalin also had reason to believe that the postwar arrangements reflected a sphere of influence settlement, in which Germany would stay a sort of neutral demilitarized zone.

The question remained: Would this neutral zone be controlled through a common four-power policy or would it dissolve into several separate areas of control? On this issue Soviet policy was more complex. Stalin put it rather crudely to Milovan Djilas, when he said that the result of the war was that where the armies stopped, the victorious power would impose its social and political order; but he also said that Germany would revive and that after twenty years we would have "another go" at it.

What, then, was Soviet policy in regard to the internal order of occupied Germany? There is a fairly clear line from the creation of the various national committees in Russia during the war to the establishment of a German Communist apparatus in the Soviet zone. There is little doubt that the Soviet authorities pressed for the establishment at various levels of a Communist-dominated political and administrative apparatus. What is not so clear is what evolution was expected: toward an independent East German state, or toward a popular front in a united Germany on the East European model. Perhaps it was not an urgent question for the USSR. As long as Soviet military forces remained in control of the eastern zone, the question of local political control through German Communists was academic. Soviet behavior in the four power councils suggests, in any case, that maintaining a voice in all aspects of Germany was the initial objective.

Yet there was a definite dualism in Soviet policy: Stalin wanted a weak Germany and a major Soviet voice in its future, but at the same time he wanted optimal control over his own sector. There was a potential contradiction here, but it was obscured for a time. It is worth noting that even in 1947, when Washington was becoming enthralled with the containment doctrine of George Kennan, General Lucius Clay objected to Kennan's analysis because he felt that the Soviets were behaving in a cooperative manner in Germany. Moreover, even as Stalin swept aside the remaining obstacles to full Soviet control in Eastern Europe, East Germany remained in a special category. By the late summer of 1948, most Western observers saw little likelihood of a definitive German settlement. The chief premise of U.S. policy—solutions by the two powers—had broken down whereas Kennan foresaw a German settlement, the only question being when. At the outset of the Berlin blockade, the dualism of Soviet policy emerged more clearly. Stalin must have concluded the *real* partition of Germany between East and West was well advanced. Since Berlin was in the Soviet sphere, it was time for the Allies to end this anomaly. The alternative—that the West could be held hostage in Berlin—apparently never occurred to Stalin. He preferred to force the West out of the former capital and hoped to make his zone a plausible claimant to the German national heritage. The net result was a failure for Stalin, but the political partition of Germany was greatly accelerated.

Lost Opportunity?

The period that followed the blockade up until Stalin's death is one of the more intriguing bits of Soviet history. No one (including Nikita Khrushchev) is in a position to testify to all that happened. But it was during this period that some revisionist historians believe a "lost opportunity" for German unity may have occurred.

The thesis is that by 1952 international tensions had reached a point that prompted the Soviets to reexamine their policy. A provocative ideological indicator was Stalin's *Economic Problems of Socialism,* in which he reaffirmed the inevitability of war between capitalists. He speculated that Germany would revive and sharpen capitalist contradictions. Most important there was the famous peace note of March 10, 1952, which offered a unified, rearmed Germany, and, in a later clarification, free elections.

The various arguments about a lost opportunity need not be reiterated. Suffice it to say, Germany confronted Stalin with a dilemma: if Western policy ran its course, Germany would become more deeply divided, a process that the Soviets had abetted. But for Germany to remain weak, rearmament had to be forestalled or clearly controlled. In this case Stalin would have to sacrifice (or at least offer to sacrifice) the division of Germany in return for guarantees of its neutralization and rely on indigenous Communists to exert some influence on a central government.

This was a strange period. There was Stalin's supposed threat to retire at the nineteenth Party Congress, which elevated Georgi Malenkov as his successor. The doctors' plot was unveiled; the Slansky trial began; there was a possible purge of Vyacheslav M. Molotov and Anastas I. Mikoyan. In terms of German policy, we will probably never know whether Stalin was merely trying to buy time or was seriously contemplating a change. In any case, his opening was never seriously tested. The West was still committed to the idea that it was insufficiently strong to negotiate and that the building of strength had to take priority. Adenauer said that at the time, "Our policy must be to help make the West strong enough to induce the Russians to want to compromise." In his view, the Soviet proposals of March 1952 were "proof" that if the West continued to build its strength, then a point would be reached when the Russians would be ready to negotiate "sensibly." It is rather incredible in retrospect that in this period the West concluded it was not strong enough to negotiate: the American strategic advantage was still overwhelming, the Western economies were rapidly reviving, and a military alliance was being created, including some form of German rearmament. In any case, although Stalin's initiative can be explained on tactical grounds, one must wonder in retrospect whether he, too, sensed that Western strength was gathering and that some alternative in Europe and in

Germany might be worth exploring.

The full story overlaps into the immediate post-Stalin period and involves the purge of Lavrenti P. Beria. Both Beria and Malenkov have been accused of harboring secret plans to betray East Germany. They were at the time supposedly planning to sell out their East German comrades and unite Germany under a neutral scheme. To be sure, there is considerable evidence of turmoil in East Germany after the death of Stalin. From March 1953 through the riots of June, Soviet policy appears to have been unstable. We know from Khrushchev's memoirs that the tensions in the new regime were extremely high and that Beria was supposedly plotting some sort of coup, with Malenkov his potential ally.

We will never know the full details, however. It was in the interest of Khrushchev and his group to blacken Beria's reputation on every count and, after 1957, to implicate Malenkov. Certain leaders of the East German party (Wilhelm Zaisser and Rudolph Herrnstadt) were purged almost simultaneously with Beria's fall, thus lending some credibility to the thesis of a conspiracy. But it was in Walter Ulbricht's interest to link them with the discredited Beria. Nevertheless, it is not inconceivable that Beria and perhaps Malenkov, caught in the midst of a power struggle, would have wanted some foreign spectacular. Preventing the incorporation of the Federal Republic into the Western alliance could have been a considerable achievement. Finally, one must remember that this was a frightened group, as Khrushchev himself has vividly described them. Stalin's death was a psychological blow. His successors were apprehensive of Western forays and the unsettling effect of his death on the population. Innovations may well have received more of a hearing in this period than any of the participants would care to admit.

Khrushchev's Pressures

In any case, the arrest of Beria appears to have put an end to a period that had begun with Stalin's peace note. None of this was clearly understood at the time, of course. The wily Churchill sensed a weakness in the Kremlin and began a campaign for a summit meeting in May 1953; he even offered the possibility of a partial settlement animated by the master thought behind the Locarno Plan. It is an interesting commentary that Western statesmen continued to believe for a long period that if they could satisfy Soviet security interests, the unification of Germany could then be settled. After 1953, this was probably a serious misperception of Soviet policy, since the division of Germany had become inseparable from Soviet security interests. The Soviets, in any case, saw through this Western probing. With Molotov back in command, Moscow began a series of maneuvers to turn the Western interest in negotiations to the Soviet advantage.

The Soviet objective was no longer to test the incentive for unity but to forestall or defeat the rearmament of Germany. This meant focusing initially on the weakest link, France. Molotov in 1954 skillfully played off French interest in an Indochina settlement against Soviet interests in Central Europe. The first step was the Foreign Ministers Conference of January 1954, which settled nothing, but led to the same group reconvening to consider Asian matters. Eventually the Soviets struck a bargain with Pierre Mendès-France. In return for Soviet intervention to help settle the remaining issues in Indochina—permitting Mendès-France to make his self-imposed deadline for a settlement—the French parliament eventually killed the European Defense Community. Even if no explicit bargain was made (Mendès-France denies it), this was the clear implication and both sides performed according to expectations.

For all the skill displayed by the Soviets in this period, what followed is still baffling. How could the Soviets permit the rapid turnabout executed by Anthony Eden and John Foster Dulles that led to the Western European Union and the rearmament of Germany wihtin NATO? One can only speculate that once again the tensions within the Kremlin, and the infighting that was almost constant until July 1957, played their role. Khrushchev clearly wanted to open up a more flexible policy, leading to the Austrian treaty and the reconciliation with Tito. Molotov resisted, according to most accounts. It may be that Molotov was wary of experimenting in Germany, lest this play into Khrushchev's hands. (Incidentally, the Soviet peace note of March 1952 occurred when Molotov was supposedly out of favor.) Or it may simply be that a collective leadership could not make any decisions that would have had any significant effect.

Nevertheless, one aspect is clear: by 1955 the Soviets had set a new course in Germany. The attempt to keep Germany weak was failing, and even the Austrian treaty had no effect on Western policy. The necessity to keep Germany divided became paramount. At the Geneva summit of 1955, the Western statesmen consoled themselves in the delusion that something had been accomplished, that war was now less likely, and that a new spirit had been created, as if the problems in Europe could be solved by atmospherics. But the consequences were more clearly spelled out by Nikolai Bulganin and Nikita Khrushchev during their stopover in East Berlin. Their statements made it clear beyond challenge that the division of Germany was now considered complete and that this had been the real meaning of Geneva.

From that point forward Soviet policy shifted more clearly to new objectives: first, to ratify the division of Germany and, second, to limit and constrain the pace and scope of German rearmament. The tactics were to vary, but the priorities were clear. Despite continuing illusions in the West reflected in the disengagement debates, there was never any real indication after 1955 that the USSR would relinquish its hold over East Germany. The problem for Moscow was to obtain recognition of its hegemony from West Germany and the Western alliance.

The intense phase of the campaign to seal the division of Germany came in the wake of the announcement of a Soviet intercontinental ballistic missile (ICBM) capability and the launch of the first Soviet space satellite in the fall of 1957. This was the period of the so-called missile gap, when a shift in the balance of power seemed to have occurred. If so, Khrushchev intended to translate that shift into political gains. It was no accident that his demands were for Western recognition of the European division as evident in the main element of Soviet proposals for a summit agenda in 1958-1959. The specific demand in his ultimatum of November 1958 was to sign a German peace treaty with both German states and create a "free city" in Berlin. The Western powers would thereby be compelled to recognize the division of Germany and symbolize their capitulation by withdrawing from Berlin. These actions would have abandoned any pretense of a four-power responsibility for Germany and Berlin. World War II, for the Soviets, would then have been finally over.

Khrushchev badly miscalculated. It may be that he was seriously misled by the various crosscurrents of politics in the Federal Republic where disengagement theories enjoyed a vogue, and where the *Atomtod* campaign seemed to signal a pacifism and neutralism that might work to Soviet advantage. But it is important to note that at no point did the Soviets seriously propose to discuss German unification. All Western statesmen understood the game, and only the apprehensions of the missile gap led them into the feckless negotiations at Geneva, then at Camp David, and finally in Paris.

The irony was that Khrushchev's intimidation of the West actually caused far greater apprehension in the East. The expectation that the division of Germany would become final, and that the opening through West Berlin would be sealed off, caused a growing panic. This reached such proportions that the Soviets had to move, which they did in August 1961.

By then Khrushchev was more and more on the defensive. His bold gamble was failing, the missile gap was evaporating, and the United States was mobilizing. He launched his disastrous adventure into Cuba, which contributed to his ultimate downfall. For Germany, however, the results were doleful. The physical division of Berlin symbolized in microcosm the political division of Germany. Vestiges of four power rights were maintained but with no real policy behind them. The West had been prepared to fight for West Berlin, or so it seemed, but not in order to prevent the further division of the former German capital. The Soviets had failed to enforce recognition of their German policy, but Khrushchev's successors could take some comfort that this step had probably become inevitable. What remained in doubt was the process and the final price.

It is probable that the seeds of the 1970 Eastern treaties were sown in August of 1961. If there was one man who was profoundly impressed by the limits of Western policy it was the mayor of Berlin, Willy Brandt. He said in December of 1961 that the crucial task for German foreign policy was "entering a new relationship with the Great Power in the East."

Strange Interlude

It is fairly clear that in the years that followed, Brandt and his associates devised an alternative Eastern policy, which was occasionally spelled out in startling terms by Egon Bahr. The Christian Democrats also recognized that there had to be alternatives to the frontal assault on the German national question. The Soviets could not be forced or charmed out of East Germany, but some Germans apparently thought that they might be maneuvered out. The remnants of the Adenauer period were gradually but purposefully dismantled, the Hallstein Doctrine being the most obvious. The road to Pankow seemed to lie through Bucharest, or so the theory ran.

Again we see the reoccurrence of the basic illusion: the assumption that if Soviet security interests could be satisfied in this way, their claim to East Germany could be softened. One must ask: if the Soviets maintained their German position in a period of major weakness, when the West had an atomic monopoly and massive strategic advantages, why would they relinquish it when their strategic position was improving in the 1960s, especially when their major adversary was entrapped in Southeast Asia?

The period between the Cuban crisis and the Czech crisis is an amorphous blur. Some of the major themes were recognizable, but the diplomatic maneuvering and exchanges elude a definitive analytical summary. In the West the view persisted that somehow a formula could be devised that would relieve Soviet apprehensions about its security; there were various ingenious semantic devices—recognizing the status quo to change it; change through rapprochement; or various agreements on the nonuse of force. The idea was that the Soviet leaders would come to understand that the West did not really harbor any design on Eastern Europe and that a period of peaceful change could be inaugurated. This theme, which found resonance in Germany, became intertwined with the American obsession with nonproliferation. This, too, reflected the view that what was needed was to relieve Soviet apprehensions of a nuclear armed Germany. The Soviet Union aided and abetted what amounted to the revival of "European security." In 1965-1967 the Soviets began to emphasize a European Security Conference, which would have as its starting point the dissolution of military blocs. As a subsidiary theme, there was a Soviet attempt to exclude the United States from participation. Doubtless this was a minor tactic to test how far the Vietnam war had gone in splitting the United States from its allies, especially in the wake of Charles de Gaulle's withdrawal from the integrated commands of NATO. It was also a period in which American leadership in Europe was lacking because of the obsession with Vietnam. Gradually, without any particular strategy that was discernible, the West came to focus on the idea of a mutual reduction of forces, following vague Soviet hints in April 1967 that withdrawal of "foreign troops" might be an issue for exploration. The formal Western proposal of June 1968 suggested mutual reductions. The conclusions of the nonproliferation treaty shortly afterward stimulated speculation that a new era of peaceful engagement might be dawning. Lyndon Johnson proceeded with summit plans.

All of this, of course, was exploded by the Czech crisis. However, one observer in Germany, Karl Birnbaum, noted that the Czech invasion "brought into focus the discrepancies that had existed *all the time* between Western and Soviet conceptions of détente in Europe."[1] The Brezhnev doctrine made a mockery of Western concepts of European security other than as a proposal for a sphere of influence policy. But in retrospect it is somewhat amazing how little all of this affected European diplomacy. The NATO countries announced a boycott of exchanges, which was lifted by April 1969, and revived the MBFR idea. Few observers noted the military consequences of five more Soviet divisions in forward positions: in any force reductions the Soviet base was automatically 15 percent larger.

What had happened was that the burden of East-West diplomacy was shifting from the older confrontation in Europe to the new superpower relationship, as reflected in SALT and the achievement of Soviet strategic parity, and to the potential triangular relationship with China, as reflected in the confrontation over the Damansky Islands and the subsequent showdown of 1969. One can only speculate how these new trends might have evolved had it not been for an unexpected event that changed the dialogue definitively—the election of an SPD-led government for the first time in the history of the Federal Republic.

The Eastern Treaties

The motives of Chancellor Brandt in concluding the Eastern treaties are beyond the scope of this essay. Some of the concepts had been tentatively tested in Moscow during the Grand Coalition. Brandt's ostensible mechanism, the renunciation of force, had its antecedents in the earlier period of the Grand Coalition and had been subjected to a series of pre-Czech exchanges. The idea obviously appealed greatly to the USSR. For a major member of a military alliance to renounce the threat or use of force could only be read as acquiescence in the status quo, which, after all, was the Soviet aim as spelled out in innumerable documents. For the major revisionist member of the alliance to renounce force was an added gain. It implied that there was only one remaining avenue to the solution of the German question — a formal merger of two independent states, reflecting the Soviet position. Finally, the Soviets must have been sensitive to the psychological implications of bilateral Soviet-German negotiations, at a time when the West was uncertain over its own future, with the EEC bogged down, America embroiled in Vietnam, and the nuclear balance shifting toward equality. If the Eastern alternative was sufficiently attractive, then perhaps currents of neutralism associated with SPD could be revived.

It is not surprising, therefore, that the Soviets were prepared at the end of 1969 to respond rapidly to Brandt's initiative. Moscow had already quietly put aside the proposals for dissolving the military blocs. Soviet relations with Nixon were still uncertain and a "selective détente" beginning with Germany seemed a productive alternative. The resulting maneuvering, however, led to a much more complicated situation than the Soviets had envisaged.

First of all, as a result of Bonn's encouragement, the Nixon administration had made a formal overture to Moscow suggesting negotiations on Berlin. The idea was that certain concrete security issues should be resolved before entering into the vaguer Soviet proposals for a European Security Conference. If Berlin could not be settled, then what was the meaning behind the grandiose Soviet concept for European détente? The Soviets stalled, keeping the Berlin question alive but making no major reply. Obviously, bilateral negotiations with Bonn were more attractive, especially since the Soviet proposals for nonuse of force had included a provision that Bonn would recognize Berlin as a "special political entity." Thus, Soviet-German negotiations, after preliminary exchanges, opened in Moscow on December 9, 1969, with Berlin negotiations still in abeyance. To Washington this seemed a reversal of priorities. Berlin should precede, not follow, German bilateral negotiations. How could the three Western allies negotiate for Soviet guarantees of transit to Berlin, if as a result of West Germany's diplomacy, East Germany's legitimacy and sovereignty was recognized?

As a result, Moscow had to pay at least lip service to the Western insistence on Berlin negotiations, especially since the United States had succeeded in making it a prerequisite for any European Security Conference.

Accordingly, Berlin negotiations formally began in March 1970 but remained low-key, for by that time German-Soviet talks were gathering speed. Bahr's negotiations in March 1970 had already yielded results that were being considered by both governments. Moreover, Brandt had already taken a monumental step by traveling to the GDR and meeting with his counterpart, Willi Stoph.

Clearly a gap was developing in Western policy that was being exploited by the Soviet Union. Bonn was receiving support from its Western partners, especially since Brandt had the prudence and foresight to revive his Western policy, pushing for the admission of Britain into the Common Market. Nevertheless, there was no great enthusiasm in the West for his *Ostpolitik,* and rumors of disagreements circulated. One reason for these uncertainties was that the USSR, while being conciliatory in its dealings with Bonn, was far from conciliatory in its dealings with Washington. Tensions in the Middle East were growing at the very moment that Brandt was completing his negotiations, Moscow and Washington were on the verge of a dangerous confrontation over the Syrian invasion of Jordan, and there were difficulties over a Soviet probe for a submarine base in Cuba. This was clearly a selective détente. In any case, the Soviet-German treaty was the centerpiece of Soviet diplomacy in this period. It must have been regarded as a major accomplishment of Soviet policy, for it clearly states what Moscow had asserted for years, namely that the contracting parties

- undertake to respect without restriction the territorial integrity of all states in Europe within their present frontiers;

- declare that they have no territorial claims against anybody nor will assert such claims in the future;

- regard today and shall in future regard the frontiers of all states in Europe as inviolable, such as they are on the date of signature of the present treaty, including the Oder-Neisse line that forms the western frontier of the People's Republic of Poland and the German Democratic Republic.

To be sure, this treaty was surrounded with diplomatic verbiage. But to the leaders in the Kremlin, Western qualifications must have seemed as minor background noise, and indeed, their subsequent evaluation has been that this treaty marked the end of an era. The division of Germany was final, or at least as final as any political settlement could be. The USSR had achieved its aim; but the question remained: What would the course of West German policy be?

The Revival of European Security

Among the motives and expectations of the Soviet leaders, there must have been some hope that the rationale for German policy ascribed to Egon Bahr would prove to be exploitable. Reports that Bahr envisaged acceptance of the status quo as only one stage in a process leading to a unified neutralized Germany could not have been overlooked in Moscow. Indeed, Soviet policy in the wake of the German treaties moved along the lines of the so-called Bahr scheme, with emphasis on broader European security arrangements and negotiations for military withdrawals. This produced a strange conjunction of events: when Washington was struggling to defeat the Mansfield amendment in May of 1971, Brezhnev announced his willingness to negotiate troop reductions. This incident illustrates that Soviet willingness to cultivate an independent German initiative had its limits; without American consent no final settlement could be definitive. From 1971 forward it was Washington that held the key, not Bonn. The lack of any definitive second phase was indeed a defect in *Ostpolitik*. It was unclear what would happen after the Moscow treaty. Bonn could not negotiate on the broader military questions, but without some movement in this realm *Ostpolitik* might become sterile.

Moreover, the riots in Poland in December 1970 pointed up the dangers of selective détente. The German recognition of Polish borders proved of little value to Wladyslaw Gomulka and indeed, may have stimulated demands for an improvement inside Poland. In any case, Poland was a warning that a purely German settlement was insufficient; a pan-European ratification was still necessary. This policy led eventually to Helsinki and was a central feature of the peace program announced by Brezhnev at the twenty-fourth Party Congress in March 1971. It turned out, ironically, that at the moment the USSR achieved one of its most constant objectives, circumstances were changing. Less had been solved than met the eye. There was an additional price to be paid in September 1971 in the Berlin negotiations; and in paying this price the USSR mortgaged some of its freedom of action, as was demonstrated in May of 1972, when Moscow proceeded with the Nixon summit in the face of the bombing and mining of North Vietnam.

One reason for the Soviet decision was that the Eastern treaties were still hanging in the balance in the West German *Bundestag;* to kill the Nixon summit might well have endangered, if not destroyed, the accomplishments of August 1970. This the Soviets decided they could not or would not do. Indeed, it apparently involved a minor purge of the politburo — the removal of Pyotr Y. Shelest — in order for Brezhnev to prevail.

At the 1972 summit, the next phase of Soviet diplomacy opened with the renewed drive for a European Security Conference. The aim clearly was to crown the bilateral acceptance of the status quo with a pan-European and American acceptance. But it was ironic that as Moscow gathered in the confirmation of the European territorial status quo, it had less and less meaning. No one really disputed the European territorial settlement (except perhaps Hungary and Romania). Its acceptance had long since been implied in Western policy, although out of deference to Bonn it was rarely acknowledged. In the endless search for some compensation, however, the West had come to yet another approach. Cooperation became the Western price for accepting the European status quo.

At first the Soviets were slow to recognize the explosive potential of pan-European cooperation. They sought to give it an economic twist and then hoped to impede its actual operation with pettifogging qualifications. For a time they succeeded because Western opinion was slow to recognize the potential of the Helsinki conference. The Soviets not only had left themselves open to future charges of bad faith, but they also had given the West a rallying point for turning the next European Security Conference into a sort of court for judging Soviet performance. Naturally, Moscow rebelled and has had some success in turning away the challenge of the Belgrade Conference.

The Next Phase

Whatever its merits or defects, the Helsinki conference in effect substituted for a general peace treaty. It confirmed the territorial and general political arrangements that emerged in the postwar period. It did nothing to affect the division of Germany, except that it revealed the weaknesses in Soviet authority over Eastern Europe. Although Soviet policy had in the past exploited fear of a resurgent Germany to consolidate its control in Eastern Europe, by the time of the Helsinki meeting this fear had lost much of its effectiveness. The continuing division of Germany was becoming the status quo.

German unity thus seems to be a dormant if not politically dead issue. The process of negotiating the military dimensions of European security, however, remains alive and appears to be becoming more important, for several reasons.

First, the process of posttreaty normalization between Bonn and Moscow continues, but appears to be largely an end in itself rather than a bridge to a larger settlement. In West Germany, only a pale reflection of the original illusion survives. For example, during Brezhnev's last visit, the West German aim was described as persuading the Soviet Union of Bonn's interest in East German stability so that the USSR and East Germany might gain the self-confidence and bargaining room to permit intra-German relations to progress without becoming a security risk to the Soviet Union (*Der Spiegel*, May 1, 1978).

But the chief means of influencing the Soviet Union has become economic. Trade with the USSR still constitutes a small portion of total German trade, but its absolute volume has grown significantly — by 155 percent since the signing of the 1970 treaty. Eastern Europe and the Soviet Union have risen to fourth place in West German trade, more than trade with the United States. Massive European credits have been extended to the East by all of Western Europe.

But to what end? Moscow has persistently sought imports of technology with Western financing. As long as the flow continues, there is no reason for Moscow to revise its European détente policy, particularly since the Europeans have been reluctant to assert possible political conditions for their economic assistance. Bonn seems to have acquired its own stake in economic accommodations with the East. This had led to a strange turn. The supposed inducement for Soviet relaxation in Europe — economic ties — are apparently now as important to the German economy as to the Soviet. The net advantages are becoming blurred. (See the Alastair Buchan lecture of Helmut Schmidt on the value of Soviet economic relations, printed in *Survival*.)

The second problem is that normalization between Moscow and the Federal Republic (and indeed, all of Europe) rests on an uncertain military equation. The Soviet advantage in conventional military forces in Central Europe is not a new factor. It is one of the permanent features of the postwar period. As long as the strategic nuclear balance was clearly in Washington's favor, this inequality in Europe could be accepted. In an era of strategic parity — if not an emerging Soviet advantage — what is the meaning of a potential disequilibrium in such a vital area of Central Europe? Will the West insist that the price for a continuing détente is to redress the European military balance? This has been the import of the proposals put forward in the Vienna talks on MBFR. Thus far, the Soviets have easily resisted these demands.

The probability of reaching a SALT II agreement raises issues for both Germany and NATO. Any new agreement most likely will not affect the European regional balance, thus permitting the Soviets to continue their own buildup of European theater nuclear forces. The West is, however, considering possible countermeasures, such as cruise missiles or short-range ballistic missiles. But such moves will raise once again the fundamental paradox of Germany. To counter the Soviet military threat in Europe, the Federal Republic has always been the area for emplacing weapons systems intended to strengthen the alliance. Each step in this direction, whatever the particular weapon, not only risks a further deepening of the country's division, but also emphasized Germany's vulnerability to Soviet counterpressures. It is difficult to believe that the Soviet Union would passively accept the stationing in Germany of nuclear weapons capable of reaching Moscow.

At the same time, a significant military strengthening in Germany also would run into a significant political opposition in Germany — an opposition that seeks not to heighten the military confrontation but to negotiate with the East. Thus, even Helmut Schmidt wavered on the neutron bomb and was driven by domestic politics to urge Moscow toward new initiatives in MBFR. It may be significant that Brezhnev was in fact forthcoming in presenting a slightly new move in MBFR. It is not impossible that Moscow may now be prepared to contemplate some limited form of military disengagement, for example, troop reductions in return for limits on Western nuclear forces in Germany. The reasons might be Soviet apprehensions about the new global geopolitical balance that seems to be evolving and the increasing economic costs of maintaining a two-front military disposition.

This new world balance of power is characterized by the emergence of the quadruple entente of West Europe, China, Japan, and the United States. This coalition is in an incipient state, but one of its unifying elements is opposition to Soviet hegemony. For the USSR it must seem ominously reminiscent of encirclement. The economic potential of such an entente is staggering: its combined GNP is four times that of the USSR. Of particular concern for Russia is the prospect that the Europeans — supposedly pursuing a relaxation with the USSR — may use it as a source of economic and military assistance to the new Chinese modernization program. Multibillion-dollar projects are being discussed. Washington has given some signs that it will not block military sales by Europeans and thereby is implicitly encouraging them. Indeed, certain Chinese arms supply arrangements may be under negotiation with England and France; economic arrangements with Germany are probable.

Will the USSR tolerate such a trend? Probably not. But countermoves in Europe create a dilemma. On the one hand, Moscow might pursue a policy of further relaxation (including some force reductions) in Central Europe in return for Western restraint in dealing with China. This policy would probably be most attractive to Bonn, but not necessarily to Washington or Paris. On the other hand, the Soviet Union could exert pressures on the Europeans to halt any assistance to China. Some warnings have already been given in Paris and London. This is risky. To be effective a renewal of pressure would have to extend to vulnerable areas, especially Germany — Berlin, thereby jeopardizing the USSR's economic stake. Nevertheless, tensions that arise out of Western dealings with China cannot fail to color the Soviet position on intra-German relations and European security.

* * *

In sum, the period of consolidation that began with the 1970 treaties and ended in the Helsinki conference is giving way to a period of more intensive maneuvering. No one at this time is likely to revive the German question. But the broader question of the role of Europe in the framework of a new international equilibrium has already been raised. The position of Germany could be pivotal — certainly it will be so for the USSR. The West may be poised on the brink of a new period of building strength — in NATO and in the EEC — much as it was thirty years ago. But there also remain strong undercurrents for negotiated arrangements pointing toward Moscow. The new direction is thus still to be determined.

Note

1. Karl E. Birnbaum, *Peace in Europe: East-West Relations 1966-1968 and the Prospects for a European Settlement* (New York: Oxford University Press, 1970).

9

Adenauer's *Ostpolitik*

Hans-Peter Schwarz

Comprehensive research on Adenauer's foreign policy began in the late sixties, and since then quite a few monographs, readers, and articles have been published. But even a preliminary account of the first chancellor's foreign policy is still missing, as is a more detailed analysis of his European policies, his *Deutschlandpolitik,* or his *Ostpolitik.*[1]

My theses on Adenauer's *Ostpolitik* have benefited from the fact that I had a chance to look into Adenauer's files, which have not yet been made available to the public. It is therefore possible to assess from a new angle the picture that developed out of the documents already published. But the topic "Adenauer's *Ostpolitik*" is so broad that it is impossible to document all the theses in this short essay. Such a task is reserved for a later, more comprehensive study. Therefore only a few significant problems of Adenauer's *Ostpolitik* will be dealt with here, and I shall not try to give an exhausting or even systematic review. After stating each thesis, however, I shall juxtapose to it those of subsequent governments.

A Permanent Concern for Russia's Long-term Expansionist Policies

In its inner core, Adenauer's *Ostpolitik* was defensive but not pessimistic. He perceived the Soviet Union as a great, expansionist power for a long time to come. A few scattered remarks granting the Soviet Union a will to peace, made in later years, cannot do away with the fact that his image of the Soviet Union was very similar to Paul Valéry's image of Germany. At the end of the nineteenth century, Valéry published his well-known essay on the eastern neighbor entitled "Une conquête méthodique"—a systematic policy of conquest.

Asked about his opinion on the Kremlin's long-term policies the chancellor often advised his domestic or foreign guests—including President Kennedy—to read the book of a little-known German author, Dieter

Friede. The book was published in 1959 under the title *The Russian Perpetuum Mobile*. Friede tried to show that Russia had been the leading war-fighting nation in Europe and had always been eager to expand its power. In sum, Adenauer regarded Russian nationalism as being enforced by Soviet expansionist policies.

In the four volumes of Adenauer's *Memoirs,* there is only one map. Covering a whole page it shows the Soviet Union, extending from Vladivostok to the Polish border, with Western Europe as a small appendix of the Eurasian landmass. Squeezed in the lower part of the map are China, Iran, and Turkey (*Memoirs,* vol. II, p. 19). On the page opposite the map, a table shows all the countries the Soviet Union has annexed since 1939 — beginning with East Poland in 1939 and ending with the eastern parts of Slovakia in 1945 — a total of 492,600 km. This is put into perspective by a remark informing the reader that the Federal Republic only covers an area of 245,000 km^2. The acquisition of land by the Soviet Union since 1939 therefore equals more than twice the territory of the Federal Republic. Having mentioned that the Soviet Union subjugated the Eastern European bloc countries, the author augments this information by a list of fifty-eight treaties broken by the Soviet Union.

The suggestive description in the *Memoirs* does not stand alone. Adenauer always came back to those facts. To him Russia was the only European world power still existing — in the words of Raymond Aron, "the last classic European empire." Adenauer was convinced that Soviet hegemony, unless counterbalanced by the United States and a unified Western Europe, would extend over the whole continent. Therefore, Western unity, American presence in Europe, and the political-military balance of power were the elements of the only strategy capable of coping with the facts of the postwar European order. To many, this view seems today no less realistic than it was in 1945 or in 1960. One could even show that various supporters of the new *Ostpolitik* perceived European security in a similar way — there were others, of course, who held a different opinion.

The opposite point of view is mainly expressed by those persons and groups who based *Ostpolitik* primarily on general ideas like the *Primat der Friedenssicherung* or the postulate of reconciliation between the blocs. Those aims, as will be shown, had quite some significance for the first chancellor, too. Nonetheless, he preferred the ideas of Machiavelli, who in the fifteenth chapter of *The Prince* said, "One should not see the world as it should be, but as it is." And for Adenauer the basic fact of the European world was the threat Russia posed as a potential European hegemonial power, since from the days of Stalin it had given highest priority to military power and im-perialistic demonstrations of force.

By the fifties the discussion hinged on whether Adenauer did not overestimate Soviet capabilities to exert influence or power while underestimating the strength of the Western states. There is no empirical solution to that dispute because each attempt of a counterfactual history would be highly speculative.

Adenauer's Détente Calculus

From the outset Adenauer was preoccupied with the question of how to overcome permanent confrontation of the two blocs. He had two basically different answers to this question. During the early years of the Federal Republic, which coincided with the peak of the Cold War, Adenauer believed in the "crash theory." He believed that the European empire of the Soviet Union would fall into parts as soon as Western rearmament was completed and as soon as the more efficient community of free nations on both sides of the Atlantic was unified. The prospect of a collapse of the Eastern bloc and a rollback of the Soviet Union behind its own borders did not seem very unrealistic to him.

These were ideas that John Foster Dulles still maintained in 1955. By that time, however, he met with stiff opposition from the chancellor, who had abandoned the crash theory.[2] Since the spring of 1952, Adenauer had developed a détente concept that, although concerned with possible solutions of the German question, anticipated in many respects the perceptions and expectations common to Western thinking during the sixties. From that time until his death, Adenauer was convinced, as many learned from him in private conversation, that there was only a long-term solution to the German question. Not before the Cold War tensions had eased and the Soviet Union, for a variety of reasons, was ready to enter into negotiations, could such a solution be expected. One should never forget that Moscow's control over the *Ostzone* was closely intertwined with its control over the other states of its European empire. Only if the Kremlin could be sure that there would be no more military confrontations with the West, or if Soviet interest in relaxation of tensions between East and West were to become overwhelmingly strong, would the Soviets loosen their grip on their empire. But how to get Moscow to do this? Adenauer had a series of answers to that question, which, for purposes of clarification, can be summarized into five theories.

1. The theory of frustration. Once the West was united and strong, Adenauer reasoned, Moscow would come to the conclusion that it would not make any progress and therefore would be ready for a negotiated solution. That was the basic point of Adenauer's *Politik der Stärke.*

2. The theory of disarmament. This theory was based on the belief that the Soviet Union would in the long run not be able to stand an armaments race with the West. Facing enormous tasks at home (promoting agriculture, developing Siberia, providing better transport and communication systems, raising the standard of living, etc.), Moscow would be forced to shift its resources. Then the time would be right to settle, through general disarmament, territorial questions as well.

3. The crises theory. Adenauer always believed and during certain periods (the last time in summer 1963) was deeply convinced that the Soviet Union would have to cope with economic crises and deficiencies of the worst kind, especially in agriculture, but also in housing and consumer goods production. The Soviet Union would therefore, he reasoned, become dependent to a certain extent upon the West, which in turn, could make its economic help conditional on the fulfillment of political demands.

4. The theory of a relaxation of tensions. During his long life Adenauer had seen many ups and downs in the international system, and he regarded it a basic fact of life that tensions between groups of states or between great powers would ease after a while. Sooner or later new enemies would enter the area, or other developments would render former disputes obsolete. He was convinced that the Soviet leadership, too, would not be able to resist the forces of change in the long run.

5. The China theory. With the comeback of Red China in world politics at the Geneva Conference of 1954, Adenauer added a new point to these arguments. Due to the Chinese threat, he reasoned, Moscow would be ready to make concessions on its Western flank, although maybe only after a renewed phase of political pressure on the West. Adenauer's attention was heightened by various anti-Chinese remarks Krushchev had made during the former's visit to Moscow in September 1955. Since that time the probability of a Soviet-Chinese conflict was a constitutive factor in his détente calculations.

To the historian of détente policies, the theorems sketched above are not new. They played an important role in the détente policies of certain Western governments in the post-Adenauer era, too. The theories, however, were persuasive already during Adenauer's time. In that era as well as in later years, the Soviet Union was indeed confronted by the difficulties the chancellor envisioned as well as by some others. But she never was willing to make such far-reaching concessions as Adenauer had hoped for. Adenauer's calculus for his *Ostpolitik* was therefore much more subtle than most of his critics like to acknowledge. Unfortunately his concept had a little flaw: it did not turn out as it should have.

Mistrust of the Détente Policies of the Allies

It is not difficult to notice a basic contradiction in Adenauer's *Ostpolitik*. On the one hand, he saw no alternative to a peaceful solution of the German question except a policy of détente. On the other hand, he was always beset with mistrust whenever Washington, Paris, or London entered the road to détente. Like Bismarck's *cauchemar des coalitions,* Charles de Gaulle's Yalta complex, Adenauer had his Potsdam complex: a fear the four powers could settle their differences and — since most peace treaties are sealed by sacrificing animals to the deities — the German eagle would get plucked of its last feathers. The danger of an East-West accord at Germany's expense seemed to be obviated after the ratification of the Paris Treaties of 1955. But Adenauer knew too well that treaties — as de Gaulle put it — fade like roses and young girls. He watched every Western step toward détente with the utmost skepticism. He was alarmed by everything: French plans for a conference on the German question in the years 1951 to 1953; the Eastern policies of Mendès-France in 1954; the Geneva summit of 1955; the London disarmament conference of 1956-1957; Macmillan's trip to Moscow in January 1959; the Anglo-Saxon *Deutschlandpolitik* during the Berlin crisis; de Gaulle's rapprochement with Russia in 1965; the nonproliferation treaty negotiations between the United States and the Soviet Union, which began in 1965. The list could be expanded easily.

How Adenauer tried to prevent any damage to the Federal Republic by countering the persistent efforts for relaxation of tension cannot be described here. He had a few rules about how to offset the urge to reach an understanding with the Soviet Union. He appealed to the idea of Western unity. He never ceased to tie all the various activities of the Western big powers toward the East in a net of consultations. His call for a multi-lateralization of the détente policies mainly served the purpose of providing himself with a kind of veto position, since most of the détente negotiations directly or indirectly touched vital German interests.

On the whole, therefore, Adenauer tried to put some brakes on the train to détente. Indeed there was already in the fifties no need to encourage détente tendencies, which sprang out of the ground everywhere. And he never hesitated to point out very precisely and without any undue restraint where German interests seemed to be threatened. He did not mind becoming difficult when he presented the interests of his country, or what he thought they were, with a tenacity normally only ascribed to Gromyko or General de Gaulle. In that sense he was a rather troublesome partner for the Western protagonists of détente.

Judged by his own premises and aims Adenauer was, however, quite successful. Despite the extreme pressure during the Berlin crisis, the positions on the German question were at the end of his chancellorship still intact, Berlin once more remained unscathed, the nuclear option in whatever form was kept open, and every Soviet approach to obtaining a right of interference in Central European defense planning was fended off. At the same time, he was able, despite all the toughness of the confrontations, to establish a rather orderly relationship with the Soviet Union.

It is arguable whether the later abandonment of some positions he stuck to very closely had been unavoidable. In the late sixties it was common currency to point out that the Federal Republic, by sticking to its old positions on the German question, would maneuver itself into international isolation. Only a few remembered that from 1959 to 1962, the Federal Republic had, in relation to the German question, been exposed to stronger pressure from East and West as well as from within than all other West German governments in the following years. If ever a danger of becoming isolated existed, it was during those years. Adenauer knew how to avoid isolation and in addition was able by apt diplomacy to create the preconditions of German-Soviet normalization.

Utmost Care with the German-Soviet Bilateralism

There are very early indicators that Adenauer was convinced of the importance of direct contacts between the Soviet Union and the Federal Republic. In that respect he had more foresight than some of his officials in the Foreign Office. His decision in September 1955 to immediately establish diplomatic relations with Moscow, which caused criticism in the United States, developed to a large extent out of the consideration that a German chancellor must have, especially during an era of détente, his own Russian card to lay on the table.

He proceeded nevertheless in that direction only with the utmost care. He was aware of all the fears regarding a new Rapallo in the Western capitals as well as certain ideas entertained by some schools of thought in both the Foreign Office and German conservative circles that under certain circumstances could turn out as new variations of the concept of Germany as a bridge between East and West. He was firmly resolved to plan his direct contacts to the Soviet Union only as part of a common overall policy of the Western states. There must not be the slightest doubt that the Federal Republic would remain anchored in the West.

Nevertheless, Adenauer carefully established first contacts with Khrushchev and even initiated some explorations into the German question, although he still thought it better to stress four-power responsibility in the latter. Some communications flowed via Ambassador Smirnow, many via Ambassador Kroll, who was directly controlled by the Chancellery, so far as it was possible to control a personality like Kroll at all. Adenauer, however, always took pains to inform the Western heads of government of the very delicate explorations: his proposals of an Austrian solution for the GDR as well as of his later so-called *Burgfriedenspläne*. (He was bound to do so, by the way, by the Paris Treaties.) In any event he accepted the idea that the Federal Republic, which year after year was acquiring a permanently growing economic and political weight, sooner or later had to look for her own arrangements with Moscow, although those contacts should not take place without the approval of her allies. The *Burgfriedenspläne* were considered by Adenauer a kind of alternative or fallback position in case the Soviet-American Berlin talks collapsed.

The discrepancy between Adenauer's very careful proceeding and the rather uncoordinated German advances in the fall, winter, and spring of 1970 is very striking here. Distrust of Germany and of other nations perhaps could have been avoided if the example the first chancellor set in diplomacy had been followed. And indeed, the new *Ostpolitik* was soon replaced by the classic Adenauer line of multilateral détente. After a first period of the new *Ostpolitik,* German bilateral undertakings were tied again into the more secure net of careful consultations with the responsible allies. One of the continuities traceable to the Adenauer era is seen here.

The German Question in the Overall Context of Adenauer's *Ostpolitik*

Politicians seldom are willing to set clear priorities. Even in pursuing divergent goals, they prefer to live with conflicts instead of establishing a list of priorities that may be analytically convincing, but prove very embarrassing from a practical point of view. Certainly, Adenauer was no exception in this respect. All in all, however, he was a lot more willing than later chancellors to acknowledge fundamental conflicts of goals and to set priorities more or less brutally.

In the case of the German question, the order or priority was: security, preservation of peace, and reunification. To secure peace he relied, as did all later governments, on a strategy of deterrence; in case deterrence failed, he was resolved to go to war. In principle, therefore, the main goal of security had higher priority than peace. Reunification was conceived as a result both of successful *Deutschlandpolitik* and peace policy; it was connected with security policy within the Western alliance as well as with the pursuit of peace — in principle, however, it remained subordinate to both. Adenauer never would have accepted any reunification formula that implied a risk for the West German democracy. He also never gave any thought to a strategy that solved the national question in a way pursued for decades by the radical Arab states against Israel and accepted by world public opinion as a fact of life: a solution by threat of force or use of force. Thus his reunification policy was a peace policy, too.

One could say Adenauer's *Ostpolitik* was first of all a security policy. Second, it was a peace policy. Inextricably involved in those two policies, however, were his efforts to find solutions for the German question based on the right of self-determination. He never confined *Ostpolitik* to the problems of the so-called *Deutschlandpolitik,* reunification, Eastern territories, and security of Berlin. A favorable change of the status quo with its division of the German nation was a very important goal, but it never was on top of his priority list. The well-known triad — freedom, peace, unity — illustrates very well where emphasis in Adenauer's *Ostpolitik* was placed.

Until the middle fifties, therefore, Adenauer had to struggle with forces in his own camp as well as with the opposition parties, who tended to see *Ostpolitik* primarily as reunification policy. Adenauer found that view an undue simplification. Earlier than others, earlier than the SPD, too, he recognized that the German question and European security were inseparably intertwined. Since the middle fifties this perception has been common sense in all political camps. But still the chancellor had to fight for his order of priorities, as he saw it, so as not to pay for German reunification with security risks for West Germany or the entire German nation.

Is it possible, therefore, to say Adenauer did not care much about the Germans in the GDR and the national question in general? Of course not. But he had resolved to set priorities. In addition, he believed that progress in the German question needed time. Although he was willing to take high risks in his Western policy (with the acceptance of the Schuman Plan, the decision for German rearmament, and the question of nuclear armament of the *Bundeswehr*), utmost caution characterized his *Ostpolitik* and *Deutschlandpolitik.* This explains the overall defensive trait of his policy. Basic positions were vigorously established and also maintained: the political and legal aspect of the German question, the legal commitment of the Western powers to support reunification policy, his claim to being the only legitimate spokesman for all of Germany, and the theory of continuity with regard to the legal status of Germany. But in his opinion the Federal Republic still was too weak and time still not ripe for developing an offensive reunification policy based on these positions.

By the end of the fifties, the balance of power had changed so dramatically that negotiations on the German question were hardly more than a holding operation. Today we know that during that time, Adenauer, speaking to his confidants, carefully qualified by a number of reservations, wondered whether an agreement on the status quo was not about to materialize. Plans drafted by State Secretary Globke as well as the *Burgfriedenspläne,* brought into play during the explorations with the Soviet Union (of which de Gaulle and Kennedy were extensively informed) were a result of these considerations.[3] But one should not overlook the fact that those explorations never became definitive agreements. The chancellor's last word regarding the German question was not the consideration over a legal codification of a modus vivendi with the GDR, but his rather daring but in the last consequence successful refusal to pay for the security of West Berlin with an abandonment of his basic positions. Adenauer did that at the risk of most serious confrontations with the Kennedy administration as well as the Macmillan government, but in the final analysis he remained stead-fast until the danger was over.

Nevertheless, the German question limited to a degree his willingness to make concessions in his *Ostpolitik*. How far he would have been ready to go with the development of direct German-Soviet contacts during the last months of his chancellorship in 1963 must remain a subject of speculation.

All this leads to the conclusion that the goals of his *Deutschlandpolitik* did not dominate Adenauer's *Ostpolitik,* but they nevertheless had a substantial impact. The image of a chancellor paying only lip service to the national question, while pursuing in reality a *Rheinbund-Politik,* is not correct. Adenauer was a rather rare example — in the twentieth century — of a cautious German patriot. He not only knew that timing was a very impor-tant factor in political planning, but he was also able to make the right use of it. He was not willing to make advance political and legal commitments to a tough and legalistically operating adversary.

What then are the main differences in Chancellor Brandt's new *Ostpolitik*? Four points should be mentioned:

1. Adenauer in his final phase merely pondered whether there was no other way than modifying certain basic positions on the German question. Brandt, however, actually gave them up (recognition of the GDR, treaty with Poland defining the borders).

2. Unlike Adenauer, Brandt was convinced that an international con-stellation had come about for that comprehensive détente-dialogue with the Soviet Union in which the German question could be embedded. Brandt, as did Adenauer, conceived of *Deutschlandpolitik* as a part of a comprehen-sive *Ostpolitik*. But Brandt started out from far more optimistic premises.

3. Contrary to the first chancellor, Brandt did not hestitate to make some advance commitments, in order to get the negotiation process going. He accepted the theory of two states in his official policy; signed a treaty with Moscow before the conclusion of the Basic Treaty and the Berlin Agreement, as well as the framework agreement with the Soviet Union before an agreement with Poland; but contented himself with very limited concessions by the East.

4. All in all, Adenauer had been tougher, more patient, and more cautious. He also perceived the East-West confrontations from the vantage point of a nineteenth- and early twentieth-century orientation. Being familiar with the ups and downs in German history, he did not see why it was necessary to surrender to unpleasant realities so soon, after only a

couple of decades of German division. In addition, he had a highly
developed sense of national dignity. And as an enemy of the Nazi regime
who spent the twelve years of the Third Reich in Germany, several months
of it in prison, he knew all too well what impact foreign acknowledgment
and friendly treatment of a dictatorship could have on a suppressed population. This, too, was a reason not to recognize the GDR.

There can be no doubt that he paid for his tenacity with a rather high
degree of immobility regarding the German question. From the late fifties
to the late sixties, Bonn's political weight in international relations was
neither adequate to its central position in Europe nor to its economic
accomplishments, because it had to concentrate its energies to a very high
degree in the defense of its positions in the German question. Politicians of
a younger generation who were weaker and not so disciplined and who
could be found in all parties, especially within the SPD and FDP, increasingly regarded this activity as an unnecessary constraint on their political
activities.

A Moscow-centered *Ostpolitik*

With the events in Poland of 1956 and the Hungarian revolution, the
Eastern bloc became motivated. Since that time the argument whether and
how *Ostpolitik* should deal with the smaller Eastern European countries
played an important role in German politics too. The debate centered
mainly around three issues: Was it possible to establish diplomatic relations with governments who had had diplomatic relations with the GDR
since 1949 without endangering the claim to sole representation? How
could the outstanding issues with Poland or Czechoslovakia be reconciled
with a policy of normalization? Would not a more active *Ostpolitik* vis-à-vis
Warsaw, Budapest, Bucharest, or Prague endanger the desired overall
solution sought in the dialogue with the Soviet Union?

To Adenauer the last of the three considerations seemed of special importance. Basically he believed that the key to the German question, to use an
often cited phrase, lay in Moscow. He doubted there was any chance to influence the Russians through nations of their hegemonial system. In his
opinion such a policy would have been very counterproductive especially in
1956 and 1957 vis-à-vis Poland, where the program of liberalization
Gomulka had started in his first years was watched by the Soviet Union
with deep mistrust.

He was aware, however, of that special historical challenge any German
policy toward Poland had to meet. Although throughout his lifetime he was
not very familiar with the problems of Eastern Europe, he knew quite well
that Poland was a nation of European culture and had a historical con-

sciousness that made her part of the West. He knew that to normalize relations between Germans and Poles would require overcoming memories not only of expulsion and the seizure of German eastern territories, but also of cruelties committed by Germany in the years between 1939 and 1945.

But during those years when something could have been done—in 1957 and 1958—he remained impassive, mainly because of a complex mix of considerations regarding the Soviet Union, the refugees, and his basic positions in the German question and partly because of Yugoslavia's unfortunate policy in the fall of 1957. He even committed some small faux pas that further hindered the German-Polish dialogue. In the final analysis he remained a *Realpolitiker,* knowing that the smaller Eastern European countries were not able to conduct their own foreign policies freely and that all efforts in that direction would be in vain.

As we know, later governments under Ludwig Erhard and Kurt Georg Kiesinger/Willy Brandt took a different tack, but they were not very successful. Establishing trade missions and diplomatic relations with Bucharest in 1967 did not result in a breakthrough but quite the opposite: the USSR began to keep even tighter reins on the smaller Eastern bloc countries with regard to their policy toward Germany. So it came about that the SPD-FDP coalition, by starting out with negotiations for a treaty with Moscow, took up the old Adenauer line, which was to settle the basic issues with Moscow first and then establish within that framework new relations with the other Eastern European nations.

Will to Peace and Readiness for War

Did Adenauer ever expect military moves by the Soviet Union and what plans did he have in case of such an event? The chancellor never doubted that a totalitarian system such as the Soviet Union would, under certain circumstances, be willing to start a war. From his first conversations with Soviet leaders, however, he brought back a feeling that Russia too, after all the experiences she had had in the first half of the twentieth century, was as fed up with European wars as were the Germans themselves. In his opinion the Soviet Union preferred to expand her influence through a fifth column like the Communist parties in France or Italy, if necessary through diplomatic-military pressure, but not by war. During the 1950-1951 crises, when Adenauer's insights were still limited, as well as during the Berlin crises from 1959 to 1962 and the Cuban missile crisis in the fall of 1962, he feared most that a new war could be started due to miscalculations—a crisis scenario more similar to the events of 1914 than to the events of 1939.

Basically, he was determined to resist a potential military threat with toughness. Military superiority, he thought, was better than mere equality with the Soviet Union. All forms of inferiority he deemed suicidal. So he was not impressed at all by the argument raised in the fifties that the Soviet Union would be provoked by the drawing-up of a German army. In establishing a strong *Bundeswehr* during the years 1955 to 1958, he virtually used the last chance before the international climate would foreclose such a move. In 1957 and 1958 he managed against strong domestic and Soviet opposition to push through the armament of the *Bundeswehr* with nuclear launchers. During crises involving a risk of war, he stood firm but remained cautious. During the never ending discussions from 1959 to 1962 on the question of how NATO should counter a potential blockade of West Berlin, he came to the conclusion that in case an attack should prove necessary, *Bundeswehr* troops should be a part of it. Standing aloof was an option foreclosed to West Germany. In the worst case, however, he still would have tried first to establish a blockade — a much debated option — or still better a mere embargo. Franz Josef Strauss, the then defense minister, agreed with such a cautious procedure.

On the other hand, there is no sign indicating that Adenauer would have been willing to capitulate. In internal conversations on the Berlin crisis, he again and again criticized the mistakes the Western powers made during 1936 and 1939 by not being swift and tough enough in countering Hitler's moves. In his opinion, securing peace — a goal he supported as eagerly as all the later governments — required a credible deterrence. There is no indication that he would not have been willing to use all available means for defense, once deterrence had failed. The triad of freedom, peace, and unity signalizes that keeping peace ultimately had lower priority than securing freedom. But he did everything to defer as long as possible the hard decision to wage a war.

Later governments of the Federal Republic, unlike Adenauer's government, have never been confronted by a real danger of war. Thus it is difficult to make comparisons. One should note, however, the different attitudes toward Soviet propaganda campaigns that since the early fifties have been launched whenever the West tries to improve its defense posture. Adenauer was neither impressed by that nor by domestic opposition. A Chancellor Adenauer waffling in the same way as the federal government did during the neutron bomb debate in 1977 and 1978 is hard to imagine. It should be added, however, that he had to deal with an American government that was not so easily impressed by Soviet propaganda campaigns when deciding on improvements for the European defense posture.

Split Attitude Toward Arms Control

Since 1955 Adenauer declared both publicly and privately that a general and controlled disarmament should be a prime political goal of the West.

One is tempted to think that he used that argument becuase it did not cost much, but proved very helpful in controversies with the Social Democratic opposition as well as for the diplomatic business between East and West. Of course he knew about the psychological impact such catchwords as "arms control" have on the masses. When after 1970 the opposition got irritated by Brandt's so-called peace policy, it forgot that the first chancellor, too, knew how to play the tunes of peace. A careful analysis of Adenauer's diplomacy, however, proves that his very positive and pushing attitude on the question of disarmament was deeply rooted in his beliefs.

He was a bourgeois politician par excellence who had lived through enough wars during his lifetime to share all the longings for peace of the German people. He was shocked by modern mass killing weaponry, although that did not stop him from pushing for nuclear armament of German NATO troops after some sober calculations. To him a general disarmament of the big powers seemed the only way out of the dilemma created by the desire for peace and for military policy. In addition he hoped to get from a policy of disarmament some positive impulses toward German reunification.

Political reality, however, made clear again and again that his sympathy for a general and controlled disarmament was not based on a thorough analysis of the hard facts. Since the disarmament conferences in London, the Western alliance was confronted with the East's persistent attempts to use arms control as a means to achieve the goal of a demilitarized zone in Germany and especially a denuclearization of the Federal Republic.

There are few ideas Adenauer opposed as emphatically and uncompromisingly as the idea of a special status for the Federal Republic with respect to her national security, especially if that status gave the Soviet Union the right to interfere legally with German politics. Already the restrictions imposed by the Western European Union (WEU) Treaty were not very well liked by him because they ran counter to his goal of total equality within the Western alliance. But he realized that this was the price he had to pay for his buildup of the *Bundeswehr*. In any case those restrictions of armament were imposed by allies, which left a chance to remove some of them after due consultation.

Regional arms control measures negotiated with the Soviet Union and applied to Germany or the Federal Republic were, as he saw it, quite a different matter. To him there were several dangers: a possibility of separation from the NATO alliance; the opportunity for the Soviet Union to apply political pressure, questioning the sovereignty of the Federal Republic; and also a temptation for the Western allies to negotiate arms control agreements with the East at the cost of German interests. The Federal Republic, already discriminated against within the Western alliance, would have been discriminated against even more in international politics. The West, so he insisted, must never allow itself to open up through arms control measures the possibilities of direct or indirect interference by the main enemy of NATO. Above all, Germany must never be pressed into a special status internationally. In his opinion it was only a short step from a special status, as far as the security of the Federal Republic was concerned, to neutralization. And it was one of his main beliefs that neutralization was the shortest way to hell.

He could not agree with the arguments that arms control agreements required restraint from both sides. If the United States and the Soviet Union were ready for self-restraint, he thought it a useful thing, but only as long as this did not touch the interests of the American allies. But to bind a weaker partner by one or two superpowers in his opinion had nothing to do with a balanced commitment and would only surrender to the Soviet Union, which had the better leverage, the means to manipulate the Federal Republic. It is therefore no accident that he was one of the sharpest critics of the negotiations for a nonproliferation treaty from 1965 to 1967. His attitude toward arms control policy remained ambivalent and at its base rather negative until the end.

From 1956 on, this issue was central to his domestic disputes with the SPD, which already perceived itself as the arms control party. When, in 1969, the Social Democrats finally took over the helm, the new *Ostpolitik* was only the logical consequence. There are many instances the Social Liberal coalition could cite to invoke continuity with Adenauer's *Ostpolitik*. Arms control policy, however, definitely is not one of them.

Open Parlance and *Realpolitik*

In Adenauer's understanding, *Ostpolitik* had two dimensions: a political-ideological one and one of *Realpolitik*. The political-ideological dimension implied confrontation with the totalitarian Communism of Soviet provenance. This conflict had to be fought mainly on the domestic front within the West: against the fifth columns of Communist parties; against the fellow travelers; and against socialist, radical liberal, left-wing Catholic, or nationalist groups that let themselves be used by Eastern propaganda. For the chancellor an immunization at home was a decisive precondition to successfully exercising power. He not only expressed this opinion in speeches and conversations; he also came up with some rather impractical ideas for a supranational coordination of Western propaganda efforts. In his view the main addressees in the ideological-political competition should have been, besides the Western societies, the Germans in the GDR, the Poles, the Czechoslovakians, and the Hungarians.

Propaganda, however, was only one element of a political-ideological

Ostpolitik he thought essential. In order to formulate such a policy, it was necessary to conceptionalize and represent it in a persuading manner, so that broad majorities of the population would be convinced of its soundness. Therefore a clear political parlance was one of the basics.

Adenauer had no doubt that Western democracies were willing to follow their governments in fighting for their self-assertion only if the governments acknowledged permanently and without embellishment the very fact of the Soviet threat. He did not think much of restraints in the political-ideological confrontation in order not to arouse any anger in the East. Above all he thought it necessary to give both the elites and the masses a clear picture of the military balance. He accepted being labeled by the public a rigid anti-Communist. As long as he remained chancellor, he was able time and again to gain the support of large majorities for his opinions.

A judgment of Adenauer's policy based solely on his public statements overlooks a second dimension of any *Ostpolitik* that he realized very clearly: the reality of politics. In his opinion the Soviet Union was not only the center of world communism, but also a great power that pursued her specific interests within the framework of the given distribution of power. Like all states she quite often acted pragmatically. As a result, there was political-ideological confrontation on the one hand and, on the other, a chance for compromise and a certain degree of normalization. Given the effectiveness of deterrence, modern weapons technology, and the military superiority the West still had during those days, a certain pragmatic normalization seemed possible. From a rather early time on, Adenauer was persuaded by that kind of reasoning and was willing to fight for it within the alliance.

So two different pictures of the chancellor have emerged. The first based mainly on public statements is of Adenauer as an anti-Communist hardliner. The other one, evident from a careful study of his files, shows a quite different Adenauer: a *Realpolitiker* who not only believed in the possibility of agreements with the adversary, but also made concrete steps in this direction.

The double strategy in Adenauer's *Ostpolitik* in many respects looks like a mirror image of Soviet foreign policy, which also juxtaposes the function of a permanent political-ideological struggle and the necessity for a temporary peaceful coexistence. The Soviets therefore respected the chancellor as a congenial partner for détente. The differences between Adenauer's *Ostpolitik* and the new *Ostpolitik* are especially striking in this instance. Later governments hesitated to link *Realpolitik* and tough political-ideological confrontation as forthrightly as the first chancellor did. The tune of the ideological competition has changed significantly since then, not only in the West but also in the Communist bloc (but to a lesser degree in the GDR).

Ostpolitik as the Chancellor's Domain

This rather sketchy study covers only a few main elements of Adenauer's *Ostpolitik*. Thus the study could be criticized for being superficial because it assesses German *Ostpolitik* during the fourteen years of Adenauer's chancellorship as a policy of one man. Was not Adenauer's *Ostpolitik* a product of complex decision-making processes too? Did not these processes involve the chancellor and his cabinet, the Chancellery, the Foreign Office, and since 1955 the Ministry of Defense, the federal government, and the party leadership of the majority parties within the *Bundestag* as well as the Allied governments? Of course the picture of the chancellor alone making decisions is a myth that does not stand up to any serious research. However, until 1961 Adenauer had been able to personalize *Ostpolitik* to an astonishing degree. He started to develop his *Ostpolitik* in personal contacts with the high commissioners and so had all the strings in his hands from the very beginning. From 1951 to 1955 he was his own secretary of state as well. Although he was supported by State Secretary Hallstein in setting up the Foreign Office and in forming a policy of European integration, *Ostpolitik* and *Deutschlandpolitik* remained his sole domain.

When in the spring of 1955, after ratification of the Paris Treaties, Heinrich von Brentano took over the Foreign Office, Adenauer in a formal letter to the new foreign minister (of which he even informed the president of the republic) reserved for himself the right to conduct European affairs, matters concerning the two superpowers (the United States and the Soviet Union) as well as all international conference matters. Von Brentano was obliged to inform and consult the chancellor whenever decisions in those areas were to be made. In a series of sharp confrontations during the first months of Brentano's tenure, Adenauer succeeded in getting his demands accepted.

There were various groups in the Foreign Office who from time to time tried to make their own *Ostpolitik* behind the back of the chancellor and to get, in addition, the support of the foreign minister. But in such cases — as for example in the spring of 1959 when the positions of the West for the East-West conference of foreign ministers had to be outlined — Adenauer did not hesitate a second to embarrass the Foreign Office and its minister as soon as he realized that important matters had slipped out of his control.

During the tenure of Ambassador Kroll, the chancellor was especially determined to have direct control over diplomatic activities in Moscow through personal contacts or through State Secretary Globke. Adenauer's control over the *Ostpolitik* eased a little bit when Gerhard Schröder took over the Foreign Office and Erich Mende became minister for all-German affairs. The confrontations between Schröder and Kroll were more or less arguments with Adenauer about who was in charge of the Foreign Office.

But although Schröder partly prevailed with respect to his policy toward France, Adenauer by and large was able to maintain control over *Ostpolitik*, all the more so because the differences between him and his secretary of state were not large.

Indeed, during the entire Adenauer era, Bonn's decision making in Eastern policies was determined to a far larger degree by consultations with the Western great powers than by German actors who played with their own *Ostpolitik*. The opinions of Acheson, Dulles, Eden, Macmillan, or de Gaulle had more political impact than those of the foreign minister, of other members of the cabinet, or of powerful politicians within the coalition parties.

Therefore the *Ostpolitik* between 1949 and 1963 was to a far larger degree the chancellor's own policy than it has been ever since. This justifies to a certain degree a personalized approach, although even then the decision-making process was of course quite complicated and sometimes even forced the chancellor to make compromises with countervailing forces. On the whole, however, his conception of *Ostpolitik* prevailed, and he was able to realize it without large concessions and quite often without any complicated consultations. The campaign slogan *Auf den Kanzler kommt es an!* ("It is the chancellor who counts!") was quite true as far as *Ostpolitik* in the Adenauer era was concerned. Whatever future judgment is made on the Eastern policy of the Federal Republic during the years 1949 to 1963, it will primarily be a judgment on Adenauer's *Ostpolitik*.

Notes

1. For recent studies on Adenauer's foreign policy, see *Konrad Adenauer und seine Zeit. Politik und Persönlichkeit des ersten Bundeskanzlers,* 2 vols. (Stuttgart: Deutsche Verlagsanstalt, 1976); *Adenauer-Studien,* 1, 2, 3, (Veröffentlichungen der Kommission für Zeitgeschichte, Reihe B, Bd. 10, 13, 15 (Mainz: 1971, 1972, 1974; *Konrad Adenauer 1876/1976* (Stuttgart/Zürich: 1976). Surveys of the ongoing research may be found in Rudolf Morsey, "Zum Verlauf und Stand der Adenauer-Forschung," in *Konrad Adenauer 1876/1976,* pp. 139-46; Helmut Grieser, "Konrad Adenauer im Urteil der Forschung," in *Geschichte in Wissenschaft und Unterricht* 27 (1976):25-47; Hans-Peter Schwarz, "Der unbekannte Adenauer," in *Konrad Adenauer und seine Zeit,* 2:589-609.

2. Compare the letters of June 27, 1955, and August 15, 1955, reprinted in *Memoirs,* vol. II, pp. 481ff.

3. The texts of two drafts from early 1959 and of a version of November 17, 1960, are in *Adenauer-Studien,* 3:202-09. Concerning the Globke Plans, there is a posthumous account by State Secretary Globke in "Überlegungen und Planungen in der Ostpolitik Adenauers," in *Konrad Adenauer und seine Zeit,* 1:665-72.

10

The New *Ostpolitik*

Karl Kaiser

The *Ostpolitik* of the Federal Republic of Germany has entered a new phase during the chancellorship of Helmut Schmidt. But the transition to a more pragmatic style in domestic and foreign policy resulting from the transfer of power has detracted from important changes relevant to *Ostpolitik*. The rekindled debate inside and outside Germany on the German problem and on the international role of the Federal Republic (and of the GDR) is a symptom of developments that address old problems in a different context.

To an increasing extent, German *Ostpolitik* reflects the growing responsibilities and problems of West Germany's reemerging status as a European great power. Further changes were the result of various policies practiced by West Germany's leaders from Konrad Adenauer to Willy Brandt regarding the European environment and German options. Finally, there have been changes in the international and European scenes, in the American-Soviet relationship, and in the global constellation of forces, all of which pose new problems for German *Ostpolitik*.

The problems and changes at hand are not so much the result of the day-to-day politics of the SPD-FDP government led by Helmut Schmidt, though this government without doubt increasingly shapes the style, options, and content of policy the longer it stays in office. One is dealing, rather, with international conditions and problems of German *Ostpolitik* that are of a more long-term character. Once in power, a CDU government would have to face them as well. Precisely for this reason and because of both the international implications of *Ostpolitik* as well as the confused domestic debate within Germany, a modicum of bipartisanship in this area continues to be of paramount importance. In what follows I shall attempt to analyze the changes in the context and content of *Ostpolitik* and to examine the domestic and international implications.

Old and New *Ostpolitik*

A comparison of Adenauer's *Ostpolitik* with the new *Ostpolitik* introduced in some of its aspects by the Great Coalition of CDU and SPD and fully implemented during the chancellorships of Brandt and Schmidt not only interests the historian and social scientist, but also brings the problems and dilemmas of contemporary policy into sharper focus. When undertaken as part of the public political debate, it is (like many discussions on important historical issues) an indispensable part of the conceptual debate on central political problems of the present or future.

Continuity and Change

A comparison of *Ostpolitik* under Adenauer and his successors can easily be misleading if one fails to take into account the changes in the international environment within which they acted. Moreover, each chancellor created a different environment for his successor. Thus, certain options concerning German reunification that appeared realistic and sensible to pursue in Adenauer's days appeared illusory or outdated by historical developments by the time Brandt was chancellor. Through his *Ostpolitik,* Brandt, in turn, liberated the Federal Republic from numerous constraints and thus created one of the preconditions for Schmidt's greater use of West Germany's power potential in German diplomacy.

Viewed in a historical perspective, the achievement of the Adenauer era for West Germany in this respect can be summarized as having destroyed the foundations of the classical German *Mitteleuropa* position that resulted in Germany's fatal *Schaukelpolitik* ("see-saw policy") between East and West. To be sure, this was not Adenauer's doing alone, but he seized the opportunity provided by the East-West division and fully exploited the possibilities of West Germany's revival through integration in the West. His priorities in pursuing this integration were security and freedom in the Western sense.[1] Any *Ostpolitik* (which included *Deutschlandpolitik*) that implied risks for this policy was unacceptable to him and the majority of the electorate. All his unorthodox ideas in *Ostpolitik,*[2] with the exception of opening diplomatic relations with the Soviet Union, failed to lead to any serious endeavors that produced results. In fact, given the international constellation of his era, it is doubtful whether they could have, at least until the early sixties.

When the Great Coalition and to a greater extent the Brandt-Scheel government sought a new departure, the priorities of freedom and security remained the same; but they were able to conduct *Ostpolitik* from the secure basis of full integration in the West. Moreover, the West fully supported their policy. Active *Ostpolitik* no longer threw the Federal Republic's fun-

damental Western orientation into question as Adenauer had dreaded that
it might. In this sense Brandt's *Ostpolitik* would have been impossible
without the fundamental reorientation of the Federal Republic toward the
West achieved in the Adenauer era.

This is not to imply any judgment whether possibilities other than those
of Adenauer existed in *Ostpolitik.* In the perspective of the 1980s this is a
politically futile question, and it is fortunate that the Federal Republic has
been spared a debate of significant proportions on "missed opportunities."
Nor does this interpretation imply agreement with all facets of Adenauer's
Ostpolitik, which, after all, remained in essence declamatory. Moreover, it
remains questionable whether it was necessary in Adenauer's days to stick
to orthodoxy for so long and so adamantly, although, admittedly, the
Kennedy administration's somewhat adventurous Berlin policy made a
pragmatic adaptation as urgent as it was difficult.

The changes that *Ostpolitik* had undergone by the time Brandt left office
are well known and need not be analyzed in detail here: the shift from a
concept of reunification through (basically) an absorption of the GDR into
the West to an undefined solution of the German problem through a
rapprochement of the German states as the result of overcoming Europe's
division; the abandonment of the *Alleinvertretungsanspruch;* ("the claim to sole
representation"); the de facto recognition of the GDR; the shelving of the
Hallstein Doctrine; the recognition of the borders; active détente policy as a
contribution to solving the German problem (rather than the previous concept of reunification as the prerequisite of détente). These changes were
fundamental in nature and of profound importance for Europe.

In the partisan debate on the pros and cons of the old and the new
Ostpolitik, three reproaches constantly reappear that depict the new Eastern
policy in an unfavorable light compared with its predecessor: the
unilateralism and lack of multilateral Western coordination, the self-
imposed haste, and the unnecessary and unilateral concessions of the
policy. Because of the current and continued political relevance of these
issues, they deserve brief attention.

Unilateral versus Multilateral Ostpolitik

The issue of whether German *Ostpolitik* is adequately coordinated with
the Western powers remains as important today as it was in Adenauer's
days. Not only the legal situation of continued Allied powers' rights, but
also plain political realism requires a concerted approach on all important
issues of Eastern diplomacy. But so far no significant evidence exists to support the thesis that the *Ostpolitik* of Brandt was inadequately coordinated
with the West. Despite some initial reservations concerning specific
elements of Bonn's new initiatives on the part of the Nixon administration,

all major steps were agreed upon in close consultation within the "group of four." The bilateral phase of West German *Ostpolitik* was a necessary prerequisite for entering the multilateral phase of the European Conference on Security and Cooperation and of the Vienna negotiations on troop reductions, since only the Federal Republic herself could settle such sensitive issues as the territorial question or the relationship with East Germany, though in close cooperation with the West.[3]

Second, Western coordination of *Ostpolitik* in the Brandt and Schmidt period was quite a different process compared with that in the closing days of the Adenauer era and, though less so, during Ludwig Erhard's term of office. By the early 1960s the Federal Republic had maneuvered herself outside the mainstream of Western *Ostpolitik,* which had entered its phase of détente and was, therefore, to a growing degree at odds with specific elements of West German policy. The Bonn government then increasingly used multilateral coordination as an instrument to block or change Allied policies that it regarded as detrimental to the German position, a process that, needless to say, put growing strain on the relationship.

Indeed Adenauer himself laid the basis for what he regarded as a particular threat to West Germany: the danger of isolation from the West. The SPD-FDP government, as Brandt observed,[4] had to defend an axiom of Adenauer's early policy against his political heirs who adamantly opposed the new *Ostpolitik.* And even after the transition to Chancellor Schmidt, the problem persisted as witnessed in the reception of the Helsinki accords, which the German opposition rejected, making it the only democratic party in the West to do so. It was the new *Ostpolitik* that brought the Federal Republic back into the mainstream of Western policy.[5]

Finally, the implementation of various bilateral German-Eastern and multilateral moves, linked through reciprocal *Junktim,* resulted in the Eastern treaties, the Berlin Agreement, the intra-German Transit Settlement, the opening of the CSCE, and negotiations on mutual troop reductions. The recognition of the GDR by Western countries was postponed until the two German governments had negotiated their Basic Treaty. All in all the implementation of this détente program, more or less according to plan despite the extraordinary complexity and divisiveness of issues and the number of actors involved, represents perhaps the most outstanding example of coordinated Western diplomacy, although in all fairness the credit must be shared with the Allied powers.

A Policy of Haste?

To raise the question of self-imposed haste of *Ostpolitik* until 1972, and of insufficient use of all negotiation possibilities, is no doubt legitimate. But is the reproach borne out by facts? First, it is worth remembering that most of the relevant issues had been thoroughly studied in the *Auswärtige Amt* (Foreign Office) since the days of Foreign Minister Gerhard Schröder, long before the enactment of the new *Ostpolitik,* even before the Great Coalition. The complex questions connected with the mutual renunciation of the threat and use of force that were at the center of the treaty with Moscow had been examined ever since the first drafts of the "peace note" of 1966 were drawn up. The situation was similar with regard to Poland. The head of the trade mission established by Schröder in Warsaw conducted numerous confidential talks on these issues since early 1967. Second, there was objective (not just self-imposed) time pressure because of growing disagreement in the outside, notably Western, world with central elements of the German position. There was a real danger that Western countries would act unilaterally and thereby irrevocably destroy negotiating positions necessary for securing Bonn's basic interests. In some countries, namely Britain, the Netherlands, and Sweden, public pressure to recognize the GDR was visibly mounting. The final reproach — that the new *Ostpolitik* had made unilateral concessions — should be seen in the wider context of bipartisanship.

The Bipartisan Foundation of the New Ostpolitik

The great domestic battles over *Ostpolitik* in the early 1970s are over, and since then elements of bipartisanship in this area that go beyond a mere *pacta sunt servanda* have increasingly appeared. But disagreements and polemics remain, and of all the ongoing disputes over the past, the reproach of *Verzichtpolitik* and of having made unilateral and unnecessary concessions is potentially the most disruptive, for it can still be expanded and abused as a legend to feed a destabilizing revisionism in German and European politics.

For those who want to claim the entire credit of the new *Ostpolitik* for the SPD and FDP as well as for those who want to blame the SPD-FDP coalition for all alleged pitfalls of the policy, the reminder that essential elements of the new *Ostpolitik* have a bipartisan origin may be useful. As mentioned earlier Chancellor Erhard's Foreign Minister Schröder made important preparatory steps. In addition, the Great Coalition of CDU and SPD irreversibly changed crucial parts of what was once Adenauer's *Ostpolitik,* which thereby lost its internal logic and political force.

The Great Coalition made the first steps toward the "two-state theory" by establishing communication with the GDR, by proposing its inclusion in a European system of mutual renunciation of the use of force, and by accepting it as the *effective* though not *legitimate* ruler over the East Germans. The Great Coalition also shelved the Hallstein Doctrine in its dealings with Romania, Yugoslavia, and Cambodia.

Finally, SPD and FDP politicians were not alone but were joined by CDU politicians in stating that the Oder-Neisse issue could not be solved by inflicting new injustice on those who had settled in the now Polish areas. The realization was not confined to the SPD and FDP that a recognition of the border by the Federal Republic had only a limited bargaining value after the four powers had gone on record on the issue at Potsdam and public opinion in those countries had pretty much settled on nothing but the territorial status quo.

The questions remain, of course, of current importance. The reference to a future all-German entity not bound by the territorial settlement, introduced during parliamentary ratification procedure in order to gain opposition support, has become the source of renewed doubt about the ambivalence of the German territorial commitment, doubt that in turn has had considerable impact on approaches to the German problem.

The *Ostpolitik* of a European Great Power

Ostpolitik *from a Western Basis*

The *Ostpolitik* of the Schmidt-Genscher government is built on the heritage of its predecessors and reflects West Germany's changed role in a changing international environment. Adenauer's *Ostpolitik,* as explained above, aimed at a grand revision of the results of World War II and was unsuccessful; yet it kept certain options formally open. However, during his era the Federal Republic was irreversibly integrated in Western Europe, the Atlantic alliance, and the Western economy. The *Ostpolitik* of the Brandt-Scheel government, preceded by the openings of the Great Coalition, profited on the one hand from a new opportunity to pursue an active program from a secure position of the Federal Republic's integration in and full support from the West. On the other hand, it undertook an overdue revision of the previous *Ostpolitik,* which threatened to isolate the Federal Republic and jeopardize German interests.

When Brandt and Scheel left office, their successors inherited a profoundly changed constellation:

- the settlement of open territorial issues and removal of major previous sources of distrust and tension;
- a modus vivendi and ongoing dialogue with East Germany, the Soviet Union, Poland, and other East European countries;
- a redefinition of security as encompassing both defense and détente;
- an active German détente policy in numerous areas and a new image of the Federal Republic in Eastern Europe, now no longer an easy target of Communist propaganda;

- a four-power Agreement on West Berlin;
- an endorsement by the Soviet Union of a permanent involvement of the United States (and Canada) in the security of Europe;
- the multilateral process of CSCE and mutual force reductions (MFR);
- the realignment with Western détente policy (notably on the territorial issue) and thereby the precondition for and initiation of European political cooperation, i.e., the beginnings of a common foreign policy of the European Community; and
- a liberation of the foreign policy of the Federal Republic from the heavy constraints of the previous policy.

Thus the stage was set for the *Ostpolitik* of the Schmidt-Genscher government. No longer impeded by the burdens of the old policy and exploiting the heritage created by preceding governments, the new government could for the first time make full use of West Germany's resources in foreign, defense, and foreign economic policies. Moreover, in doing so it could fulfill West Germany's four systemic roles and reconcile them with each other:

- as one of the leading actors in the Western and world economic system;
- as the barrier state in the defense of Western Europe, major actor in the NATO alliance, and chief partner of the United States in the conventional defense of Europe;
- as the key economic power and one of the leading powers of the European Community; and
- as a country induced by its geostrategic position, the exposed position of West Berlin, and its links with the East Germans to act as a bridge and force of mediation with Eastern Europe.

Now for the first time, the Federal Republic fully realizes the potential of the leading position it enjoys as the result of its full integration in the Western and worldwide system built up under America's basically benevolent hegemonial leadership. Indeed, this position offers the West German government under peaceful circumstances "many of the objectives of the traditional continental option"[6] pursued by its precursors under conditions of unity to the detriment of European peace.

Of the Federal Republic's four systemic roles, three are Western oriented, indicating how deep its involvement in the West has become. The political, cultural, and economic system of the republic is primarily geared to and dependent on the West. This means no less than that the preconditions for a new Rapallo have been removed by history. Deals with the East have only occurred when there was no adequate place for Germany in the West, but such a place exists today in the Western councils of leadership. Finally, in the future there will be no serious chips offered by the Soviet Union nor any takers in Bonn.

In playing from its secure Western position its systemic role as bridge builder to the East, the Federal Republic fulfills the obligation of her geostrategic position and political past. Although to other Western states Eastern policy is but one important part in a whole spectrum of foreign policy areas, to the Federal Republic it is of crucial significance, since it relates to immediately felt and central issues of national politics: the possibility of a European conflict for which Germany is to be the likely arena (including the high priority of defense and détente policy); the security of West Berlin, a strategic but vulnerable part of German territory; the solidarity with the East Germans and the historical bonds with the smaller East European countries; and, finally, the considerable economic relationship with Eastern Europe.

Despite West Germany's Western orientation, détente policy, therefore, remains of more immediate concern to West Germany than to other Western powers. For the Federal Republic, détente policy has a more concrete substance in terms of acts affecting human beings, the movement of persons, trade, etc., in comparison with other Western countries, which tend to treat their *Ostpolitik* more in terms of general principles and strategic considerations. This makes for differences in priorities and perceptions as witnessed, for example, in the skeptical German reaction to President Carter's human rights policy.

In the framework of its Western roles, the Federal Republic increasingly uses its economic resources in *Ostpolitik*. The various deals with East Germany that the FRG rewards with Western currency for all services that help alleviate the negative consequences of the German division, and also those with Poland, demonstrate this. In fact, it was in connection with *Ostpolitik* (and subsequently with policy on the European Community) under Schmidt's chancellorship that anything like a debate on the economic costs of foreign policy first began.

The personality and political priorities of Chancellor Schmidt have, of course, played a significant role in bringing about the new phase in German foreign policy and *Ostpolitik*. As a leading Social Democrat of long standing, as former finance and defense minister as well as author on strategic questions, he brought to his new office the expertise and the familiarity with issues, leaders, and countries needed to fulfill the Federal Republic's Western functions in the European Community, the world economy, and the Atlantic alliance. In addition, he brought the self-assuredness and the sense of limits and of obligations that have helped the Federal Republic to assume the role of a European great power.

Chancellor Schmidt's devotion to Western values and the corresponding goals of German policy do not essentially differ from those of his predecessors, nor have they been questioned even by his political opponents. But his commitment to a course of active détente policy with the neighboring states in Eastern Europe has often been underestimated.

Schmidt played a crucial role in reorienting the SPD on a new course of *Ostpolitik,* notably at the 1966 Dortmund party Congress. As the parliamentary leader, he steered his faction through the difficult years of the Great Coalition when the Social Democrats were the more active partners in promoting and implementing new departures in *Ostpolitik.*

Schmidt advocated a change of West German foreign policy on the Oder-Neisse line when this was still unpopular even within the SPD. In fact, Poland always occupied a special place on his list of priorities. To complement reconciliation with France in the West (where he sees himself in direct succession to the tradition established by Adenauer) with a similar process with Poland in the East has been and continues to be one of his major goals. His dealings with the Poland of Edward Gierek have indicated this priority to which his foreign minister and coalition partner Hans Dietrich Genscher attributes equal importance.

In its new phase, *Ostpolitik* must deal with a series of built-in dilemmas to which I shall briefly turn before reviewing some of the more important problems of *Ostpolitik* in the coming years.

The Dilemmas of Growing Power and Continuing Dependence

A new debate on the German problem centering around the question of German unity has started in Europe, notably in France. Old questions, such as the danger of a much too powerful Germany upsetting the balance of power in Europe or of reversing existing alignments, have reappeared. It is worth examining the factors that unleashed this debate, for they bring into focus some important developments relevant to *Ostpolitik.*

Three factors seem to have triggered the debate. The first factor is the combination of West Germany's new resource potential with a government that, freed from some former constraints, actually employs this potential in the pursuit of Germany's interests. The difference in resource potential compared with other European states is, of course, not new; nor does the West German government pursue anything other than a strongly West European and Atlantic policy. Finally, German unity is hardly within realistic reach. But the new reality of a German government actually using resource potential for political purposes as Europe's great powers have always done in the postwar period is sufficient to raise new questions and old specters.

"Que faire de l'Allemagne?" Le Monde headlined in 1978.[7] Will not the

Federal Republic use its power to achieve unity or make deals with the East to achieve it? After all, German unity is a goal laid down by the West German constitution and shared by all political parties, and some French authors in this debate also support the idea of reunification.[8]

The new constellation in Europe has reduced the reluctance to bring into the open a tacit assumption that all of Germany's neighbors, East and West, have held for many years: given Germany's power potential, its division is regarded as a precondition for stability and peace in Europe.[9] "While West Germany fits comfortably into Western Europe, a united Germany would not. . . . No one outside Germany has an interest in Germany's unification."[10] Indeed, the combination of the German states would create an industrial giant of 80 million inhabitants with a GNP one-and-a-half times that of France, twice that of Britain, and about three-quarters that of the Soviet Union.

There is a second reason for the new debate on the German problem. If a united Germany is only a theoretical problem, the power potential of the Federal Republic in the European Community is real. Is Germany becoming the "dominant economy" of Western Europe?[11] It is not coincidence that the debate is stepped up at the very moment when direct elections to the European Parliament create the prospect of a genuine move toward more political integration. Since Britain has withdrawn as a serious weight to counterbalance Germany due to her continued anti-European posture, does that leave the Federal Republic as the dominant power of the European Community? And what would be the consequence for the relationship with the East?[12] These questions are asked most openly in France, but shared by many other Europeans.

Third, there is a debate on the German problem that is confined to Poland (with a probable echo in Moscow). It is linked to certain ambiguities in the German position on the Oder-Neisse line and the open Chinese challenge to the territorial status quo in Europe. Only portions of this debate have come into the open; they ostensibly deal with specific points in the French discussion on Germany, but, in fact, express strong Polish opposition to any move on the German problem that might call into question the territorial status quo.[13]

This argument underestimates the realities of the intricate web of dependence on the outside world that heavily circumscribes the margin of maneuver of the Federal Republic: dependence on the United States for security, on the European Community and the world economy for prosperity, and on continued détente with the Soviet Union to improve the position of West Berlin and relations with East Germany as well as other Eastern neighbors. These factors provide powerful inducements to a prudent German posture, even if there were the domestic desire for a more adventurous policy.

But the debate also points out a series of dilemmas in the three areas of European, Atlantic, and Eastern policy. They are the product of West Germany's new power potential and its increased margin of action. In the field of *Community policy,* an anti-Community posture or a renationalization of policy as taken by de Gaulle or today by Britain would immediately unleash specters of German nationalism and counteract German moves. But a pro-integration policy would have similar effects, for it would nourish the suspicion that the Federal Republic wants to dominate the Community or use it as a new power base.

In *alliance policy,* the Federal Republic faces two dilemmas. First, a passive acceptance of the deterioration of the defense posture of its allies would undermine German security as well, but an increase of the German contribution to NATO would nourish the fear that the Federal Republic will become militarily too powerful or that the multilateral character of the alliance will be increasingly eroded by a U.S.-German axis. Second, because of her geostrategic position, the Federal Republic more than any other West European country is absorbed in the difficult exercise of finding the right balance between détente and defense. Given her resource position and role as barrier state, she inevitably has to extend that exercise to other alliance members, a process that easily leads to misunderstandings or resentment. Moreover, it can happen, as is the case with relations with the United States these days, that the Federal Republic will have to press for European interests in the fields of defense and détente *simultaneously.*

Finally, in the field of *Ostpolitik,* a hawkish posture is likely to isolate the Federal Republic in the West, to threaten the achievements of détente with regard to West Berlin, East Germany, and Eastern Europe, and to hurt German interests. But an active détente policy is not without problems either, since it nurtures fears of a new Rapallo or of reproaches of being too soft vis-à-vis the Soviets, if not of "self-Finlandization."

Since these dilemmas are the result of the new constellation of forces in Europe, the Federal Republic cannot avoid them. It has to live with them and can, at best, minimize their negative impact through a prudent management of conflicting developments that persist in upholding the basic elements of an *Ostpolitik* from a secure Western basis.

Notes

1. See the contribution of Hans-Peter Schwarz to this volume.
2. On this point see Hans-Peter Schwarz, "Die nationale Frage — morgen," *Die politische Meinung,* May-June 1974.
3. For details see Karl Kaiser and Peter Roggen, "Die Ostpolitik der Bundesrepublik Deutschland im Rahmen der westlichen Entspannungspolitik," in Marion

Gräfin Dönhoff, Karl Kaiser, Paul Noack, Wolfgang Wagner, eds., *Die Internationale Politik 1970-72* (München: Oldenbourg Verlag, 1978).

4. Willy Brandt, "Konrad Adenauer—Ein schwieriges Erbe für die deutsche Politik," in Dieter Blumenwitz et al., eds., *Konrad Adenauer und seine Zeit* (Stuttgart: Belser, 1976), p. 106.

5. For a similar interpretation, see the penetrating study by William E. Griffith, *The Ostpolitik of the Federal Republic of Germany* (Cambridge, Mass.: MIT Press), 1978.

6. David Calleo, *The German Problem Reconsidered* (Cambridge: Cambridge University Press, 1978), p. 166.

7. André Fontaine in *Le Monde,* November 22, 1978.

8. *Le Monde,* August 16, September 13, November 22, 1978.

9. For the discussion of these issues in the late sixties, see my *German Foreign Policy in Transition* (London: Oxford University Press, 1968).

10. Compare the critical analysis of the argument by Joachim Hütter, "Die Stellung der Bundesrepublik Deutschland in Westeuropa: Hegemonie durch wirtschaftliche Dominanz?" *Integration,* no. 3 (1978); and Michael Kreile, "Die Bundesrepublik Deutschland—eine 'économie dominante' in Westeuropa?" *Aus Politik und Zeitgeschichte,* Beilage zur Wochenzeitung Das Parlament, July 1, 1978.

11. William Pfaff, "German Challenge: Problem to Europe," *International Herald Tribune,* December 1, 1978.

12. See Fontaine, *Le Monde.*

13. See the article of the editor in chief of *Polityka,* Mieczyslaw Rakowski (also member of the Central Committee of the UPWP), *Polityka,* October 21, 1978; and Ryszard Frelek (Central Committee of the PUWP), "Polska w zmierionym swiecie" [Poland in a Changed World], *Sprawy Miedzynarodowe,* no. 12, 1978.

11

The Role of Public Opinion in West German Foreign Policy

Peter H. Merkl

The role that public opinion plays in the making and understanding of foreign policies is hardly new in political science. There have long been models of communication systems, such as that of Karl W. Deutsch, that have emphasized the flow of communication and information into and out of the policymaking system.[1] There is also an ever growing literature on bureaucratic decision making in foreign policy that has always assigned an important role to contributions from the media and from the larger public, even though it has rarely used public opinion data as such.[2] The analysis of public opinion polls on policy matters and general attitudes often raises additional problems of interpretation before it can be plugged into a policymaking model. Due to timing and structural constraints, we can never assume that perfect knowledge exists between the policymakers and public opinion. The presence of mediating structures (such as the press and other media, in particular) will inevitably distort the message on its way from the public to the policymakers, who for their part often are hard of hearing and may take a skeptical view of the level of public information and judgment. Still, there remains the task of clarifying, at least after the fact, what the public felt and of relating it to actual government policies. A democratic foreign policy, if such a thing is indeed desirable, requires the understanding of the patterns of interaction between public opinion and government decision makers.

Fortuna, Necessità, e Virtù

The larger public interested in international politics and foreign policy usually interprets the complexities of foreign policy chiefly in the way Niccolò Machiavelli perceived it in the days of Columbus: the statesman or prince finds himself in ever changing situations that challenge him to the utmost. Fortune (*fortuna*) may bring opportunities or threats to the survival of his state. Iron necessity (*necessità*) may test his skill and perseverance in

the face of severe odds. In the end it will be his ability (*virtù*), the leadership
of a lion or the ingenuity of a fox, that will be the key to his success and to
the survival of his state.[3] Machiavelli's vision of what matters in foreign
policy is still essentially correct although it may well need further elabora-
tion. Even Machiavelli was aware, for example, of the importance of public
opinion in the autocratic states of the prince. He carefully distinguished
between how the prince and his actions should *appear* to his public and his
antagonists and what he and his actions should be in reality—which was at
least the compliment of hypocrisy that vice pays to virtue. But there was
also an element of respect (or rather of fear) toward public opinion, which
in a more democratic age the makers of foreign policy can ill afford to ignore.

Whose Opinions, Which Public?

Machiavelli's awareness of perceptions and appearances serves well our
consideration of the role of public opinion in foreign policymaking. We
need only to separate it from his model of political action and provide
greater detail about its application. Most of all, it is necessary to consider
the different levels and kinds of public whose opinions and attitudes are
relevant in varying degrees to the making of foreign policy.

In the case of West Germany, at the apex of the policymaking apparatus
are the equivalents of Machiavelli's prince, the foreign policy leadership in
elective or appointive positions dictated by the political structure: the
chancellor, foreign minister, those cabinet ministers and state secretaries
whose relevance changes with the content of the policy at hand, the
Bundestag committees on foreign affairs, defense, all-German affairs,
borderland questions, refugees, and the budget, the *Bundesrat,* the
Chancellery, and intracabinet councils such as the Federal Defense Council.[4] It is a truism to say that the opinions and attitudes of this small group
of people are crucial as they face the challenges that *fortuna* metes out to
their country. History is replete with examples of gross misperceptions of
the situation by such leaders—cases where they mistakenly perceived a
necessità that was not really there, or where they were skillfully deceived.
The impact of their opinions and attitudes on actual foreign policymaking
is obviously the most direct, misperceptions and all. Since they are making
policy, moreover, they feel compelled to act, and their actions and opinions
may easily form a vicious circle: they may misperceive a hostile attitude on
the part of a neighboring state and, in reaction, initiate such measures as
will make that neighbor respond and confirm their own prejudices.

Most observers would hesitate to consider the study of the opinions of
foreign policy leaders as a kind of public opinion study because they are

accustomed to expect a certain audience quality. However, policy leaders have opinions, too, that are closely related to the opinions of other public groups, which are discussed below. Their opinions are frequently studied especially in relation to actual past policies and differ from those of less potent public groups only in their close link to the implementation of policy and thus to the creation of new situations.

The next level of elite opinion more clearly constitutes a public and has been studied with methods of quantitative public opinion research. This level is comprised of the opinion leaders of the elite, as distinct from the policymaking elite. Two West German elite studies of the 1960s illustrate the range of definitions of such an opinion elite in political science research.

A 1964 interviewing project of Karl W. Deutsch, Lewis J. Edinger, Roy C. Macridis, and Richard L. Merritt,[5] which concerned itself particularly with foreign policy attitudes, defined the West German political elite as follows:

1. political (partisan) elites
2. military leaders
3. communication (media) elites
4. civil servants
5. business and business association leaders
6. other professions (including the churches, labor, and professional associations)

In five of these six groups, the researchers intended to interview a like number (thirty) of respondents and half that number among the military. Generally speaking, the bulk of this elite sample was about forty-five years of age and occupied highly influential positions in society and government, although not the top positions in the latter. If there was a choice, the interviewers preferred ascending, younger elite persons to those near retirement. Only a small fraction was in formal policymaking roles, but it can be assumed that most of the basic foreign policy attitudes of the larger political elite were shared by both policymakers and influential persons.[6]

The second elite study was conducted by Rudolf Wildenmann at the University of Mannheim in 1968 and aimed at a similar group distinguished by its formal rank. This project had singled out about 800 respondents as follows:

- 191 party leaders, mayors, land ministers, chairmen and vice-chairmen of federal and land legislative committees
- 89 high federal or land civil servants
- 129 economic and managerial elites

- 150 communications media elites
- 88 functionaries of business associations
- 78 trade union leaders
- 90 university, church, and other associational elites

Wildenmann omitted members of the federal government, fearing a high rate of refusal and seeking to avoid the bias introduced into a measurement of opinion by loyalty to government policies. His definition of elites is "persons or groups who are capable of imposing their own views and guidance within recognizable social formations."[7] Like the Deutsch-Edinger sample, the Wildenmann sample consisted of respondents mostly over forty-five years of age and highly educated, which deviates markedly from the "attentive public" for foreign affairs (discussed below), not to mention the West German public at large.

This elite level should always include party, media, and mass organization leaders outside of the government, especially those that are in opposition to the broad outlines of government policy. This entire group of several hundred persons has, of course, less influence on actual policy, yet it still wields leverage on government leaders and the general public that is out of proportion with its numbers. The influence that the group primarily exercises is a kind of veto power over official policy and is more effective in mobilizing support against rather than for a given policy. In either case, its opinions should be analyzed even if it is difficult to show just how each of its members is influencing opinions.

From the elite level, we proceed to the levels of mass opinion, beginning with the concept of the attentive public, which is defined as that well-informed part of the adult public that really follows foreign policy through the mass media. By common consensus, West Germany's attentive public for foreign affairs is rather large. A recent cross-national study by Daniel H. Willick found 27.1 percent of West Germans "very interested in international affairs," as compared to 16.9 percent of Englishmen, 11.9 percent of Frenchmen, 8.7 percent of Japanese, and 4.4 percent of Italians.[8] Richard Merritt and Ellen Pirro have supplied comparably high indicators of media attention and media exposure to foreign affairs for West Germany, also in contrast to other European countries. Indeed, the newspaper-reading public is very large, with nine out of ten reading a paper at least once a week and more than half reading the paper daily.[9] The attentive foreign policy public forms the well-informed mass audience that critically observes and evaluates government foreign policy. Its approval on the issues of "grand politics" (foreign policy) most likely is crucial to the re-election of the government. However, unlike the opinion elite, the attentive public cannot get its detailed views across very well except in public opinion polls in which they will be weighed along with nearly three times their numbers of poorly informed voters. Their votes cannot indicate satisfaction or dissatisfaction with specific policies; they are limited to the choice of "turning the rascals out" or leaving them in office.

This definition of the more potent part of the general voting public overlaps with another such public — the mass membership of political parties, trade unions, farm organizations, and other massive groups. This mass membership has a privileged position in relevant policy decision not because it is well informed, but because it is organized along interest-specific lines. The individual member of a trade union has little leverage on government policy beyond that of an unorganized worker, but the trade union federation has very considerable clout if it chooses to make an issue of a particular policy. And the members' influence with their union is greater than their influence with the government, which must serve a more varied clientele. There has not been much research on the foreign policy views of trade unionists and not much more on those of party members,[10] but the positions adopted by these organizations (and their leaders) with some input from the membership are generally known. Examples of West German groups with particular interest in certain foreign policies have been the Farmers League (DBV), various refugee groups, industrial and employers' associations, and the Trade Union Federation (DGB). Cases in which, for instance, the refugees advocate a certain policy toward Eastern European countries also illustrate linkages and trade-offs between foreign and domestic policy goals. When the bulk of Eastern refugees was economically integrated into West German society during the Adenauer years, the government had to forgo a revanchist foreign policy stance in exchange for generous credits and subsidies. When the Brandt coalition decided to launch its *Ostpolitik* over refugee protests, it risked determined opposition and enmity on domestic issues as well.

Such trade-offs may also be present (if less openly and clearly) at the broadest public opinion level, that of the adult voting public — which will be our primary concern here. The general voting public is more poorly informed on questions of foreign policy than are the elites or the attentive public. It is crucial, therefore, not to regard its judgments and public responses as necessarily rational choices made on the basis of adequate information. Its judgments, instead, need to be scrutinized for their level of knowledge (cognition), the salience of certain issues, the feelings and prejudices they reveal (affect), and in particular their tolerance or intolerance for actions or inaction in matters the public hardly understands anyway. Irrational fears or an excessive sense of trust in the international environment are among the various primary feelings and orientations that underlie the mysterious processes of evaluation by which a half-informed public judges foreign policies.

There is still another level of public opinion in foreign affairs that shall not concern us here any further though it should be mentioned: foreign opinion as received and perceived from inside a system. Not only are West German foreign policymakers quite aware of the images that other countries have of the Federal Republic and the Germans, but so are the various elites and, at least, the attentive foreign policy public in Germany.[11] The opinions of foreign officials, as relayed through diplomatic channels, are major factors in the situation in which a government makes its decisions. Foreign media images and public perceptions similarly have considerable impact on policymakers as well as on opinion leaders and the attentive public. West Germans have been particularly aware of what *das Ausland* thinks of them, and by comparison, have worried more than most nations — with the possible exception of Americans — about why they continue to be the target of pronounced hostile prejudices stemming in large part from the misdeeds of earlier German generations.[12] On the other hand, new generations of Germans, who were less than fifteen years old in 1945 (two-thirds of the population today), have increasingly developed a healthy disregard for any unreasoning phobias they encounter. Still, the awareness of other people's perceptions can be a major constraint on foreign policy action and choice, since the actors will strive to avoid confirming the popular stereotypes about themselves.

Mass Opinion

When we deal with the mass level of public opinion on a subject as difficult and complex as foreign policy, we need to ascertain first the answers to certain crucial structural questions. Even where exposure to the media is as high as in the Federal Republic, the first question is, Do the people really care? Not everyone who watches television a lot is interested in politics — even in Europe, with the more political and news-oriented media.[13] The second question deals with the manner in which foreign policy issues present themselves to the mass public and how it can respond to them.

Interest in Foreign Policy Issues

Figure 1 shows the amazing rise of interest in politics over the first three decades of the Federal Republic. The most remarkable feature of the rising curve of interest is that the affirmative responses grew evidently at the expense of those who had not been at all interested in politics before, rather

FIGURE 1.   Are you interested in politics, generally
speaking?

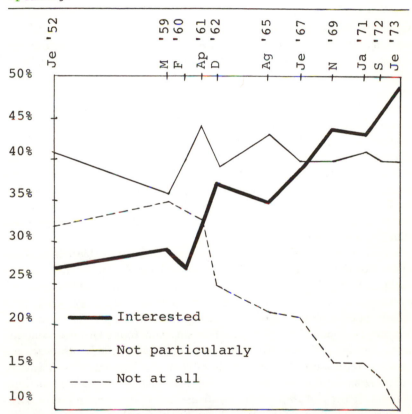

Source: Dieter Just and Lothar Romain, Auf der Suche nach
dem mündigen Wähler. Bonn: Bundeszentrale für politische
Bildung, 1973, p. 186. This diagram was plotted from data
in JOM, 1973, p. 213. The sample is representative of West
German and West Berlin adults.

than at the expense of those who were not particularly interested. Only one-tenth of the mass public (as compared to almost one-third in 1952) still is not at all interested in politics, a figure that roughly corresponds to the proportion of nonvoters in federal elections. We can take for granted that West Germans would include foreign policy issues prominently among the political questions that interest them, although foreign policy interest must fluctuate considerably in interaction with domestic issues and priorities. After the 1961 elections, for example, Viggo Graf Bluecher wrote persuasively that "the most salient issue among the electorate is the *grosse Politik* [foreign and world politics]," which is also far more stable and lasting than domestic issues tend to be. Only the small number of people highly involved and interested in politics, he claimed, tend to pay equal attention to domestic issues.[14] Nevertheless, he had to admit, such issues as access to Berlin and the desire for peace rose to high levels of saliency only after the alarming events of that year, beginning with the Kennedy-Khrushchev meeting in Vienna. Reunification, however, was the issue of highest salience every year from 1955 to 1963,[15] an issue of abiding if "cold" enthusiasm. In October 1960, four-fifths of the respondents expressed their strong support for reunification, yet only one-third was prepared to "do anything to attain it." Nearly all respondents regarded reunification as a matter of family or personal deprivation, a "nondiscussable fundamental value" in their lives.

But how long will people keep longing for the unattainable? In 1964 the saliency of the reunification issue began a sharp downturn after having reached a high (when 41 percent of respondents regarded it as "the most important question facing Germany today)." The DIVO survey of late 1964 already rated inflation higher,[16] although the surveys of the Institut für Demoskopie continued to give reunification a generous edge over economic issues for another year. In 1966 and in January 1967, however, the economic recession in the Federal Republic had eclipsed the importance of reunification in the perception of the public, with 62 percent naming economic issues and 18 percent reunification.[17] Other foreign policy issues rarely rated a higher saliency than domestic issues either, except when accident or Soviet heavy-handedness happened to stir up East-West crises at nearly every federal election. The 1949 elections were overshadowed by the Berlin blockade and those of 1953 by the crushing of the East German revolt of June 17, 1953. The elections of 1957 were in the wake of the abortive Hungarian and Polish revolutions and the demise of John F. Dulles's doctrine of rolling back the iron curtain. The 1961 elections were preceded by the construction of the Berlin wall, and those of 1969 may well have been influenced by the invasion of Czechoslovakia by the Warsaw Pact nations or the collapse of the Bonn policy toward Eastern Europe. Only the 1965,

1972, and 1976 elections were undisturbed by foreign policy crises.[18] Even the 1972 elections took place among intense foreign policy agitation that polarized the public for and against the *Ostpolitik*. Since measurements of voter interest in foreign policy are most likely to occur at the time of elections, the claims of high West German attentiveness to foreign affairs may well have been exaggerated.[19]

Specific Policy Approval or Disapproval

The intensity of the interest[20] stirred by the *Ostpolitik* debates of 1972 soon gave way to a certain disillusionment with its effectiveness as people became impatient for concrete results and more aware of the price that had to be paid for reconciliation with the East.[21] By the time of the 1976 elections, foreign policy issues had slipped far down the list of priorities of the West German voter. Topped by such issues as inflation, unemployment, crime, vocational education, health care, and abortion, the highest-ranking foreign policy issues were only twelfth (European unification) and fifteenth (German reunification) on the list. This is not to deny that European unification was favored by 79.4 percent of the respondents and German re-unification by 63.9 percent. But the public evidently considered many other issues more pressing.[22] It is worth noting, however, that mass opinion expressed about specific past or present policies is only one kind of public opinion — the most overt kind — and not necessarily as effective as a public protest against a given policy.

The Politics of Fear

More important than popular opinions on everyday political issues are some of the basic deeply seated concerns that the masses share with the policymaking elites. Because these concerns do not generate specific, immediate actions, they are not easy to pin down. In essence, they amount to underlying attitudes that determine at least the masses' first reactions to new policy proposals. Wolfram Hanrieder expressed one of these fundamental concerns in the following words: "the Cold War struggle between two opposing alliances not only gave birth to the Federal Republic, but also imposed upon West Germany a fundamental concern with its security from external threats."[23] What at the elite level may take the form of specific policy recommendations appears as a largely inarticulate climate of fear at the mass level or, as I have called it elsewhere, a "lack of trust in the international system."[24] At the broadest interpretative level, there is a curve of responses to the annual New Year's Eve question of the Allensbach pollsters, "Is it with hopes or with fears that you enter the New Year?" The result is a kind of compound angst curve that mirrors, along with economic

FIGURE 2.   Is it with hopes or with fears that you enter
the year?
_____

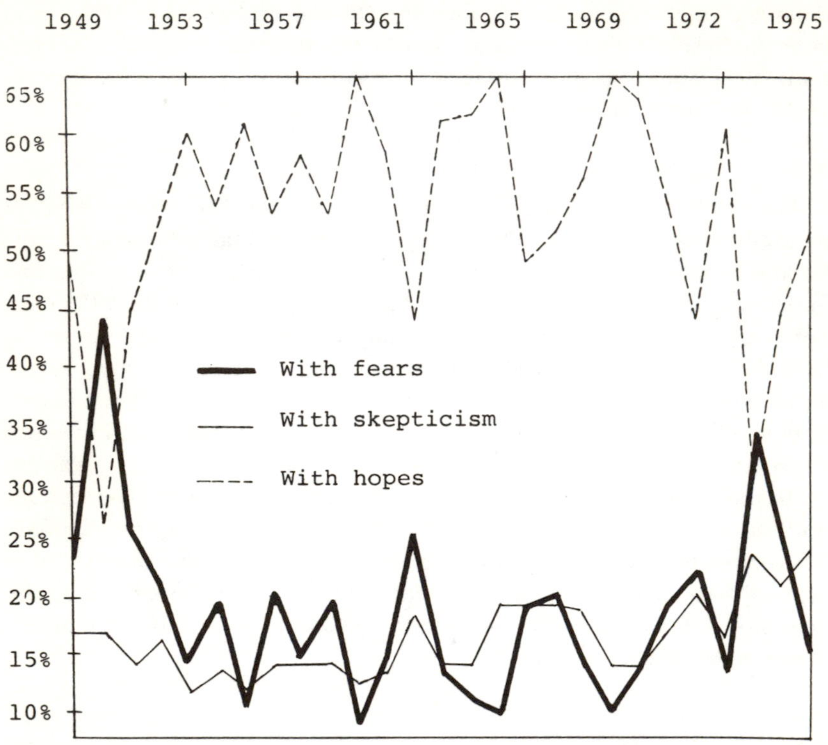

    1949   1953   1957   1961   1965   1969   1972   1975

Source: 1976 New Year's card of Institut für Demoskopie.

indicators, the fear of instability brought into West German life from the
international environment (see Figure 2). Witness the peaks of angst at
such crucial foreign policy junctures as 1950, 1956, 1961, and 1966. The
skeptical responses faithfully follow the peaks and valleys of anxiety and, if
added to the anxiety curve, would greatly emphasize them.

A Fear of War

A more selective indicator than this generalized angst is the fear of a major war and, more specifically, *Angst vor dem Russen,* the fear of Soviet attack. The fear of major war includes the deep-rooted German fears that, no
matter what the Federal Republic does or what might be the cause of the
conflagration, the two Germanies are likely to be laid waste in the process.

     In the first decade of the Federal Republic, in particular, there were 10 to

18 percent who expected a major war "within the next three or four years," according to DIVO polls.[25] The percentages resemble those of the generalized angst curve, including a sharp peak in the *Sputnik* year of 1957, the year after the Hungarian crisis. Even more startling are the Allensbach polls of the 1960s—supposedly the period during which international tensions in Europe, at least between the Soviet Union and the Western Allies, were systematically reduced. Between 1961 and 1967, 35 to 46 percent of West German adults (over sixteen) said they did expect another world war, while 43 to 57 percent believed that "no one would risk such a war."[26] Even the optimists had not specifically excluded the possibility of a world war starting by accident.

Angst vor dem Russen

As for the fear of the Russian, the anxieties show a notable change from the high point of November 1968, after the Czechoslovak invasion, to the onset of Willy Brandt's *Ostpolitik* in September of 1969.[27] However, when one observes the total curve (see Figure 3), it appears that the temporary resurgence of fear was an aberration in the long-range downward trend of the diminishing fear of Russia. And again, the younger and the better educated respondents turned out to be considerably less frightened of the Russians than were the rest.[28] The post–World War II generation and the well informed evidently did not share the guilt and fears related to the war experience. And yet, even at the height of the *Ostpolitik* debate in 1971, as many as 50 percent would not credit the Soviets with the goodwill to bring about a rapprochement with West Germany (versus 34 percent who did). Forty-five percent believed "the Russians had not changed" (vesus 34 percent who thought they had).[29]

Who Is Stronger, East or West?

To get to the bottom of this mystery, we need to recall that there has been an ominous change in the popular assessment of Soviet power among West Germans. Back in 1953, the pollsters began to ask their respondents whom they expected to be stronger fifty years from then, the United States or the Soviet Union (see Figure 4). At that time, the image of U.S. strength was still stronger (32 percent) than both alternatives combined—a stronger Soviet Union (11 percent) and equality between the Soviet Union and the United States (9 percent)—even though 48 percent professed that it was impossible to predict. By 1966, the combined responses for Soviet superiority and equality (21 percent and 16 percent, respectively) already exceeded the proportion of those envisioning American superiority in the future (29 percent). By 1973, 32 percent thought the Soviets would be more powerful in fifty years while 14 percent thought the United States would have the edge.

FIGURE 3. Do you feel threatened by Russia or do you
not feel threatened?

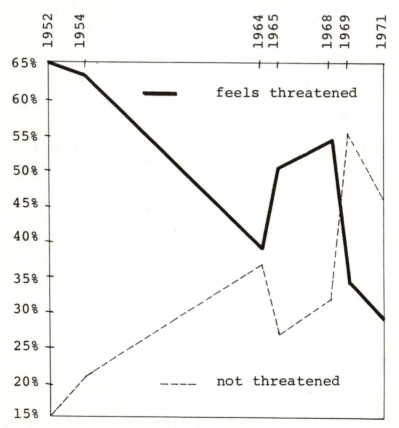

Source: Allensbacher Archiv, IfD Umfragen, nos. 077,
1094, 2001, 2046, 2056, 2071.

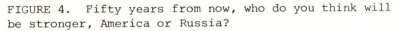

FIGURE 4. Fifty years from now, who do you think will be stronger, America or Russia?

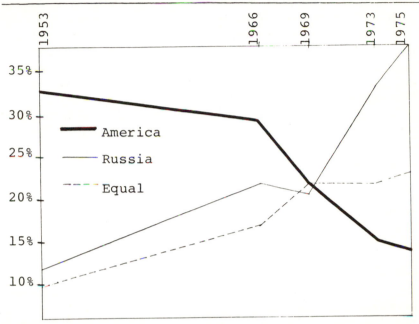

Source: Allensbacher Archiv, <u>IfD Umfragen</u>, nos. 065, 2015, 2048, 2092, 3015.

By 1975, the ratio between visions of Soviet and American superiority was nearly three to one, with more people anticipating a stronger USSR (37 percent) than those who expected a stronger America (13 percent) or equality between the superpowers (22 percent), combined.[30] In 1963, the question, Who has the stronger armaments (now), the West or the East? still drew a 34 percent response naming the West, 15 percent naming the East, and 26 percent considering them equal. In February 1976, the same question was answered in favor of the West by only 6 percent, for the East by 57 percent, and for equal strength by 24 percent.[31]

Better Red than Dead

What conclusions does the German public draw from this perception of growing Eastern military superiority? In July 1969, 64 percent of the young voters of the Federal Republic were hoping for better relations with the East. Even among respondents who identified with the CDU-CSU, 63 percent were hoping for a peace treaty between the Soviet Union and Germany, and 70 percent placed safety from Eastern aggression high on the agenda for the 1969 elections.[32] But if it should come to the final battle to protect Europe from Soviet conquest, only 25 percent of West German adults said in 1975 they would "fight even an atomic war to defend our way of life," while 49 percent preferred "above all to avoid war even if we had to live under a Communist regime." German responses to this question in the fifties had been nearly evenly balanced between those who would rather be dead and those who would rather be red.[33] Thus mass sentiment, at least in 1969, has emphatically turned to an accommodation with the East, while the West German leadership, perhaps with better insight into the situation, prefers toughing it out on the side of the West.[34] For the masses, moreover, the threat of the East has not lessened in recent years, even in the wake of *Ostpolitik.* In February 1976, 51 percent professed being worried about the menace from the East while 37 percent were not.[35] What is there to keep the next set of West German government leaders from turning to neutralism or to a Finlandization of West German foreign and defense policy?

Mass Opinion and *Ostpolitik*

How did West German mass opinion react to the *Ostpolitik* initiatives of the new Brandt administration at the outset of the 1970s? In July 1970, the Institut für Demoskopie presented West German adults with a collection of opinion cards with which the respondents could express various degrees of agreement (see Table 1). The overlapping majorities for mutually exclusive opinions revealed the confusion of the public, although there was also a solid sense of the need for new approaches.

It is logically impossible, it seems, that 70 percent (question 3) considered the postwar situation not final while 63 percent did consider it final (question 6).

At any rate, in March-April of the following year, 57 percent expressed their approval of the Eastern treaties with the USSR and Poland (versus 15 percent who did not). More significant yet, new majorities had finally begun to accept the fact that the eastern territories beyond the Oder-Neisse line were lost forever and that the disputed border there with Poland might as well be officially recognized (Figures 5 and 6). Since this was a major implication of the Eastern renunciation-of-force treaties, a close correspondence of elite and mass opinions with actual governmental policies had occurred.

The final clincher, and also a case of close correspondence, was the long-range change of mind regarding the diplomatic recognition of the East German state. To be sure, Willy Brandt only meant to recognize the DDR as

TABLE 1.   Questions Posed to West Germany by Institut für Demoskopie Poll

	Agree fully	*Agree partly*	*Dis-agree*	*No opinion*
1. "Twenty-five years after the end of the war, we simply must draw a line through the past. We can proceed in politics only on the basis of the present realities."	51%	24%	13%	12%
2. "For twenty years, nothing was done to bring about a relaxation of tensions with the East. It is high time that something is done."	45%	25%	17%	13%
3. "What happened after the war in the East is not final. A peace treaty will decide what things will be like."	41%	29%	14%	16%
4. "We would betray the right to self-determination of the German people if we recognized the DDR government even though it still oppresses the people and will not permit free elections."	37%	23%	22%	18%
5. "We can offer the East whatever we want, recognition and the reunciation of force. They will give us nothing in return, only suspicions and hostility."	36%	29%	19%	16%
6. "The German division and the loss of the Eastern (Oder-Neisse) territories are results of the lost war that we cannot undo. There is no point in pretending they are not final."	32%	31%	22%	15%

one of the two states within the German nation and not in the diplomatic sense. Once the Hallstein Doctrine had been dropped and there were regular contacts between East and West Germany, however, there was no stopping the international stampede to grant diplomatic recognition to the DDR and to acknowledge its eventual admission to membership in the United Nations. However, considering the earlier West German emphasis on reunification and the insistence that Bonn was the sole legitimate representative of all Germans (*Alleinvertretung*), the issue of West German recognition of the DDR indeed looks like a bellwether of West-East German relations during this crucial period. According to 1970 polls, moreover, 9 percent of West Germans have close relatives in the DDR, another 21 percent have distant relatives, and 14 percent have friends. Twenty-five percent send parcels to East Germans and 21 percent frequently or occasionally correspond with East Germans.[36] Thus to many West Germans, these issues are very close to their hearts.

FIGURE 5.   Will Pomerania, Silesia, and East Prussia
ever be returned, or are they lost forever?

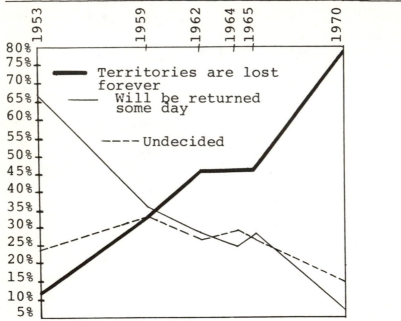

Source: Noelle and Neumann, <u>The Germans</u>, p. 482, and
Allensbacher Archiv, <u>IfD Umfragen,</u> no. 2067.

Figure 7 shows the long-standing reluctance of the German public until
the mid-sixties to yield any ground on the issue of recognition of the DDR.
Even at the height of the West-East German negotiations leading up to the
Traffic and Basic Treaties of 1972,[37] there was not exactly a popular majority for recognition of what West Germans had for so long considered an
illegitimate regime.[38] Somehow it always seems harder to come to a
generous settlement with neighbors whom one knows too well not to despise
than with countries farther away.[39]

We can conclude that the underlying attitudes of fear made the West
German mass public anxious to come to an agreement with the East on
such particulars as the renunciation-of-force treaties with Moscow, Warsaw, and eventually Prague and that it did so largely before the *Ostpolitik* of
the Brandt government was launched. This is not to deny that the momentum generated by the *Ostpolitik* contributed to the public acceptance of
policies that, a few years earlier, had not enjoyed popular majorities. Can
we now expect the level of West German fears to decline? Evidently not,

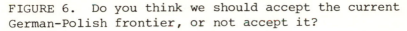

FIGURE 6. Do you think we should accept the current German-Polish frontier, or not accept it?

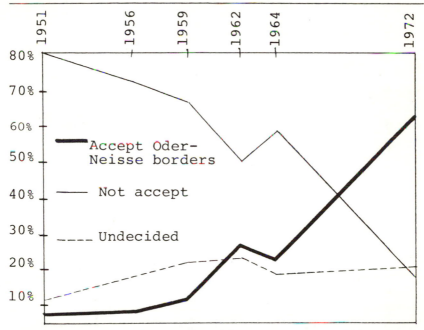

Source: Noelle and Neumann, The Germans, p. 483, and Allensbacher Archiv, IfD Umfragen, nos. 1093, 2082.

although there may well be qualitative changes at work here: the pre-1969 fears seemed to be highly related to the age of the respondents; in other words, a generational phenomenon that stems from memories of World War II. Perhaps now the younger generation is learning to fear the powerful neighbor on the East, too, as the evidence of the level of Soviet armaments sinks in. And, of course, West Germans are not alone in being motivated by fear. The Soviet Union itself most probably was moved toward a settlement in Eastern Europe by fear of China.

Instruments of Policy

My remaining topic is the instrumental identification of the West German public with various institutions for foreign policymaking. The most prominent foreign policymaker in the public view, as well as in reality, is the chancellor. We lack longitudinal public opinion data on how much the public has identified the chancellor with foreign policy,[40] but we can

174

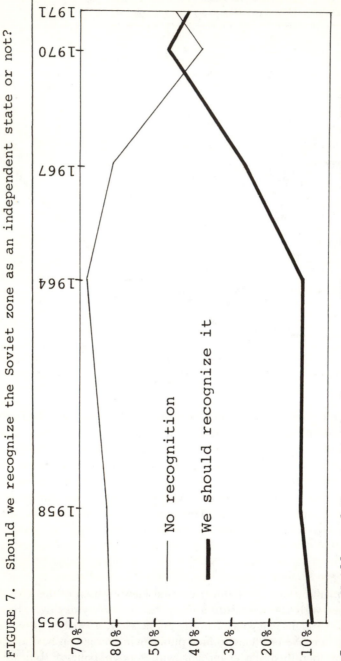

FIGURE 7.   Should we recognize the Soviet zone as an independent state or not?

— No recognition

━━ We should recognize it

Source: Noelle and Neumann, The Germans, p. 478, and JOM, 1973, p. 510.

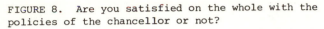

FIGURE 8. Are you satisfied on the whole with the
policies of the chancellor or not?

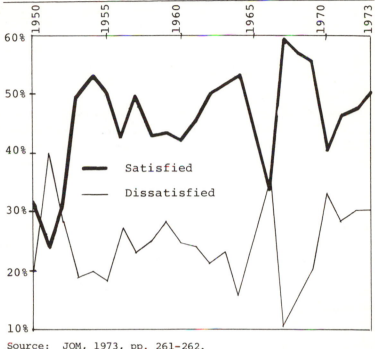

Source: JOM, 1973, pp. 261-262.

assume from other evidence that Adenauer and Brandt, at least, were
viewed principally in this fashion. Thus we can take a diagram of general
policy support for all the chancellors in succession (see Figure 8) — Konrad
Adenauer (1949-1963), Ludwig Erhard (1963-1966), Kurt Georg Kiesinger (1966-1969), and Willy Brandt (1969-1973) — as an indication of the
peaks and valleys of the chancellors' foreign policy support. The public
identification with Brandt, the chancellor, was far lower than that for the
team of Kiesinger and Brandt (1966-1969). We have to remember,
however, that this was the period of the Grand Coalition when the party
faithful of both the SPD and the CDU-CSU may have felt compelled to en-
dorse the government. From the fall of 1969 on, there was again competition between the major parties. On the other hand, there was also a longitudinal measurement over the entire 1966-1973 period that was based on the
question Do you have a good (or not so good) opinion of Willy Brandt?
(Table 2). The tabulation shows more clearly the positive image of Brandt
during the years of the *Ostpolitik*.[41]

TABLE 2.   Do you have a good (or not so good) opinion of Willly Brandt?

Good opinion	Dec. 1966	July 1967	March 1969	Oct. 1969	March 1971	Feb. 1973	July 1973
(percent agreeing)	43	51	57	55	63	72	61

Such a question, naturally, had partisan overtones as soon as party competition reestablished itself. The last poll of the Grand Coalition period, the
one of March 1969, elicited favorable opinions even from the 51 percent of
the respondents who identified with the CDU-CSU, a feat Brandt was
unlikely to repeat after he became chancellor.[42]

Parties as Instruments of Foreign Policy

Political parties, too, can be viewed by the public as instruments of
policymaking, as evident from Figure 9, which follows the public assessment of how good either one of the two major parties was at foreign
policy.[43] The rising curve of the SPD and the falling one of the CDU-CSU
in the post-Adenauer era clearly show how the public shifted its instrumental identification from the latter to the former. In fact, it is probably at

FIGURE 9.   Which party is better at foreign policy
(SPD or CDU–CSU)?

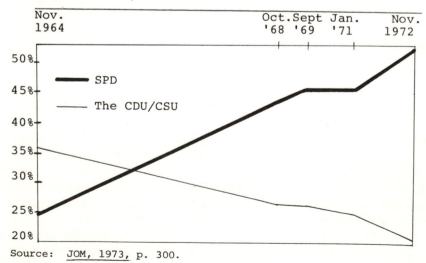

Source: JOM, 1973, p. 300.

this point that the calculations of SPD Vice-chairman Herbert Wehner regarding the effect of Social Democratic participation in the Kiesinger cabinet become clear. Even in coalition with the CDU-CSU, the SPD had an opportunity to show its ability in several policy areas, including foreign policy.

Given this instrumental identification among SPD adherents, furthermore, it is not surprising that just before the 1972 elections in August, they aligned their party most of all with the *Ostpolitik* and the maintenance of peace. Ninety-two percent of SPD adherents shared this image of their party, while CDU adherents instead identified their party with the maintenance of peace (82 percent), firmness toward the Russians (78 percent), European (EEC) cooperation (72 percent), and military security (68 percent). On all but the first policy goal, CDU voters expressed stronger preferences than did those of the SPD.[44] The CDU-CSU image stressed firmness and security.

Concluding Remarks

This brings us to the end of our study on the changing attitudes of the West German mass public over the years. As I stressed at the outset, this is not the only level of influential opinions in foreign policymaking, nor are its opinions more than one of several factors the policymakers take into account. On the other hand, the formal influence wielded through the ballot assures mass opinion at least some measure of attention. Elective foreign policymakers cannot in the long run afford to ignore mass opinion or act contrary to it. In fact, it may be their best strategy to make sure that the voting masses share as much of the policymakers' information as possible. The mass public should better understand their proposed course of policy rather than relying primarily on its fears and prejudices.

Notes

1. See Karl W. Deutsch, *The Analysis of International Relations* (Englewood Cliffs, N.J.: Prentice-Hall, 1968) and Bernard C. Cohen, *The Public's Impact on Foreign Policy* (Boston: Little, Brown, 1973).

2. See, for example, Graham T. Allison, *Essence of Decision: Explaining the Cuban Missile Crisis* (Boston: Little, Brown, 1971); Michael Brecher, *The Foreign Policy System of Israel* (New Haven, Conn.: Yale University Press, 1972); Howard H. Lentner, *Foreign Policy Analysis* (Columbus, Ohio: Merrill, 1974); James L. Payne, *The American Threat: The Fear of War as an Instrument of Foreign Policy* (Chicago: Markham, 1970); and John D. Steinbruner, *The Cybernetic Theory of Deci-*

sion (Princeton, N.J.: Princeton University Press, 1974).

3. See Machiavelli's *Discourses on the First Ten Books of Titus Livius* (1521) and *The Prince* (1513).

4. See also Merkl, *German Foreign Policies, West and East* (Santa Barbara, Cal.: Clio Press, 1974), pp. 201-08.

5. Karl W. Deutsch, et al., *France, Germany and the Western Alliance* (New York: Scribners, 1967), p. 14. See also the elite literature cited there, p. 5, n. 1.

6. See also the approach used by Deutsch and Edinger in their earlier book, Karl W. Deutsch and Lewis J. Edinger, *Germany Rejoins the Powers* (Stanford: Stanford University Press, 1959), Chapters 5-9.

7. Rudolph Wildenmann, "Eliten in der Bundesrepublik" (Unpublished manuscript, August 1968).

8. Daniel H. Willick, "Public Interest in International Affairs," *Social Science Quarterly* 50 (September 1969):274.

9. See also W. Phillips Davison in Hans Speier and W. Phillips Davison, *West German Leadership and Foreign Policy* (Evanston, Ill.: Row & Peterson, 1957), pp. 242-81. Deutsch and Edinger in *Germany Rejoins the Powers,* p. 112, cite a 1955 figure of 39 percent attentive to foreign affairs.

10. See, for example, Merkl, "Ideology, Attitudes, and Politics of Party Members" in Merkl, ed., *Western European Party Systems: Trends and Prospects* (New York: Free Press, 1979), which includes questions on European intervention, Vietnam, and the recognition of the German Democratic Republic.

11. See, for example, Hans-Adolf Jacobsen and Mieczyslaw Tomala, *Wie Deutsche und Polen einander sehen* (Düsseldorf: Droste, 1973) and Jörg Peter Menzel and Wolfgang Pfeiler, *Deutschland Bilder, die Bundesrepublic aus der Sicht der DDR und der Sowjetunion* (Düsseldorf: Droste, 1972).

12. See, for example, Hermann Ziock, ed., *Sind die Deutschen wirklich so Meinungen aus Europa, Asien, Afrika und Amerika* (Herrenalb/Schwarzwald: Erdmann, 1965).

13. Television ownership in the Federal Republic has grown from 11 percent of the households in 1958 to 32 percent in 1961, 73 percent in 1967, and 95 percent in 1973; 54 percent watch the news daily and another 25 percent watch it several times a week. Elisabeth Noelle-Neumann, *Jahrbuch der öffentlichen Meinung, 1965-1973* (Allensbach: Institut für Demoskopie [hereafter *JOM, 1973*], 1974), pp. 193-195.

14. Viggo Graf Bluecher, *Der Prozess der Meinungsbildung* (Bielefeld: Emnid, 1962), pp. 14-15.

15. Institut für Demoskopie, *Jahrbuch der öffentlichen Meinung, 1958-1964* (Allensbach: Institut für Demoskopie, 1965) (hereafter cited as *JOM* with the last year polls were taken).

16. The respondents ranked the issues as follows: inflation, reunification, social security, crime, honest government, protection against the East, lower taxes, good relations with the United States, better housing, European integration, and better relations with the Soviets. By way of contrast, Wildenmann's elite sample ranked the "most urgent priorities of the government" of 1968 as follows: sound public finances, educational reform, economic growth, better East-West relations, economic reforms, better U.S.-German relations, diplomatic relations with Eastern Europe, including England in the EEC, better transportation, better relations with

East Germany, better Franco-German relations, plurality voting, etc.

17. *JOM, 1967,* p. 387.

18. Werner Kaltefleiter, "Konsens ohne Macht," *Verfassung und Verfassungs-wirklichkeit,* 1969, pp. 18-20.

19. Using reunification as an indicator of attentiveness to foreign affairs raises an additional conceptual problem. As late as 1964, a DIVO study unearthed the fact that half of the respondents of a national sample considered reunification a domestic rather than a foreign affairs issue. DIVO, *Der Wähler vor der Bundestagswahl* (November 1964) (Stuttgart: Deutsche Verlagsanstalt, 1965), p. 57 (hereafter cited as DIVO with the last year of the polls taken).

20. All three of the major parties at the time reported a tremendous influx of new members. Political interest in general, and particularly in the issues at hand, was highest among young Germans. Throughout 1976, polls gave the governing coalition (SPD-FDP) of Willy Brandt a considerable edge over the opposition (CDU-CSU). See Dieter Oberndoerfer, *Die Ausgangslage der Parteien vor der Bundestagswahl 1972 und 1976* (Sozialwissenschaftliches Forschungsinstitut der Konrad-Adenauer-Stiftung [SFK], 1976).

21. See the polls of 1973 in *JOM, 1973,* p. 299, on the effectiveness of the Eastern treaties. By 1975, 47 percent (versus 23 percent who did not) expressed disappointment. Allensbacher Archiv, *IfD Umfragen,* no. 2172 I.

22. See Dieter Oberndoerfer, *Umfrageergebnisse des SFK von Mai/Juni 1976 zu wichtigen politischen Aufgaben* (SFK, 1976), pp. 2-4. Some 53.1 percent wanted to see the defense forces of the Federal Republic strengthened.

23. See his *The Stable Crisis* (New York: Harper & Row, 1970), p. ix. The title of the book also reflects this "fundamental concern."

24. See Merkl, "Politico-Cultural Restraints on West German Foreign Policy," *Comparative Political Studies* 3 (January 1971):446-47.

25. See Ibid., p. 458. Between 52 percent and 69 percent did not expect a major war, at least not that soon.

26. Ibid. and *JOM, 1973,* p. 542, where the polls of 1967 are broken down by age and occupation. By 1965, the respondents under thirty were notably more optimistic than their elders.

27. In 1968, 44 percent feared (versus 49 percent who did not) that the Soviet Union might make good its threat of armed intervention on the basis of the "enemy state" clause of the United Nations Charter. *JOM, 1973,* p. 598.

28. See *JOM, 1973,* p. 575.

29. See *JOM, 1973,* p. 576, and also p. 534, which for 1970 contrasts the low level of trust in the Soviets with the high level of trust in the United States. However, it should be noted that in 1965, 66 percent of West German adults saw "no reason to be less distrustful of the Communists" (versus 17 percent who advocated trust) than in the past. See Elisabeth Noelle and Erich Peter Neumann, eds., *The Germans, Public Opinion Polls 1947-1966* (Allensbach: Verlag für Demoskopie, 1967), p. 560.

30. By this time, the share of the undecided also had declined to 26 percent. See Elisabeth Noelle-Neumann, "Die Verklärung: Adenauer und die öffentliche Meinung 1949-1976," mimeographed (Allensbach), Table 25.

31. Ibid., Table 27. See also *JOM, 1973*, pp. 544-45. Already in 1973, 48 percent thought the East was stronger in Europe, (versus 7 percent who gave the edge to the West) Ibid., p. 551.

32. See *JOM, 1973*, pp. 322-23. In June 1976, 48 percent of the voting public wanted to see safety from Eastern aggression high on the election agenda. Allensbacher Archiv, *IfD Umfragen*, no. 3030 I-II.

33. In February 1955, 38 percent wanted to fight (versus 34 percent who wanted to avoid war); and in March 1959, 32 percent wanted to (versus 33 percent). See Noelle-Neumann, "Die Verklärung," Table 28.

34. By way of contrast, it should be pointed out that West German appreciation of NATO has risen considerably in the 1970s. In 1960, 37 percent did not think NATO could hold off a Soviet attack (versus 19 percent who did). By 1973, 37 percent still did not think so, but the optimists had risen to 27 percent. *JOM, 1973*, p. 551. The presence of American troops, on the other hand, was welcomed far more in the 1960s and 1970s than back in 1956 when 51 percent wanted to see them withdrawn (versus 22 percent that did not). *JOM, 1964.*

35. Allensbacher Archiv, *IfD Umfragen*, no. 3024. In 1961 and 1965, respectively, 42 percent and 37 percent opted for neutrality versus 40 percent and 46 percent who wanted to remain allied with the United States. Noelle and Neumann, *The Germans*, p. 523.

36. *JOM, 1973*, p. 515. See also an earlier poll (1965) in Noelle and Neumann, *The Germans*, pp. 474-75.

37. See Merkl, *German Foreign Policies*, pp. 175-77.

38. In 1970, 65 percent saw clearly that the Basic Treaty would lead to many more Western countries granting diplomatic recognition to the DDR, a fact the Bonn government was still officially denying. *JOM, 1973*, p. 520.

39. See also the detailed opinions on options of the Berlin settlement. *JOM, 1973*, pp. 523-24.

40. See, however, the data on Chancellor Kiesinger and his foreign minister and on Brandt's foreign policies in 1967. *JOM, 1973*, pp. 273, 276. The pollsters had a grading system for respondents that resulted in very few *A*s (ones) for Brandt, but 56 percent *B*s and *C*s (twos and threes).

41. *JOM, 1973*, p. 265.

42. This is not to say that his *Ostpolitik* did not also enjoy a good deal of Christian Democratic support. In fact, substantial agreement emerged on such questions as Did Brandt treat the Russians the right way? which was popularly understood to refer to the linkage between the Berlin Agreements and the ratification of the Eastern treaties. *JOM, 1973*, p. 268.

43. See also *JOM, 1973*, p. 325, on the perception of the SPD by its adherents as an instrument toward the achievement of the goals of *Ostpolitik:* 68 percent of SPD adherents thought it so, 55 percent of CDU-CSU adherents expected the same of their own party, only somewhat less than those who expected it to combat inflation and unemployment. *JOM, 1973*, p. 325.

44. See *JOM, 1973*, pp. 332-34. Policy approval for Brandt in October 1972 stood at 46 percent versus 31 percent who did not approve.

12

Germany and the Third World: The Politics of Free Trade and the Free Hand

Ernst-Otto Czempiel

The history of West Germany's relations with the Third World provides interesting insights into the political learning process. Traditionally, Germany has had no relations with the extra-European world. It always has been a European state, continental in outlook and tradition. From this point of view, the loss of its colonies in the wake of World War I was no political accident. It ended a very short period in German politics: roughly twenty years—too short to change orientation. Germany emerged from World War I in its traditional shape as a European middle power with continental interests only.

In 1949, when the Federal Republic of Germany was founded, the situation was more or less the same. What had been tradition appeared now as a welcome gift of history. Having no colonies, the Federal Republic did not have to share the white man's burden. The Federal Republic could keep its German identity as a European power. It could cooperate with the West, but only in the European framework. The Atlantic Community did not go beyond the traditional European region; the Pacific as well as the Indian Ocean remained outside. Germany's problems were of the old and well-known order: reunification, economic reconstruction, and reconstitution of political relations with its European neighbors. Despite two world wars, the first half of the twentieth century had changed neither the psychological nor the operational environment of Germany.

I

The change came during the 1950s. In the wake of the *Wirtschaftswunder*, Germany's economy expanded into the world—a world with an increasing number of new sovereign states, rapidly augmented as a result of accelerating decolonization. With 1960, the "year of Africa," the Old World definitely had become a new world. Answers to the German question had to be found not only in Europe but also in this new world. In addition to the (at least temporary) awakening German self-interest in the Third World, there was pressure from the Western Allies. Above all, the United States urged West Germany to participate in giving economic aid to the new countries. Thus Germany found itself at the end of the fifties in a completely new situation. Its economic interests and its political obligations had become worldwide in substance and in character. Germany had developed into an economic world power and had been forced to become a political world power too. It was a member of almost all specialized agencies of the United Nations and was, as observer, a de facto member of the United Nations itself.

This change during the fifties was sudden and dramatic. Germany was confronted with a whole set of new problems for which no ready answers were at hand. There was a lack of experience, personnel, and knowledge. Economically as well as politically, new politics had to be invented from scratch. How did the Federal Republic react to this challenge?

As a rule, countries have considerable time to adapt to changing circumstances. They can try several strategies and select the most pertinent ones. The Federal Republic, however, had no time. It was forced to react more or less immediately. Bonn's reaction toward this fundamental challenge was twofold. For the political part of the problem it went back into its stored memories and looked for a strategy suited for difficult and highly volatile situations. It found, and reactivated, the strategy of the "free hand." This stragey had been invented during the last quarter of the nineteenth century in order to implement the foreign policy of the newly created big-power Germany. The strategies of the free hand are obviously expedient for newcomers that dare not, or will not, take sides.

For the economic part of the problem Bonn could not consult memory. For the first time in its history, Germany had become an economic power of overwhelming strength. Under these circumstances, the Federal Republic imitated the behavior of the United States. As a strong economic newcomer on the world market, the United States had in a comparable situation invented the strategy of "free trade." After World War II the United States had intensified this stragey with considerable success. During its reconstruction period West Germany had learned a great deal from the United States—why not learn about foreign economic policies as well?

With this combination of traditional and borrowed strategies, West Germany rose to the challenge posed at the end of the fifties. These, however, were not the only answers available. History had taught some lessons with regard to free hand and free trade. Domestically, the Federal Republic made some use of those lessons. It developed the *Soziale Marktwirtschaft* in order to combine economic freedom with social responsibility. A corresponding foreign policy would have meant a strong engagement against all forms of colonialism for an economic world order that would (at least to some extent) protect the weak and the poor against the strong and the rich. But Germany opted for the "classical" approach. It did not extend its progressive domestic policies into its foreign policy. Those areas were kept completely separated. Germany started its role as a world power with a Janus face: although progressive domestically, it looked toward the Third World with the classical view of a traditional European power.

The decision for a politics of free hand and free trade marked not the end of the political learning process but its beginning. Since then, the Federal Republic has been faced with two questions. First, will it be possible to continue indefinitely the separation of the two areas or will one influence the other? And second, is the Federal Republic strong enough to uphold the principle of free trade and simultaneously keep its hands free? This paper primarily tries to answer the second question. Does the Federal Republic still follow the classical approach it adopted during the fifties, or has it altered its relationship with the Third World?

II

At the outset, it is necessary to distinguish between the economic and the political dimensions of Germany's relations with the Third World—with the former divided into the issues of foreign aid and foreign trade. Historically, the relationship has undergone three phases. From 1949 to 1955 (the beginning of the Federal Republic until the regaining of sovereignty), Germany's interests were mainly focused on its own problems. The Federal Republic made considerable contributions to multilateral development institutions,[1] but had no development policy in the proper sense. A policy started more or less in 1955, when the Federal Republic resumed diplomatic relations with the Soviet Union and thus opened up the possibility that the GDR would gain recognition by other states, socialist or neutral.[2] During this phase (roughly until the end of 1966 and the beginning of the Great Coalition), the main German interest was to keep the developing countries from diplomatically recognizing the GDR.[3] Bonn gave foreign aid and shaped its attitudes in the United Nations primarily in view of this goal. It was the period of the famous Hallstein Doctrine. After this policy was scrapped in 1965 and the Great Coalition formed, the third phase in Germany's relations with the Third World began. It was, and still is, dominated by the aspect of development in its proper sense. Freed from narrow political considerations, confronted with a decolonized Third World, and promoted by the interest of an ever-expanding industry, the Federal Republic had to find its way between its own interest in free trade and the interest of the developing world in economic growth and independence.

Generally speaking, the Federal Republic found a rather good way. Consequently, it has gained a good reputation not only within the First, but also within the Third World. Former Chancellor Willy Brandt was elected chairman of the Independent Commission for International Questions of Development;[4] in July 1978, Bonn was host to the fourth summit of the Western heads of state, where they again committed themselves to spending more in development aid; and in 1977, the Federal Republic gave 13.3 billion DM to the developing countries, which is roughly 1.12 percent of the German GNP.[5]

However, the view one gains from statistics is not the only one, and perhaps not even the most pertinent one. If one takes a closer look at the details of the relationship between Germany and the developing world, the Federal Republic does not appear as the most generous and benevolent spender. On the contrary: it is at the bottom of the scale ranking the Western industrialized states according to their behavior toward the developing countries. In trade matters, the Federal Republic is well known as one of the last hard-liners that fight for the principle of free trade. In the field of foreign aid, the Federal Republic appears more as a good salesman than as a generous donator.

The formation of the Federal Republic's development policy was encouraged either by open pressure or by good examples of other countries. Germany's foreign aid program of the sixties did not start before the United States intervened rather strongly in Bonn.[6] It did not, in 1978, cancel some Official Development Assistance (ODA) debts of poor developing countries before Canada, Sweden, Switzerland, and Great Britain had done so. And Germany was the last of the industrial countries to reverse its stand in the question of an integrated raw materials program.

Germany's official policy statements reflect this reluctant attitude. For the federal government, the idea behind development policy is "to promote international cooperation and to counter a confrontation between industrialized and developing countries."[7] The German government aims at contributing to the development of an international economic order, "based on the principles of a market economy in which international solidarity and the protection of the weaker partners are kept in mind."[8] In contrast to this official program, which, although four years old, is still valid, the Bundestag found perhaps more pertinent words for the goals of the German development policy, interpreting it as part of German peace policy — Germany's intention to eliminate, together with its neighbors in the European Community, the causes of the economic disputes between the industrialized and the developing countries.[9] The Bundestag argued for the autonomy and independence of the developing countries.

The difference in the pronouncements between the government and the *Bundestag* does not necessarily make for a difference in substance. The *Bundestag* does not seem to be very much interested in development policy. There have been only two debates within the last two and a half years concerning this subject. In both discussions,[10] Germany's economic, political, and structural interests received at least as much attention as the concern for helping developing countries. In his first speech before the *Bundestag,* the new minister for economic cooperation, Offergeld, tried to combine the goal of economic and social development in the Third World with the central goal of Germany's interests in security, raw materials, and general foreign economic policy.[11] But states should not only serve interests; they also should have moral obligations. The crucial question, therefore, is what kind of mix between benevolence and *Realpolitik,* between aid and interests, between free trade and development policy, the Federal Republic has developed. In order to answer these questions we have to look into some details regarding Germany's policies toward aid and trade.

* * *

In 1976 the Federal Republic gave 5.3 billion dollars as foreign aid to the developing countries. Only the United States gave more: 12.5 billion dollars.[12] From 1950 to 1976 the Federal Republic spent a total of 107.5 billion DM for the developing countries.[13] More than half of this amount was provided by private business interests; and since business usually is concerned with profits, more than half of what is being claimed as Germany's foreign aid obviously has benefited the German economy. This demonstrates the significant role private business plays in the official conception of foreign aid. The "heavy emphasis on the 'free market economy' with a minimal role for Government" is, in fact, the "unique feature of present-day German thought on development aid."[14] The government acknowledges and stresses the "great importance of private capital transfers" to the developing countries and on the international scene acts as speaker for the private economy.[15] Thus, it is no accident that the German economy pays more than half of what is called foreign aid. It is part of an official program.

The program is also pledged to enlarge the share of ODA to 0.7 percent of the GNP, as developing countries have demanded.[16] But the share of ODA in Germany's foreign aid has steadily declined. It fell from 0.45 percent of the GNP in 1962 to 0.31 percent in 1976, and 0.27 percent in 1977.[17] This is one-third of the percentage the developing countries are demanding and the Federal Republic has pledged. Even in 1976, when the Federal Republic spent 0.31 percent of its GNP for the Official Development

Assistance, it ranked far behind Sweden and the Netherlands (0.82 percent each), France (0.62 percent), Denmark (0.57 percent), and Canada (0.47 percent).[18]

According to Economics Minister Graf Lambsdorff, the Federal Republic will not reach the goal of 0.7 percent until 1984.[19] Since, altogether, the Federal Republic is spending more than 1 percent of its GNP for the developing countries, the government obviously does not feel obliged to change the internal composition of this aid. If the transfer of private capital is being understood as aid, there is, in fact, no need for such a change. Although private business contributes to economic development, this contribution is not enough and a transfer of real values from the developed countries to the developing ones has to take place in order to permit and facilitate development. There always has been free trade in terms of capital export. What is needed is capital transfer in terms of aid, i.e., grants and soft loans. In this regard the Federal Republic is far behind the expectations of the developing countries.

But even within the category of ODA, the FRG does not live up to the expectations of the recipient countries. They prefer aid given through multilateral institutions because this form of distribution enhances the voice of the recipient countries and keeps intervention of the donor country to a minimum. The Federal Republic, however, has preferred bilateralism.[20] On the average, between 1950 and 1976, three-quarters of Germany's development aid was given bilaterally and one-quarter multilaterally, based on the government's decision to limit the share of its multilateral aid to not more than 30 percent.[21]

The reasons for this preference are manifold. For one, the donor country can select the countries it would like to aid. During the sixties, Germany's ODA was concentrated on South Asian states and Brazil. Six countries of these regions received more than 60 percent of ODA in 1965.[22] In the mid-seventies, Arab countries and Black Africa received the lion's share of Germany's foreign aid. Bilateralism also permits a more precise channeling of aid. In the bilateral arrangement details can be worked out on how to make use of the credits and grants. Bilateral aid can be tied to political and economic interests. Finally, bilateralism facilitates the flow-back of orders. Officially, Germany's foreign aid is not tied to a "Buy German" policy, although German industry always has been interested in a formal tying of foreign aid to the procurement of German goods and services. During the sixties, a sharp debate over this issue arose in Germany — the ministry of economic cooperation argued for tying and the ministry of economics against it.[23] In 1966, 32 percent of Germany's foreign aid was formally tied to the procurement of German goods and services. Since then the percentage has gradually diminished. Today, there is no formal tying whatsoever.

In practice, however, there are many forms of unofficial, informal tying.[24] In 1966, when 32 percent of Germany's aid was tied, 80 percent was bound to German products. In 1977, with practically no formal tying, the "vast majority of orders" went to German firms.[25] In effect some 40,000 jobs in Germany have depended on foreign aid.

With this kind of foreign aid, Germany contributed to the alarming debt problem of the developing countries. The FRG, of course, did not create the problem; and the softening of its loans according to the recommendations of multilateral bodies has certainly eased the burden of the developing countries. Generally speaking, however, the Federal Republic helped produce the causative factors involved. Of these, the most predominant are the export credits of the private economy. To push the share of the private economy in developing aid, to hold down ODA, amounts to increasing the burden of debt. For instance, if all industrialized countries had paid the 0.75 percent of their GNP in terms of grants or soft loans in 1976, the transfer would have amounted to 41.4 million dollars instead of the 13.7 million dollars that actually were transferred.[27] For these reasons, Sweden, the Netherlands, Canada, Switzerland, and Great Britain have canceled some of the debts of the most seriously affected countries. The Federal Republic of Germany, here again behaving as one of the most orthodox representatives of the principle of market economy, hesitated until the autumn of 1978. The government decided in October of that year to change loans into grants for the thirty poorest countries.[28] However, eliminating those debts will not happen once and for all in a single act. Instead, each case will be dealt with separately and on its own merits in a lengthly procedure stretching far into the eighties.

A more detailed look into the practices of Germany's foreign aid does not offer a very favorable image of the Federal Republic. One of the richest countries in the world, with a constant and considerable surplus in its current account, the FRG nevertheless has pursued a policy of orthodox neoliberalism. It has pursued a policy of classical free trade in a world that is dominated by the perennial conflict between the rich and poor. The experience that provoked Germany to develop the social market economy domestically did not affect its foreign economic behavior. On the contrary, this behavior followed the most traditional and most conservative interpretation of free trade capitalism. While it is true that a strong and expanding economy has to look for new markets, it can, however, afford a more progressive treatment of its weak partners. The Americans demonstrated this strikingly in the Marshall Plan. Although the Europeans were much stronger then, they were treated by the United States much more progressively than have the developing countries by West Germany.

Theoretically, the government knows very well that the rapid industrial development of the Third World would be the best device to create jobs in the Federal Republic of Germany and in all other industrialized countries. In practice, however, the government gives way to the short-term interests of an economy that is tuned to high rates on exports of goods, services, and capital. There is no domestic debate that could turn the tide and accentuate the long-term interest against the short term. The Trade Union Federation is well aware of these connections, but remains preoccupied with the short-term aspects.[29] The Catholic and Protestant churches, which do their best to channel their considerable amount of aid to individuals in the developing countries, keep to their business and do not speak up in public. The public still considers foreign aid a waste of the taxpayer's money and cares little about somewhat ambiguous long-range interests.[30] An information campaign, which had been started by the ministry of economic cooperation in 1977, has not been too successful. Within the political parties, it is only the young people who try a new approach and criticize the traditional free trade position. Usually, they are subdued easily.

The private economy is too interested in short-term business to allow it to think ahead. Since 1971 new investments in the developing countries have increased rapidly. Together with reinvested gains, about 2 billion DM were invested in 1976. Investment in the developing countries follows the general trend of foreign investment of the German economy. The interests behind these investments are, as usual, directed toward securing export markets.[31] Encouraged and promoted by the government, which facilitates the entry of German direct or portfolio investments into the developing countries wherever possible, West Germany's industry has expanded. These investments have contributed to the larger share of finished products in the exports of some developing countries, notably Brazil and Tunisia.[32] Those countries certainly do profit. But this does not justify calling foreign aid what has been the traditional practice of capital export.

Measured by its proper amount of about 0.30 percent of the GNP, foreign aid is nothing more than a small part of West Germany's foreign economic policy. It benefits the German economy at least to the same degree as the economy of the developing countries. A symmetric distribution of value within a fundamentally asymmetric structure unavoidably favors the stronger part. In not correcting this asymmetry, the Federal Republic indicates to what degree it follows the traditional path of a strong economy. Its main interest is its free entry into the market of the world. Free trade is its goal since it offers the means to facilitate economic expansion. This policy is equitable within a symmetric structure of the international system. Between the United States and the EEC there can be free trade only. But in the asymmetric relationship between the Federal Republic and the developing countries, free trade should be complemented with sufficiently large and effective foreign aid—exactly as the principle of private enterprise has been balanced by a policy of social justice within the Federal Republic. With this element lacking in its relationship with the Third World, the Federal Republic pursues a traditional free trade approach within a nontraditional world.

In the field of foreign trade, the result is similar. The Federal Republic argues against all regulations that limit the range of freedom of the German economy. However, it is not easy to isolate analytically the Federal Republic, since as a member of the European Community Bonn as a rule does not act unilaterally. It can be said that within the context of the EEC, or the OECD, or outside of these, the Federal Republic's behavior in trade matters is as traditional as in the matter of foreign aid.

In 1958 the Federal Republic hesitated to include the French colonies in Africa in the EEC scheme. Bonn did not wish to shoulder the burden of colonialism and participate in the consequences of a past it had not created. Finally, the Federal Republic acquiesced—partly because it wanted its own special arrangement with East Germany. Although it was never a colonial state the Federal Republic follows the traditional pattern in its trade relations with the Third World. It imports mostly primary commodities from the developing countries and exports mostly finished products to them. There is a certain tendency to change this pattern. Exports of finished or semifinished products from the developing countries into the Federal Republic have increased more than those of raw materials. Nevertheless, in 1977 60 percent of all German imports from developing countries were either raw materials or primary products like coffee or tea.[33] Germany's most important trading partners in the Third World, Brazil and Argentina, which at the same time belong to the group of the most industrialized developing countries, export predominantly primary commodities (80 percent and 10 percent, respectively) into the Federal Republic. Only Hong Kong exports more or less only finished products to Germany.

This is not an unavoidable but an intended pattern. The Federal Republic shares in full the trend of protectionism that characterizes the industrialized world. In October 1978, the president of the World Bank, Robert McNamara, criticized once again the kind of protectionism that keeps the developing countries from industrializing and from ending their dependence on external aid.[34] Usually, protectionism is justified by the need to maintain levels of employment. However, since it is well known[35] that, generally speaking, employment levels are not reduced by imports from developing countries, protectionism can only be explained as a special cover for noncompetitive industries. Whatever the reasons, the Federal Republic fully joined in the protectionist measures of the European Community against textiles, footwear, steel, petrochemicals, and other imports.[36] Without any objections from West Germany, the European Community added additional quota restrictions on imports from Brazil, Hong Kong, South Korea, and Taiwan. The Common Agricultural Policy of the European Community covers more or less all agricultural production, and the Lomé Convention and the treaties of cooperation with the Mediterranean countries also provide special protectionism. A closer inspection of these conventions demonstrates the degree to which the industrialized countries of the European Community, West Germany included, protect themselves from the importation of competitive products.

The Federal Republic, a declared free trader, has abandoned the principle of liberalism often and severely. Only a detailed analysis can demonstrate whether the reason has been a necessity for compromise with its Western neighbors or a special interest of the German industry. It is safe to assume that the latter has been more important than the former. No official German voice has been heard criticizing the protectionism of the industrialized countries. No endeavor has been made on the part of the Federal Republic to interpret generously the schemes agreed on. Since the traditional German trade relations are with countries outside the Lomé scheme, the Federal Republic has had sufficient possibilities to soften protectionism. Since this has not happened, one has to conclude that the principle of free trade is being treated by the Federal Republic as a one-way street. Its behavior is not worse than that of the other Western industrialized countries; it is well in line with them. Economically the second important country of the Western world, the Federal Republic shares a special responsibility. It is not sufficient to declare good intentions as the Federal Government undoubtedly has done.[37]

On the other hand, the Federal Republic has driven the principle of free trade to the point of isolating itself. Since 1974 the developing countries have argued in favor of a New International Economic Order (NIEO), the center of which is the Integrated Commodity Program with a Common Fund. The arguments in favor of and against this scheme cannot be repeated here. The problem is very complex. The developing countries need a certain stabilization of the earnings of their primary exports; an integrated program will, on the other hand, favor the industrialized countries more than the developing ones and will amount to a huge international cartel. Since the United Nations Conference on Trade and Development (UNCTAD) IV in Nairobi in 1976, most of the Western industrialized countries have abandoned their opposition to NIEO. Only the Federal Republic upheld its opposition. Consequently, it drew much criticism from the developing countries. In Nairobi, West Germany was termed the reactionary hard-liner of the Western world—in spite of the quite substantial argument it made. The developing countries perceived only that the

Federal Republic was against the stabilization of commodity prices, against agreements between producing and consuming countries, against the stabilization of their foreign exchange earnings, and finally against the restructuring of world production, which would bring the share of developing countries from the present 7 percent to 25 percent in the year 2000. The Third World did not understand that the Federal Republic, as part of the big and powerful cartel of the Western industrialized countries and as member and user of so many specialized cartels concerning such commodities as sugar and tin, was against regulating the markets that are of decisive importance for the developing countries. This selective use of the free trade principle drew the hardest criticism from the Third World.

It took the Federal Republic more than two years to realize that it could not continue the selective application of the principle of free trade and that the heart of the matter was not economic but political. Even economic arguments that were valid and worthwhile[38] were useless as long as they failed to convince the developing countries. In the autumn of 1978 the Federal Republic gave in. Shortly before the new round of deliberations in Geneva started, Foreign Minister Hans-Dietrich Genscher asked for a new orientation in Germany's relations with the South.[39] Obviously, the Federal Republic is now prepared to finance individual buffer stocks and to accept the Common Fund as a clearing pool for commodity agreements. Whatever the details, the Federal Republic has abandoned the principle of free trade in favor of an organized trade system commonly agreed to. Bonn has given up the traditional notion that the market forces alone could, and would, produce development. A new chapter in Germany's relations with the Third World has begun.

Undoubtedly, political insight has turned the page. Germany's social market economy had been devised for political, not for economic, reasons. A comparable phenomenon has shaped German thought about the international economy. For a more detailed view, we have to look into Germany's political relations with the Third World.

III

In the past, the Federal Republic had only a few connections with countries of the Third World, notably in Latin America. After 1949, the Federal Republic was occupied more or less with European problems. Given the burden of the Third Reich, the Federal Republic was not interested in, and could not think of, a new *Weltpolitik*. It was content to remain a political dwarf at the same time it was becoming an economic giant. Germany made business, not politics. If it was confronted with political alternatives, it reinvented the familiar strategy of the free hand. In the United Nations, if the Federal Republic, in its observer status, was faced with sensitive issues, it preferred to abstain from involvement, if it could not remain silent.[40] Surely, Germany since 1919 had not been a colonial power and the new Germany was distinctly against colonialism. But Germany's Western neighbors had considerable colonial liabilities. Facing the dilemma of deciding between two equally acceptable sides, the Federal Republic chose the free hand. The same is true in the field of disarmament. Surely, the Federal Republic is in favor of it. However, in 1954, Germany renounced for itself the ABC weapons, still a unique precedent. Chancellor Schmidt proposed before the United Nations in May 1978 to share Germany's experience in the field of controlling devices with other countries.[41] But Germany was (and still is) at the heart of the East-West conflict and had to arm itself considerably. Germany always has been against arms transfers to the developing countries and has pledged not to deliver arms to regions with high degrees of tension.[42] Chancellor Schmidt suggested before the United Nations an international convention for the limitation of arms transfers.[43] On the other hand, the Federal Republic ranks fourth in the world's leading exporters of arms.[44] German arms are very much in demand worldwide.

Given those contradictory interests, West Germany in fact was tempted to play the politics of the free hand. It offered the best of all worlds in a situation where the responsibility for the West more or less was shouldered by the United States, Great Britain, and France. As this situation changed, West Germany found itself forced to take sides more often. Three developments produced this change: the growth of interdependence, the limitation of American foreign policy after Vietnam, and, finally, the developments within Africa.

As a result of economic expansion, Germany became acquainted with nearly all parts of the world. The European Community worked both as a channel and as a cover for the developing world politics of the Federal Republic, but, of course, Germany had to respond to all kinds of problems in nearly all parts of the world.[45] Development presented itself not only as an economic, but also as a political, problem with many facets.[46] In an interdependent world, Germany could not remain independent.

The pressure upon Bonn became greater the more the United States limited its own engagement after Vietnam. The Federal Republic seemed particularly capable of filling the role. Like the United States, it was without any colonial past, and in contrast to the United States, it was without the Vietnam war. Thus the Federal Republic gained considerable standing within the Third World. Perhaps only Willy Brandt, the former chancellor, could head an international independent commission on problems of development. The United States, of course, did not withdraw completely. Wherever its vital interests are concerned, the United States is, and will, remain present. In the Middle East, West Germany (and the European Community) play only a minor role. In Latin America, West Germany is only economically present. Here it dares to oppose the United States with a hard-nosed export policy on nuclear reactors. Politically, the United States is still dominating the region.

The situation is different in Africa; obviously the third factor has generated a change in Germany's world policy. The United States traditionally had only selective minor interests in the black continent. Germany, on the other hand, via the European Community became heir to the French, British, and Portuguese tradition in Africa. The memory of a short but distinctive former German presence in Africa intensified the interest, which was strongly backed from the economic side. Germany's industry has invested heavily in the Republic of South Africa. With the United States still abstaining from an active African policy, the Federal Republic has to play its role within and outside the European Community context. It is Africa that has challenged Germany's preference of a politics of the free hand.

This rather recent experience started in the mid-seventies; after the end of Portuguese colonialism, Cuban, Russian, and Chinese influence were felt heavily in Africa south of the Sahara. At the same time, the conflict between the races in the Republic of South Africa began to explode. The conflict over Namibia, the former German colony of German Southwest Africa, was intensified. The Federal Republic could no longer afford to sit in the balconies of world politics.

Since then, Africa has become the heart of German world politics. Foreign Minister Genscher went to Africa several times. In June 1978, Chancellor Schmidt visited Black Africa, the first German chancellor ever to do so.[47] Within Germany, problems of the Third World, of support for national liberation movements, of the role of investments, of economic, ideological, and military intervention are discussed mostly with respect to Africa. The black continent is Germany's focus on the world. Africa has become the centerpiece of Germany's world politics.

If anything, Africa has forced Germany to give up its preferred politics of the free hand. Since many of the poorest countries in the world are to be found in Africa, it seems to be the African experience that has provoked the German stand concerning the New International Economic Order. Africa demonstrates that the problem of the Third World is not primarily economic but political. Political considerations must soften the impact of economic interests. It became evident that in international politics a similar mix of freedom and obligation has to be applied as in domestic matters.

If we are correct in assuming that West Germany has given up its preferred politics of the free hand, what kind of alternative behavior will it choose? Will it take sides and with whom? It is too early to answer those questions. It can be stated only that a change has taken place since early 1978. Germany has engaged itself; it plays an active role in Africa. For the time being, it looks as if Germany has taken over the role of the "honest broker," again a classical requisite within the history of Germany's foreign policy behavior. It is, so to speak, halfway between the politics of the free hand and the politics of engagement. The Federal Republic looks for peaceful compromises that will solve the Rhodesian problem and that of Namibia. Bonn has invoked the European Community Code of Conduct for Western firms investing in the Republic of South Africa. Because the Federal Republic is against economic intervention there, it has managed to lower its own investments considerably. Obviously, Bonn looks for compromises and hopes for the best. As a temporary stage in its relationship with the Third World, such a position is sufficient. It will not remain so, however, if the Federal Republic does not succeed in solving the crucial problems of the North-South conflict.

Notes

1. M. Y. Cho, "Politische Probleme der westdeutchen Entwicklungshilfe," (Diss., Bonn, 1965).

2. See Wolfram F. Hanrider, *West German Foreign Policy, 1949-1963. International Pressure and Domestic Response* (Stanford,Cal.: Stanford University Press, 1967).

3. See Ernst-Otto Czempiel, *Macht und Kompromiss, die Beziehungen der BRD zu den Vereinten Nationen 1956-1970* (Düsseldorf: Bertelsmann Universitätsverlag, 1971).

4. Fritz Fischer, "Die Unabhängige Kommission für Internationale Entwicklungsfragen ('Brandt-Kommission')," in *Europa-Archiv* 33, no. 21 (November 10, 1978):703 ff.

5. Presse- und Informationsamt det Bundesregierung, *Jahresbericht der Bundesregierung 1977* (Bonn, 1978), p. 658.

6. Klaus Bodemer, *Entwicklungshilfe — Politik für wen? Ideologie und Vergabepraxis der deutschen Entwicklungshilfe in der ersten Dekade* (München: Welftorum Verlag, 1974), p. 36.

7. Bundesministerium für wirtschaftliche Zusammenarbeit, "Die entwicklungspolitische Konzeption der Bundesrepublik Deutschland (Fassung 1975)," *Dritter Bericht zur Entwicklungspolitik der Bundesregierung* (Bonn, November 1977), pp. 55 ff.

8. Ibid.

9. "Entschliessung des Deutschen Bundestages zur Entwicklungspolitik, 27.10.1977," Bundesministerium, *Dritter Bericht*, p. 51.

10. See the excerpts of the speeches in *Das Parlament,* November 12, 1977 and July 22, 1978.

11. *Stuttgarter Zeitung,* June 23, 1978.

12. Bundesministerium, *Dritter Bericht,* pp. 144-45.

13. Ibid., p. 127.

14. Jack L. Knusel, *West German Aid to Developing Nations* (New York: Praeger, 1968), p. 178.

15. Bundesministerium, *Dritter Bericht,* p. 58.

16. Ibid., p. 69.

17. Presse- und Informationsamt, *Jahresbericht der Bundesregierung,* p. 658.

18. Conference Table 24 in Bundesministerium, *Dritter Bericht,* p. 145.

19. *Frankfurter Allgemeine Zeitung,* March 13, 1978.

20. See Karel Holbik and Henry Allen Myers, *West German Foreign Aid, 1956-1966. Its Economic and Political Aspects* (Boston: Boston University Press, 1968), pp. 51 ff.

21. Presse- und Informationsamt, *Jahresbericht der Bundesregierung,* p. 647.

22. Bodemer, *Entwicklungshilfe,* p. 219.

23. See the details in ibid., pp. 276 ff.

24. For an interesting discussion see John White, *German Aid: A Survey of the Sources, Policy, and Structure of German Aid* (London: Overseas Development Institute), pp. 107 ff.

25. Presse- und Informationsamt, *Jahresbericht der Bundesregierung,* p. 633.

26. *Das Parlament,* July 22, 1978, p. 5.

27. Hans J. Petersen, "Die Verschuldung der Entwicklungsländer als Problem der Nord-Süd-Beziehungen," *Europa-Archiv* 33, no. 21 (November 10, 1978):694.

28. Ibid., p. 702, n. 35.

29. Gerhard Leminsky and Bernd Otto, eds., *Gewerkschaften und Entwicklungspolitik* (Köln: Bundverlag, 1975).

30. Bundesministerium für wirtschaftliche Zusammenarbeit, *Einstellung der Deutschen zur Entwicklungshilfe, 1975 und 1977* (Bonn, 1978).

31. Statement of the Institut der Deutschen Wirtschaft, in *Frankfurter Rundschau,* April 12, 1978.

32. "Kreditanstalt für Wiederaufbau: 29," *Jahresbericht, Geschäftsjahr 1977* (Frankfurt, 1978), pp. 26, 28.

33. Ibid., p. 26.

34. See "Beschäftigungswirkungen von Importen aus Entwicklungsländern nicht dramatisieren," *Deutsches Institut für Wirtschaftsforschung* 1 (1978):ff.

35. See ibid.

36. *The World Bank: World Development Report 1978* (Washington: International Bank for Reconstruction and Development, 1978), p. 15.

37. "Entwicklungspolitisches Konzept der Bundesregierung," in Bundesministerium, *Dritter Bericht,* p. 67.

38. See the article by Minister of Development R. Offergeld "Anmerkungen zum Thema Neue Weltwirtschaftsordnung," *Die Neue Gesellschaft* 9 (1978):700 ff.

39. See "Die dunklen Worte des Ministers," *Die Zeit,* November 10, 1978, p. 19.

40. Czempiel, *Macht und Kompomiss,* pp. 129 ff.

41. See his statement before the *Bundestag,* June 1, 1978.

42. For details see Helga Haftendorn, *Abrüstungs- und Entspannungspolitik zwischen Sicherheitsbefriedigung und Friedenssicherung. Zur Aussenpolitik der BRD 1955-1973* (Düsseldorf: Bertelsmann Univeristätsverlag, 1974).

43. Chancellor Helmut Schmidt in ibid.

44. U.S. Arms Control and Disarmament Agency, *World Military Expenditures and Arms Transfers, 1967-1976* (Washington: ACDA, 1978), p. 10.

45. See the collected speeches of the German foreign minister, in Hans-Dietrich Genscher, *Deutsche Aussenpolitik* (Stuttgart, 1977).

46. See the papers of the *Sozialdemokratische Fachtagung: Entwicklungspolitik der SPD* (Wiesbaden, 1977).

47. *Frankfurter Rundschau,* July 3, 1978.

13

Foreign Policy and Monetary Policy

Gerhard Zeitel

I

The distinction between foreign policy and economic policy, which in the past has always been rather succinct, is now blurred by an increased penetration of national markets due to a greater international division of labor. The relationship between foreign policy and economic policy has thus gained in intensity, and their interdependence has acquired greater importance as well as complexity. This state of affairs can be substantiated by the development of international trade and payments flows as a result of the development of living standards and national product as well as by the efforts toward security treaties.

The effect of this generally intensified relationship varies, particularly with respect to the formation of regional and/or regulative as well as security blocs — an increasing global trend. The EEC, the Andean Pact, the ASEAN Alliance, and, on a global scale, the North-South alignment are examples of blocs determined by regional factors. The EEC and Comecon can be cited in turn as blocs characterized predominantly by different social and economic systems. The same applies to the tendency toward the formation of security blocs. As the examples show, relations within the blocs are determined by overlapping and cumulative factors. Therefore, they are the most pronounced if the regional, regulative, and security factors are directed along similar lines or are even identical. The same consideration applies to the relationship between monetary policy and foreign policy.

In addition, ever since the end of World War II monetary policy has been influenced by international institutions to a greater extent than in the past. Proof of this is the International Monetary Fund (IMF) and the World Bank as well as the global regulative initiatives of these institutions. In an historically unprecedented fashion, the foreign policy of individual countries is influenced integratively by the anticipatory effects of international monetary policy. The United States and the Federal Republic of

Germany were particularly closely linked and committed to these efforts
relating to monetary and economic policy. In foreign monetary and
economic relations the result was, and still is, that the U.S. dollar assumed
a leading responsibility and simultaneously enjoyed a particular privilege.
When sterling relinquished its role, the U.S. dollar became the decisive key
currency, which it still is today. In this context one cannot fail to notice that
the fundamental change in the importance of sterling is not merely by
chance a sign and manifestation of the change in the United Kingdom's
foreign situation. There is obviously a link between the monetary and
foreign policies of a country.

In recent times, international monetary policy and the resultant effects
on foreign policy are being increasingly shaped by another factor. This
takes the form of private international money and capital markets that are
gaining in importance, particularly the so-called Eurodollar market. This
market influences national monetary policy not only with respect to the
control of the money supply and interest, but also as regards the associated
exchange rate policy. In view of the quantities involved, the effect on the
latter is frequently counteractive or erratic. Investor confidence in foreign
and monetary policies plays a decisive role. This is illustrated by the investment policy of the OPEC countries. Unlike the influences of international
"monetary authorities," which can be controlled, it has until now been
largely impossible to control, on either a national or an international basis,
the developments of international money and capital markets. The investment and payment processes transcend the sphere of influence that individual member states of the IMF might have. Among other
developments, the international money and capital markets are also increasingly becoming the area of operation for Comecon countries, whose
activities had a completely bilateral orientation in the past.

II

The remarks made so far suggest that, in the final analysis, monetary
policy must be seen and assessed as part of a country's overall economic
policy. This applies to both domestic and foreign economic policy. How
much of an integral part it is depends mainly on the nature of the institutions responsible for the political sectors. In other words, it can be integrated to varying extents, depending on the central bank's decision making
relative to the government's, even if it can be assumed that the central bank
and the government are, in principle, striving to cooperate. Examples from
the United States and the Federal Republic of Germany illustrate that the
two sides clash repeatedly over monetary policy, with the emphasis being
on either domestic or foreign economic policy considerations.

Therefore, the relationship between monetary and economic policies is differentiated both with respect to the interdependence due to the objectives and the formative powers of the institutions and also in individual sectors. When speaking of foreign or domestic economic orientations, it is generally safe to assume that the domestic economic policy will be given priority. This is the case in the United States and the Federal Republic of Germany, even though the intentions do not always correspond. In the United States they are determined to a greater extent by the actual market situation (where foreign trade amounts to only 6 percent of GNP, compared to 29 percent in the Federal Republic), and in the Federal Republic by stability considerations.

The links between monetary policy and foreign policy also exist at several levels, since foreign policy covers various sectors. These include not only security policy aimed at protecting the existing order and social aspirations, but also, in particular, improved foreign trade relations in order to raise the standard of living.

The formation of foreign relations is a preserve of the government, even though, in a liberal political system with open frontiers, social groups and organizations are able to maintain contacts that might be of importance to the country's overall foreign position. In this context, any conflicting objectives or policy formation by the various bodies is of less significance than the conditions of domestic stability and a continuity of the objectives pursued.

Thus, this is proof of the great influence of the basic social, governmental, and economic system on the links between monetary and foreign policies in general and in international relations. In countries with socialist systems, monetary policy is clearly an aid in fulfilling the development intentions in the goods sector planned by the central controlling agencies. Their fulfillment is conditional upon the sealing off of foreign trade in order to exclude the counteractive effects of domestic and foreign policy precepts existing in open market systems. In this way, monetary policy is made to serve foreign policy, whose formation is in turn less affected by international trade links. This results not only in fewer economic links between countries with different economic and social systems and, conversely, closer relations between countries with similar structures, but also in foreign policy being clearly given priority. The primacy of foreign policy in relations between democracies with free market economies is less apparent and more dependent on foreign monetary and trade relations. These relations are not only closer between such countries, but are also frequently the actual "pacemakers" of foreign policy.

Therefore, foreign policy can be supported directly by monetary and economic policy measures. That is the case, for example, when various types of government subsidies are granted or loans are given to other countries or international institutions, particularly under special terms. The extent to which support can be granted is determined decisively by the economic orientation. The relationship between monetary policy and foreign policy can be of a more indirect nature, whereby, under certain circumstances, the monetary policy alters the scope for foreign policy considerably owing to its influence on economic stability, growth, and the balance of payments. In socialist countries, the direct relationship between monetary and foreign policy predominates, and in free market economies, the indirect relationship. The foreign relations of the Federal Republic of Germany with the United States on the one hand and with the Soviet Union on the other illustrate this difference.

The links between monetary and foreign policies are closest when the individual countries are committed to political and/or economic integration. Under such conditions, the monetary and economic policies become factors that shape and simultaneously support foreign policy. The EEC is an excellent example of this tendency. The complex system of links outlined in the preceding remarks is important for assessing the developments in the Federal Republic of Germany.

III

The foreign policy of the Federal Republic of Germany is characterized by an orientation to the West and by Western integration, which developed during the country's initial stages. Before the country even possessed its own government agencies, it was already a member of the Organization for European Economic Cooperation (OEEC). The Federal Republic's membership in the OEEC resulted in its subsequent membership in the European Payments Union (EPU) set up by the OEEC. The clear priority set in foreign relations corresponded to the domestic intentions, and not least to the monetary policy. The development of the governmental, social, and economic system in the Federal Republic led in turn to intensive Western integration. In terms of monetary policy it is, and was, linked most closely to the United States, finding its expression in the Marshall Plan.

The spheres of influence in Europe became more solidified in the mid-fifties and accelerated Western integration. This was accompanied in terms of monetary policy by the Federal Republic's transition to a convertible-currency country (1958). As a result, not only the Federal Republic's economic integrative trend but also the support of the foreign policy by the monetary policy was considerably strengthened.

The failure of the European Defence Community (EDC) resulted in 1955 in the integration of the Federal Republic of Germany into NATO.

The accession to this military alliance entailed the renunciation of the classical sovereign right of freely deployable armed forces as well as various armaments limitations. The accession brought about even closer links with respect to monetary and economic policy, as demonstrated by the foreign investments in the Federal Republic of Germany and the foreign exchange transactions due to the stationing of foreign troops in the country. Therefore, the Federal Republic's development of relations with the United States was determined by alliance and security interests and involved a high degree of dependency on the United States. This asymmetry of the relations is reflected by the monetary policy pursued throughout the entire period. The development of relations was characterized by distinct dollar surpluses and the accompanying key role of the dollar, as well as by close monetary cooperation between the United States and the Federal Republic of Germany.

This close cooperation in the field of monetary policy between the United States and the Federal Republic was consolidated by institutional means, that is by the Federal Republic's membership in international monetary institutions (the IMF and the World Bank). Due to the favorable balance-of-payments trend in the Federal Republic, the deutsche mark became not only an increasingly important international liquidity aid, but also a decisive support for the dollar itself, owing to the quantity of national reserves held in dollars.

The conclusion of the treaties with the Soviet Union, Eastern European countries, and the German Democratic Republic, which involved the recognition of the latter, introduced a new era of "orderly coexistence" (*geregeltes Nebeneinander*) for the countries in question. Since 1970 the Federal Republic's trade links with these countries have been expanded considerably. Their development has involved a disequilibrium since they have been promoted by credit granted unilaterally by the Federal Republic. The significance of monetary policy in this context is the safeguarding of private credit, particularly long-term credit for financing exports. As a result of the trade links, the "material basis" of these countries has been widened; i.e., the production potential has been expanded, the utilization of which is decided according to political objectives. The frequently quoted possibility of a change in the structure of the socialist countries due to convergence of the Eastern and Western systems as a result of the increased trade links has to be considered hardly realizable, not least because of the monetary limits to the granting of further credit for the purpose of expanding trade. It is also worth noting the increasing extent to which these countries are obtaining credit not on a bilateral, but on a multilateral basis by making greater use of the international money and capital markets.

Furthermore, it is hard to justify the hope that the arms limitation talks between the United States and the Soviet Union (SALT), the talks on troop reductions (MBFR), and the results of the European Security Conference (CSCE) will lead to a change in the existing setup of different systems. A significant intensification of the trade links cannot be expected unless more credit is granted. Instead, it seems probable that a further stabilization of the existing conditions will result. In particular, improved living conditions in the countries concerned will no doubt contribute to this stabilization.

Greater importance with respect to international monetary and foreign policy should be attached to the People's Republic of China, which is currently opening up its frontiers, economically and politically speaking. The size of the country, especially of the population, the urgent need for foreign advanced technical know-how, and an additional requirement for the provision of capital are the basic prerequisites for the realization of the economic targets the Chinese have set for themselves. The transfer of resources involved will probably be achieved to a large extent by way of bilateral credit granting or borrowing from the international money and capital markets. Although the figures known to date must be considered with certain reservations as far as the likelihood of their realization is concerned, the scope of credit transactions with China will, in the future, probably exceed those with the Soviet Union and thus have a considerable influence on international monetary policy. The Federal Republic of Germany has a good starting position in the goods and nonmonetary sphere for the prospective increase in trade and credit relations with the People's Republic of China, even though China will probably do most of its business with Japan for geographical reasons.

Similar considerations apply to the relations with the Third World. These have become far more complex and difficult, especially since 1973, due to the policy of cartelization and price increases pursued by the countries producing petroleum and raw materials. The trend in the raw material prices has led to a schism in the developing countries. This has been the cause for increased development aid to the poor developing countries. Owing to the fact that numerous countries are already in debt, payments moratoria and/or debt remissions are almost inevitable in many cases. This state of affairs is not only a burden to international monetary relations, but also encroaches upon the internal monetary and budgetary policy of the main creditors, particularly the United States and the Federal Republic of Germany. This effect is being aggravated by the demands for increased development aid amounting to at least 0.8 percent of the national product, as laid down in the Pearson Report.

On the one hand, the financial problems of the developing countries lacking raw materials have worsened, while, on the other, there has been a redistribution—of no less than gigantic proportions—of international liquidity reserves in favor of the petroleum-producing countries. Admittedly, the trend toward surpluses in the producing countries and corresponding deficits in the purchasing countries is definitely on the decline and is also accompanied by additional assistance granted by the surplus countries to the poorest deficit countries. However, in view of past and future investments, this trend has proven to be a potentially disturbing factor on national and international money and capital markets—a fact deserving particular attention. The same applies no less to the possibility of "errratic exchange rate fluctuations," as already experienced by individual currencies.

Until now the monetary policy of the Federal Republic of Germany has not been affected to any great extent by this trend on account of its favorable balance of payments situation, particularly with respect to the surplus countries themselves. On the other hand, the position of the American dollar and the monetary basis of operations for American foreign policy have been radically altered. Unless there is a decisive change in the predominantly domestically orientated American monetary and economic policy, the development toward an extensive decline in the role of the dollar as a key currency is already traced out. The monetary solution to the resulting problem may appear simple, such as the transition to an international key currency based on a "basket of currencies." However, an obvious conclusion is that this might also result in a reduction in the room for maneuver within American foreign policy and the possibility of increasing conflicts between American and European monetary policy, especially that of the Federal Republic.

Since 1970 and to an increasing extent since 1974, one can observe a certain trend of supplying development aid politics through the expansion of international liquidity. The general quota increases and the granting of special drawing rights have gradually caused a shift in the function of the International Monetary Fund. It is threatening more and more to degenerate into another development aid institution. The special funds that have been established provide further proof of this trend. The Federal Republic of Germany has always opposed such a trend because it brings about the danger that a global inflationary trend could cancel out the efforts directed at domestic and foreign economic stability.

The developing countries consider the additional liquidity made available to them as their internationally guaranteed claim to the national product of the industrial countries. The negative effects of such an internationally approved policy become apparent when the production capacity of the industrial countries is exhausted. Then, if demand is to be met while existing resources are scarce, this can only be achieved under conditions of inflation.

Warding off the coordinated efforts of the developing countries to gain more influence on the international monetary institutions in order to create more liquidity (which in turn results in inflation) will probably become the crux of international monetary and foreign policy. This applies particularly to the United States and the Federal Republic of Germany, whose identity of interests in this field is no longer as pronounced as in the past and may in fact be the cause of another conflict of interests.

The intensification of the joint European monetary efforts, as attempted in the form of the European Monetary Union (EMU), is a logical step in view of the trends already outlined. It is also in keeping with efforts directed at increased European integration. The question is whether all the countries involved will succeed in subordinating their domestic monetary policy to the demands of the foreign policy course embarked upon. Past experience is not exactly encouraging. When there was a conflict between balance of payments remedies and domestic stability, the tendency to take the (superficially) easier course of inflation usually predominated.

IV

As already mentioned, the foreign policy and monetary policy arrangements in the West are characterized by the fact that the individual countries do not all belong to the same international organizations and associations (e.g., NATO, Club of Ten, OECD, European Community, etc.). Membership in an international organization involves, to a certain extent, extensive foreign exchange obligations and burdens in the goods and services sector, especially in the case of the United States and the Federal Republic of Germany. Not all countries are willing or able to incur the obligations and bear the burdens to an equal extent. The foreign and monetary policy of the Federal Republic of Germany was, and still is, directed at the fulfillment of international obligations. By pursuing such a policy the Federal Republic was repeatedly forced into the role of a "troublemaker," but maintained a definitely export-orientated basic attitude.

From the outset, domestic stability was given priority in the Federal Republic's monetary policy. This clear decision was hardly surprising in view of the two currency reforms required because of two instances of national bankruptcy with extensive national debt remission experienced in the past. The monetary and credit policy of the federal central bank was therefore directed at influencing the economy and promoting growth with the objective of a high degree of stability of the deutsche mark, which was in fact achieved. A similar policy was not possible in the United States because of the national indebtedness. At least, it was impossible if one wanted to avoid excessive fluctuations in the interest rates and market performance of government bonds and their corresponding budgetary effects.

A review of thirty years of German monetary policy shows that there were only a few phases that were not determined by balance of payments disequilibria and an attempt to curb imported inflation. The stabilizing policy of the Federal Republic was adversely affected by the gap between domestic and foreign interest rates. From time to time (e.g., 1950-1951, 1959-1960, 1965-1966, and 1973), special stabilization measures were initiated in order to ward off an impending inflationary surge. Each time this resulted in a differential between domestic and foreign prices and demand, which improved the foreign trading position in the Federal Republic. Due to the resulting balance of payments surplus any headway made toward achieving stability was partly canceled out. Time and time again the stabilization policy proved to be self-defeating.

Close connections betwen the world's main money and capital markets, the internationalization of banking, the money transfers of international companies and also the increased significance of international trade and payment flows compared to those at a national level—all these factors ultimately produced conditions under which, due to the existence of fixed exchange rates, the monetary system of most countries could be influenced to a high degree at any time as a result of interest- and monetary-induced transfers of capital from abroad.

Thus, between 1951 and 1973, the Federal Republic of Germany had to make net purchases of foreign currencies, mainly dollars, equivalent to DM 112 billion. During these twenty-three years, the liquidity created as a result of the foreign currency inflow considerably exceeded domestic requirements, even if one considers the increase in turnover, which was partly due to inflation. Thus, the money supply was largely determined by foreign trade factors, in accordance with the federal central bank's policy.

This development was further aggravated by speculative money flows, resulting in intense national and international discussions since the early sixties about the utility of fixed exchange rates, as set up through the Bretton Woods monetary system. The discussion was different at the national and international levels, i.e., the positions taken varied at the two levels. The supposedly chronic "dollar shortage" up to the end of the fifties turned into a chronic "dollar surplus" at the start of the sixties. The severe criticism voiced by the Kennedy administration in 1961 regarding the gold and foreign currency reserves amassed by other countries did little to diminish the increasing loss of confidence in the dollar.

After occasional revaluations of the deutsche mark (1961 and 1969), and after a renewed massive increase in the foreign assets of the German central bank (primarily dollars), the conflict reached its climax in May 1971. The May 1971 crisis was caused basically by the excess liquidity created by the United States. This was only the prelude to the actual dollar crisis, which, after the cancellation of the convertibility into gold of the dollar in August, ultimately led to the devaluation of the dollar and an exchange rate reform in December 1971 (Smithsonian Agreement). In the turmoil of currency speculation between the end of January and the start of March 1973, the carefully constructed system of monetary parities collapsed. This was due to the fact that the American monetary authorities, without consideration for maintaining the new dollar parity, considerably eased their monetary policy for domestic reasons, while the German central bank was attempting to support the new system by means of a foreign-trade–oriented interest and foreign currency policy. To ward off further dollar inflows, it was decided to set up the European Monetary Union in April 1972 and to float the European curencies jointly against the dollar from 1973 onwards. The British and Italian central banks had already in the past floated their own currencies. Thus, the Bretton Woods Agreement, which had shaped the early postwar developments, was relegated to the past; simultaneously, however, confidence in the dollar had been shattered with lasting effects.

The resulting change in the role of the deutsche mark, which had until then been a currency dependent on the dollar as key currency, cannot be fully explained by referring to the difference in inflation rates. Between 1952 and 1972, the Federal Republic of Germany enjoyed an advantage in stability only over other major European countries. These differentials made themselves felt repeatedly during European balance of payments and monetary crises and during major exchange rate shifts. On a longer term basis, the price trend in the Federal Republic was not appreciably better than that in the United States; if the labor costs per unit of output are compared, the Federal Republic actually comes off considerably worse. There was no inflation differential between the United States and Germany. Before the collapse of the parity system, a comparison shows a particularly favorable American position with respect to the increase in money supply. Between 1952 and 1972, the money supply in the United States barely increased at a faster rate than the actual national product, whereas it increased at almost twice the rate in the Federal Republic of Germany.

The deficits in the American reserves, aggravated by the Vietnam war, particularly from 1970 to 1973, hardly affected the American money supply. But owing to the intervention obligation of the central banks in the countries receiving dollars, American deficits resulted in the creation of more central bank money and, in most cases, an inflationary effect on the money supply. This made it possible for the United States to internationalize the burdens stemming from the Vietnam war, and strained the arrangements made on the basis of the Bretton Woods monetary system.

A completely different development occurred with respect to American export prices compared to German ones. The attitude of American industry is important in this respect. It attempted to avoid price competition on the increasingly competitive foreign market by investing in European industrial countries. Instead of exporting goods, American industry shifted its production sites abroad. The "American challenge" was a feature of that era. This investment policy was also promoted by a structural liquidity and interest differential in favor of American industry. Not least due to the establishment of the Common Market, a trend of extensive structural capital export by the American economy, which was not covered by a corresponding surplus in the balance of payments, began late in the 1950s. For domestic reasons (in the interests of the construction industry) American interest rates were not increased to a level needed to correct balance-of-payments deficits. The interest equalization tax, and control measures for curbing the export of capital, proved to be inadequate. The high direct investments made by American industry in Europe (particularly in the Federal Republic of Germany) have been a major contribution toward reducing the enormous income differential. At the same time, the influx of American capital meant technical progress for the Federal Republic of Germany. The accompanying rise in productivity permitted an almost unprecedented recovery of lost ground. In the early fifties, real income per capita in the Federal Republic was approximately only one-third of that in the United States, in 1960 it was still only 45 percent, but now it is almost the same as the average American income stated in real terms. An appreciation of the deutsche mark against the dollar by about 100 percent, which has taken place in the period since 1961, was necessary in order to provide an adaptation process for the growth of incomes without creating excessive inflation.

Until quite recently one could describe the American balance-of-payments policy as one of benign neglect. For a long time the German central bank and government provided protection for this policy, especially by means of foreign exchange equalization agreements and by German willingness to hold extensive international reserves in dollar assets. Unlike other countries (e.g., France), the Federal Republic did not make use of the possibility of converting these assets into gold. With its favorable attitude toward the United States in the field of monetary policy, the Federal Republic of Germany devoted considerable effort to its foreign position and security situation and proved its responsibility for maintaining the existing monetary system. However, as a result of this policy, an important instrument for limiting and controlling international liquidity was weakened considerably. Furthermore, this led to conflicts with other European countries, particularly France, who pursued different foreign and monetary policies.

In the meantime, the changes in the international monetary system have been supplemented by the global links of private liquidity equalization and private credit granting, which can no longer be controlled by individual countries. Faced with the worldwide network of international money and capital markets, the only means left at a national level is to regulate and limit capital movements and thus restrict convertibility (compare the Netherlands and Switzerland). Until now the attempt to internationalize the control measures affecting the national banks has failed, not least because some countries intentionally consolidate their pivotal position. In the future, too, they will have little chance of success.

Beginning in 1973 the balance-of-payments equalization through the provision of private monetary reserves has been gaining in importance. Rivalry between official and private institutions is clearly visible, leading to a division of labor in which the IMF is responsible primarily for balance-of-payments equalization by granting loans to less efficient national economies, leaving balance-of-payments equalization efforts between industrial countries to private sources. This has made it more difficult to pursue an independent national monetary policy, which the Federal Republic always pursued in the past in the interest of domestic stability.

The attempt to pursue a more autonomous monetary policy by means of floating exchange rates was only partly successful. In contrast to the past, interest differentials are more likely to affect exchange rates rather than monetary reserves. An interest policy without regard for the exchange rate policy leads, however, to exchange rate distortions, making for disintegrating effects. In recent years such effects were clearly detectable in relations between the Federal Republic and the United States. This development is also aggravated by speculative capital movements of unprecedented proportions and, partly, by regional systems of fixed exchange rates.

The monetary policy of the Federal Republic has beem aimed, within the scope of the country's efforts toward domestic stability, at supporting and advancing European integration. This applies particularly with respect to the considerable foreign currency and budgetary burdens and the associated transfer of resources, primarily in France's favor. In addition, German monetary policy has repeatedly promoted joint action on the part of the countries involved (e.g., floating in 1971) with the objective of accelerating the creation of a monetary union. Following the first unsuccessful decision in this direction (1969) and the only partially successful formation of the "snake" (1972), which became a "minisnake" when the United

Kingdom, Italy, and France abandoned it, a new attempt, based on foreign policy considerations, has now been made to create a European monetary system (EMS). The creation of a European monetary bloc with its own currency unit (ECU), joint currency reserves, and fixed exchange rates has to be seen not only from the aspect of European integration, but also as a reaction to the dwindling key role of the American dollar. In view of past experience, the question whether the decline in the dollar results in the expected degree of increased collective action on monetary and foreign policy has to remain unanswered until it can be shown that a satisfactory solution has been found to the previous conflicts between the foreign and domestic monetary stabilization efforts in the individual countries involved.

The commitment of the Federal Republic of Germany must also be assessed in the light of the increasing significance of the deutsche mark as a replacement for the dollar. At present, approximately 8 percent of the official world monetary reserves are held in deutsche mark. In view of the current excess of dollars, it is to be expected that other currencies will increasingly be used as reserve currencies. This could result in additional pressure to revalue the deutsche mark upward, which can be countered more easily within a monetary union.

V

In view of the trends outlined, one can state that, especially since the early seventies, American foreign policy has lost the considerable support that it had obtained from monetary policy until the 1960s. This fact was partly hidden by the painless deficits that were connected with the role of the dollar as a key currency. Since the oil crisis this fact has become more obvious in the form of high deficits, resulting in the loss of confidence in the dollar and thus the shattering of the dollar's role as a key currency. The deeper reason for this trend is the American failure to take the balance-of-payments measures needed to rectify an inadequately stability-orientated economic policy and the associated loss in international competitiveness of American companies. At the same time, the ability of American foreign policy to resist the increased pressure of the developing countries has been weakened and, on the whole, the monetary basis for foreign policy operations has been reduced. Unless the balance-of-payments trend is reversed by means of a more stability-orientated domestic monetary policy and, simultaneously, a stepped-up promotion of the international competitiveness of American companies, a further decline in the dominating role of the dollar has to be expected. Seeking to avoid the problem through protectionist measures would most likely accelerate the deterioration of the foreign policy position of the United States.

Global monetary cooperation or integration — for example by means of a rapid raising of quotas and accelerated expansion of the system of special drawing rights, coupled with granting the IMF functions similar to those of a central bank — can hardly be expected in the near future. Instead, such measures are more likely to result in excess liquidity with strong inflationary trends. The effectiveness of special drawing rights would therefore be reduced and the importance of individual national currencies would be increased. It is wrong to place high hopes on these measures because the economic and monetary policies of the countries involved differ too much. Instead, it is to be expected that the weakening of the U.S. position will cause the developing countries to push even harder for an inflationary trend, which is useful in their eyes, not least in order to obtain increased financial means in return for the raw materials agreements demanded by them. A well-functioning European economic and monetary community could at least partly offset the diminished reserve role of the dollar. However, for reasons already outlined, it is questionable whether the European countries involved can act collectively. Furthermore, one should not ignore the possibility that such a development might lead to new conflicts with the United States and a disintegration of relations between European countries and the United States. This would not be in the interests of the Federal Republic of Germany. This disintegration could be avoided if American economic and monetary policy were geared more toward foreign trade requirements and if the European countries would aid the dollar, in particular by means of direct investment, capital exports, and by removing trade barriers.

In the event of a further decline in the leading position of the dollar, it must also be expected that the OPEC countries will abandon their close link to the dollar in their trade and payment transactions and seek a different unit of account, and that they will reexamine their foreign investment policy, as well. This would result in further disintegrative effects on an international scale, which the European Community would hardly be able to counter.

On the other hand, it seems not very likely that the socialist countries will be able to make greater use, economically and financially speaking, of the monetary uncertainty that has arisen. Increased economic integration of these countries results in even greater difficulties in this respect than the ones already outlined for the Western countries. These difficulties stem from the economic systems of the countries. They are attributable to the de facto bilateralism that characterizes their economic and monetary transactions and the lack of a controlling effect of domestic prices on trade arrangements and accounting procedures. They can only be overcome unilaterally by the dictate of those in power. For this reason the ruble cannot be considered a potential international reserve and payment medium on a global scale. This is supported by the fact the dollar is still the primary unit of account in the trade relations among the Eastern bloc countries themselves. There are also limits to an increased use of the international money and capital markets by the Eastern bloc countries, even though this possibility will probably be utilized more extensively than in the past.

On the whole, monetary and economic blocs are likely to gain in importance. In view of the increased significance of monetary and economic factors in international politics, this development would also have an effect on foreign policy. The collapse of the dollar might thus signal extensive decentralization in the field of foreign policy operations, which would no longer be dominated so clearly by the two superpowers. For the Federal Republic of Germany this would result in a more complex and difficult context for the formulation of its foreign and monetary policy.

14

Economic Growth, Economic Policy, and Foreign Affairs

Julia Dingwort-Nusseck

I

Growth of the Federal Republic in the Past Thirty Years

During the three decades since the establishment of the Federal Republic of Germany, its gross national product has quadrupled — an impressive rate for an industrial country. In the same thirty years, the gross national product in the United States has tripled and in Great Britain a little more than doubled. This development must be regarded as a singular event in economic history, the result of phenomenal growth (on an average of 10 percent per annum) in the first few years, followed by a phase of consolidation with an average of 7.5 percent up to 1970, and thereafter by a distinct slowdown, interrupted by even a real regress.

The rapid economic development in the early years of the Federal Republic would have been unimaginable without the 1948 Currency Reform, which abolished the devalued *Reichsmark* and established the deutsche mark, and, of equal importance, established the so-called social market economy. The Currency Reform of June 1948 created the basis of what the world began to call the German *Wirtschaftswunder* ("economic miracle"). Without this economic miracle the young republic's political stability, with its great national and international impact, could not have developed. The economic development during the first three decades of the Federal Republic stems from the Currency Reform. The reform stopped inflation — a situation in which an immense surplus of money, created to finance the war, was in circulation — and was followed by a drastically reduced supply of goods. Before the Currency Reform, price controls and rationing could not ensure for every inhabitant even the daily subsistence allowance. The results of this strategy (nobody could have expected anything else) were numerous illegal markets, where the American cigarette became a sort of currency. Shortly before the Currency Reform one single American cigarette cost forty *Reichsmark* on the black market.

With his bold step out of a controlled economy into a market economy, Ludwig Erhard, father of the so-called *Wirtschaftswunder,* set free the stimulus for an economic recovery that is unique.

For Ludwig Erhard, however, the long-time minister of economics and subsequent chancellor of the Federal Republic, who died in 1977, the evolution since 1948 was not a miracle, but the natural consequence of economic reasoning. For him it was more astonishing that there were even rudiments of economic order before the Currency Reform. In the spring of 1948 he said, "It is almost a miracle, and it bears evidence of great discipline of our people that the regulations of rationing and price-stops maintained the economic structure and external order for so long; but to expect, on this basis, watertight economic control and a just distribution at that, would presume that not men, but angels and gods are at work."

The German *Wirtschaftswunder* was a most impressive example of what a state-controlled economy cannot do and what the market can do. It is true, however, that the thirty-year history of the Federal Republic of Germany would have been more turbulent if the social component of the market economy had not played a larger role from the very beginning—a particularly important role in a society where the hazards of war had created highly uneven economic starting conditions: some families had lost a breadwinner while others had not; some who were expulsed from the former territories in the east or were caught in the air raids had lost all their belongings while others had not. Given these unequal individual circumstances, a market system without a strong social component would not have been justifiable.

It is true that in the course of the last thirty years some structures in the legal need for the protection of handicapped groups, but also in the desire of particular interests. Some drops in growth in the last few years can partly be explained with well-meant but in the end not always effective limitations on the market economy by dirigisme.

The decision for the social market economy and thus for incentives as central factors of economic growth in 1948 was the basis for later development, but of course it was not the only cause. One reason for the early impressive growth rates is statistical: in the first few years after the war, the economic output in West Germany was on such a low level that high increases expressed in percentages could be achieved more easily than, for instance, in the United States, which came out of the war with full employment in its economy. Hence high growth rates in those countries that had been drastically affected by the war were not remarkable. In addition to that, damaged machinery in the Federal Republic could be made usable with relatively low capital expenditures and this generated a high increase in capacity.

Some other significant causes for the postwar economic development in the Federal Republic were international aid, especially from the United States; the strengthening of the labor force, at first by expellees and refugees and later by foreign workers; the establishment of the European Community; the general liberalization of world trade; and, last but not least, the growth-promoting attitude of management and labor.

European Recovery Program (ERP)

The speedy German reconstruction would have been impossible without the Marshall Plan. When one thinks about the problem of the dollar today, one can hardly imagine that in the early postwar years the greatest handicap of Western European countries in general (and of the West German economy in particular) was the so-called dollar gap. The United States was able to provide supplies to a Europe badly in need of them, but the Europeans were not capable of obtaining enough dollars by exports of their own. This is where the European Recovery Program created assistance, the importance of which can scarcely be overrated. The help consisted mainly of free payments in kind (predominately food, raw material, machinery, and transportation), which amounted to more than $1.5 billion from 1948 to 1952. Of equal importance was the establishment of the Organization for European Economic Cooperation (OEEC) for the purpose of distributing ERP resources. This was the first organization to succeed in strengthening European integration and to lay the groundwork for the liberalization of European trade and the convertibility of currencies. At that time the popular expression "Americans are the best Europeans" arose.

Not all expectations connected with the Organization for European Economic Cooperation could be fulfilled. Franco-British rivalry in this organization prevented it from becoming the basis of a European Community, as had been hoped. Instead, on the basis of mainly Franco-German cooperation, the European Economic Community (nowadays European Community) was established. But the Organization for European Economic Cooperation — later called the Organization for Economic Cooperation and Development and extended to include the United States, Canada, and Japan — has retained up to the present day an important function as an overall organization of important free nations.

The German economy benefited not only from grants of commodities to the European Recovery Program, but also from an important source available for favorable loans. The deutsche mark values of the (predominantly free) supplies from the United States were paid, by the recipients, into a German capital fund, which granted loans, at favorable interest rates, for the reconstruction of the economy. Through continuous recrediting, this aid has continued up to the present day. As German companies embarked on rapid recovery on an extremely low equity capital basis, credit aid must be mentioned as one of the reaons for the quick economic growth.

Extensive population movements were among the special factors in the economic growth of Germany. Until 1961, millions of expellees and refugees from former German Eastern territories and from what is now the German Democratic Republic fled into the Western part of Germany. What at first was felt to be an intolerable burden in a densely populated area, where the basis of life and economy was to a great extent destroyed, later on proved to support the growth: the necessity of starting from scratch was a strong incentive for the new citizens; the pent-up demand for consumer goods and housing facilities backed up the demand far into the 1960s. Many of the refugees from the German Democratic Republic were young and had special abilities.

Following the erection of the Berlin wall in 1961, the immigration of refugees ceased. Millions of foreign workers took their places. These workers came mainly from Italy, Yugoslavia, Greece, Turkey, and Spain. The labor-market policy of that period is open to debate. For years no one would decide whether it was more advisable to enlist foreign workers for a relatively short time (rotation enlistment) or to integrate them and their families into German society.

The recession of the 1970s made a political decision unnecessary. Millions of foreign workers lost their jobs in the Federal Republic and went home. Since that time foreign workers from outside the European Community have no longer been enlisted. Inside the Common Market there are no restrictions on workers to find jobs in a country of the Community.

Workers from countries outside the Common Market who remain in Germany will be gradually integrated into German society. Their age distribution — on the average they are younger than the original German population — and their higher birthrate will slow down the rapid decline in population of the Federal Republic.

The employment of foreign workers prohibited losses of growth in a phase of overemployment; but the permanent social and economic damages for those affected have been high. For the Federal Republic, too, the pressures to change infrastructure, generated by the immigration of foreign workers, outweigh a part of the economic advantages. The new practice in policy (to bring jobs to the people and not people to the jobs, that, is, to invest in countries with structural weaknesses) holds greater promise of success in the long run for all participants. This strategy prevents workers from being uprooted, families from being separated, and foreign workers from having difficulties with their reintegration at home when they have lost their jobs in Germany. Above all, the investments in regions with economic deficiencies help to make up the backlog to the industrial nations.

Technical progress and a relatively fast change in the structure of the economy have been important determinants of the economic growth in the Federal Republic. The technological gap, which existed during the 1950s and 1960s between most of the industrial countries and the United States has been closed. Taking over American techniques by licenses or assignments of patents, or just by imitating new techniques, other countries could reach high productivity within a short time. During recent years, however, this procedure was no longer needed. Like other countries, the Federal Republic was able to depend on its own capability to develop new technologies. Year after year, the growing external interdependence became a more important stimulus to economic growth. During some of the domestic recessions, exports also stabilized. For the first time, the Federal Republic suffered from a very deep and lasting leveling off, when international and national business cycles ran on parallel lines.

The Federal Republic has profited in particular from the liberalization of world trade, the reductions of tariffs and other barriers of trade, which have been carried out in the GATT negotiations. In addition to this, the foundation of the European Community in 1957 has assisted the Federal Republic in rapidly becoming one of the most important partners in world trade. German concessions concerning agricultural pricing are of course not compatible with the philosophy of world trade. But we have to admit that only by these compromises could the quick progress in reducing tariffs inside the Community and with it the German success in exporting industrial goods be effected. Nowadays, nearly half of German foreign trade is with countries of the Common Market. In addition, the competitive power of the German export business, which has hardly been in danger even up to now, can be explained by two phenomena that have made, for a long time, the German development different from those of the other industrial countries: the growth-promoting attitude of the German trade unions and the internal price stability.

During the first two decades after the foundation of the Federal Republic, the German trade unions pursued a wage policy that had a decisive effect on reaching full employment because it encouraged the development and utilization of industrial capacities. This policy was connected to the fact that private consumption needed no stimulus by high wage increases because the pent-up domestic demand for consumer goods existed for years. Due to price stability, the real wage increases were nevertheless remarkable. A nearly complete industrial peace contributed to growth without significant friction.

This development was interrupted in 1969. At that time, two sets of expectations led to moderate wage agreements:

1. a lasting unsatisfactory economic activity with an insufficient development of profits in the enterprises, and
2. continuous moderate price increases.

Neither of the expectations was fulfilled: business activity and profits accelerated. Management and trade unions obviously did not perceive in time, or did not appreciate correctly, the unrest in the employees that arose at that time. Many wildcate strikes led to a considerable loss of union leaders' authority.

Since that time, the trade unions have fought fiercely for large wage increases and other assurances regarding wages. The more tough-minded attitude in wage policy is also marked by a change in command of the leading trade unions. The development of the labor unit costs proves this dramatically. Since 1970 the real revaluation of the deutsche mark (that is, the increase of the exchange rate after eliminating differences of the inflation rates) amounts to 20 percent versus the rest of the world, and even 70 percent versus the United States measured in terms of labor unit costs. The consequences are known: the Federal Republic, for years a favorite spot for American investments, is now trying to find possibilities for relocating production to the United States because the labor costs (especially if one takes into account the additional costs of labor—for instance, the social security contributions) are lower there.

The German success in exports, during twenty-five years of the Federal Republic up to the floating of exchange rates in 1973, has been especially supported by the undervaluation of the deutsche mark. A lower increase in prices than in most of the industrial countries, connected with only few and moderate revaluations, led, in the course of the decades, to drastic undervaluations of the deutsche mark. Long before the beginning of "floating," farsighted economists pointed to the damaging consequences of the low exchange rate of the deutsche mark. During a difficult reconstruction phase undervaluation indeed gave German enterprises a better start. But later it threatened German price stability (making for "imported inflation" in Germany), and it also helped subsidize German foreign trade. Protected by the competitive advantage of a low exchange rate, numerous branches of industry did not have to compete on the basis of realistic exchange rates—not to speak of competing on the basis of an overvalued deutsche mark.

However, two events indicated how difficult it was to implement this farsightedness into political reality. In 1961 the minister of economics, Ludwig Erhard, revalued the deutsche mark by a frugal 5 percent and was reputed to be the "grave digger" of German foreign trade. In the spring of 1969 the minister of economics, Karl Schiller, could not succeed with his plan to revalue the deutsche mark because of the opposition of his own government. In spite of the undervaluation of the deutsche mark, during the first decades since 1949, the terms of trade improved nearly all the time, because of moderate prices for raw materials in general and low energy prices in particular. With respect to oil, this situation changed abruptly at the end of 1973.

I have already talked about the German price stability as a cause for social peace, moderate wage increases, and international competitive power. In this context the role of the *Deutsche Bundesbank* (German central bank) should also be mentioned.

American occupation authorities, who constructed the new German central banking system, based it on the model of the American Federal Reserve System. The *Deutsche Bundesbank* was established in 1957, and the structure has been changed to fit the German political system. But through the institution of the *Zentralbankrat,* the council of the highest competence, it has retained a federal structure. Above all the central bank remained autonomous in relation to the federal government.

The Federal Government is responsible for the exchange rate, as far as fixed exchange rates exist. For example, they are present in the so-called snake and will exist in the new European monetary system. As a matter of fact, the *Deutsche Bundesbank* does not depend on directions from the government concerning its monetary policy (in contrast with most of the other central banks in Europe). In order to reach and maintain price stability, this independence has often proved useful when the federal government, thinking about the next elections, has shied away from unpopular decisions. The German economy and its importance for the world economy have benefited well from this structure.

II

Factors Slowing Down Future Growth

I have tried to illustrate the somewhat unique factors that have determined the Federal Republic's above-average growth during the past three decades. The effect of these special determinants has now ended. In addition, we have to observe the *negative* factors that will obstruct growth in the Federal Republic more than in most other countries.

Demographic development will play a special role. While worldwide overpopulation is a serious problem, the Federal Republic expects sharply decreasing population figures. According to present estimates, in the year

2000 the world population will have grown 150 percent (6 billion people instead of today's 4 billion people); the Federal Republic's population, however, will probably decline nearly a tenth of its level. Thus it will be at the lower far end of birthrates among all the countries in the world. In comparison, by the end of this century a population growth of 18 percent is expected in North America and 7 percent on the average in Western European countries. Some calculate that, in the year 2030, only 39 million inhabitants will live in the Federal Republic—the same number that lived there 100 years ago. Sixty-two million live in the Federal Republic today; the resident population in the year 2000 will be only 56 million. The decrease would be more drastic if the birthrates of foreign worker families living in the Federal Republic were not above the average. Thus it can be assumed that in the year 2000, in spite of expected migration losses, there will be nearly 4 million foreigners—as much as in 1975—living in the Federal Republic.

There is no doubt that in a country with decreasing population the gross national product will, other things being equal, grow less quickly than in countries with a growing population. Thus a real 3 percent increase per annum of the Federal Republic's gross national product for the next decades will have to be valued as a great success. Therefore a comparison with the growth rates of other industrial countries—including the United States—is subject to special qualifications.

How a decreasing population affects the per capita economic growth is debatable. Most economists think that, with cyclical unemployment being steadily reduced in the future, the per capita gross national product will be stimulated by the decreasing population. At first the number of gainful workers will grow, as in the course of the next years those born in the early 1960s will complete their education and look for jobs. In the future, since families will have less children than today, more wives will want to be employed and will be employed. Later on the decline of the birthrate will indeed diminish growth of the per capita gross national product, because the pensioner's share of the total population will rise decisively.

The negative consequences on the Federal Republic's economic growth, which will be produced by the falling number of gainful workers, could be compensated for through considerably increased productivity. However, I do not believe that we will be able to encourage productivity sufficiently. For one, there is the trade union's strategy to achieve a gradual shortening of the work week. We must further take into account that the gainful worker's active working life will be shorter due to longer education and earlier retirement. In addition, losses of growth have to be expected because of declining exports, which will be induced by a rise of labor costs, affecting German competitiveness. As older employees and pensioners have a higher propensity to save, there may also be a loss of domestic demand.

Technical progress is of course another option, but I do not feel competent to evaluate the extremely contradictory opinions about the possible technological developments of the next decades. Some experts fear the end of a technical era with only marginal progress, whereas others hope that the tempo of technological progress at least will not slow down, compared with the development of the past three decades. Even if the optimists are right in the end, there will nevertheless be difficulties in transforming technical progress into practical use because the trade unions object to rationalization In 1978, the Federal Republic experienced strikes in connection with the introduction of labor-saving techniques in newspaper production. These may be viewed as symptomatic of the trade unions' attitude.

In this regard the Federal Republic's enterprises are involved in a trade-off: the employment of new technologies may bring them into conflict with the trade unions, while only advantages in technology will help to defend the strong position in exports against high labor costs. That a whole nation can live from exporting blueprints has been proved an error. A successful export of blueprints presumes that the developed technologies have been industrially tested and used. A great degree of specialization may possibly improve competition, but, on the other hand, it raises the risks by changing the structure of the market.

The deterioration of the Federal Republic's terms of trade will endanger growth because its dependence on imports of raw materials is higher than in nearly every other industrial country. The FRG is not self-sufficient in tin, manganese, nickel, wolfram, and molybdenum, and for many other raw materials it has next to nothing. If the supply of key raw materials fails, all growth predictions would be cast to the winds.

For Germany—as for the United States—the supply of energy is particularly problematic. In the Federal Republic, so-called administrative impediments play a peculiar role. Authorizations of long duration, lawsuits, and parliamentary conflicts retard the construction and the putting into operation of nuclear power plants. The German population's growing consciousness of the necessity for a clean environment has become a political factor. The awareness of ecological neglect has contributed to many remarkable improvements, designed to protect the environment. Yet the mentors of environmental protection have partly lost control over initiatives, for instance, those directed against atomic energy. Administrative and political impediments have obstructed planned but not released projects, which amount to many billion deutsche mark. These impediments choke the commercial propensity to invest, and the readiness to accept economic, technical, and juridical risks is low because German enterprises have remarkably small capital resources. The ratio between equity capital and balance sheet total has declined from 30 percent on the average in 1965 to 23 percent in 1976, which is below the average of comparable industrial countries. In the United States, the corresponding figure is 50 percent.

In anticipating the German economy's future growth rates, it is to be observed that we have not proceeded as far as the United States has in the emergence into postindustrial society. In 1970 the United States tertiary sector produced 63 percent of the gross national product. In 1975 the corresponding share in the Federal Republic amounted to just 40 percent. So Germany has to expect changes, which will also be connected with a slowing down of productivity increases, as practice has proven hitherto. However, we do hope that innovation breakthroughs—especially through the employment of electronic data processing—are near, even in the tertiary sector.

III

Political Consequences

I have tried to point to the internal and external determinants of the Federal Republic's future economic growth. The facts prove that we can no longer expect explosive growth rates. Yet the political aspects—and especially those referring to foreign affairs—not only raise the question of how much growth *can* occur, but force one to think about how much growth *may* occur and how much growth *must* occur. The revolt against growth, reflected in "limits to growth" studies, also found its adherents in Germany. Soon after, growth in fact declined, although it was not a result of voluntary self-restriction. An army of jobless, not only in Germany, drastically demonstrated to the world the consequences of stagnation. Of the same insistency are other effects of growth decline: the jeopardy of social peace, the increasing state indebtedness, the aggravation of structural problems, and the protectionist tendencies in international trade.

Yet the discussion of a voluntary halt to growth has not ceased. The advocates of a limitation to growth can rightly appeal to the imperfections of the measurement of economic growth. The most important statistical indicator for the economic progress that has been reached in a year is the gross national product, which records the total production of goods and services and the income derived from them. But it does not realistically measure growth and shrinking wealth. For example, increasing leisure, induced by a shortening of working time, diminishes the gross national product, as far as production has been reduced, yet enlarges wealth. The requisite costs of repair and if necessary the medical attention following an accident multiplies the gross national product. Certainly nobody will assert that the victim's wealth has grown.

The proponents of qualified growth point out these difficulties. The lower demand for goods and paid services, compared with the early postwar years, indicates that an increase in real wages no longer has exclusively been used to procure additional goods. Instead, the immaterial contents of wealth are desired: better conditions of work — so-called humanization of labor, a better work environment, and above all more leisure (longer holidays, a shorter work week, or earlier retirement). This thesis is greeted with a relatively positive response from the population, especially the younger generation. Last but not least, the readiness of German steelworkers to strike for a shorter work week gives evidence of this attitude.

I think that, in spite of this basic feeling, the Federal Republic especially cannot renounce additional growth. Our political role in Europe and in the world is of a kind that does not allow a dispensation from growth. Such a dispensation would hinder the Federal Republic from achieving interior political stability and meeting the political and economic liabilities in the world. For example, to deliberately slow growth would mean that training facilities for those born in the early 1960s, which was a period with a high birthrate, could not be created.

Unemployment in the Federal Republic is, above all, a matter of regional and sectoral deficiencies. Handicapped groups are especially affected (for example, persons without professional education or women who are looking for part-time jobs). With respect to the problem of regional underemployment, there is less readiness in the Federal Republic (compared to the United States) to relocate. Shortening the work week would predominately affect those branches that already have a lack of skilled workers, as, for example, the construction industry.

Public responsibilities also presume sufficient growth. The Federal Republic has a dense social security screen. In the future, the population will be top-heavy with older people and only satisfactory growth rates will allow the society to pay for increasing numbers of retirement pensions.

Above all, with respect to foreign affairs, growth cannot be abandoned because of the need to help finance the Western alliance. The Federal Republic's security depends on internal social and political peace and the preparedness to defend this order. At the same time, the Federal Republic hopes to ease its economic burdens by arms control and gradual disarmament. The West German economy cannot serve as a "locomotive" for an economic upswing in the world because it is not sufficiently powerful. A forced increase of the Federal Republic's gross national product — even if this growth could be managed, which we do not believe — would bring very few positive impulses for our economic partners.

If our growth had been 1 percent higher than the 3 percent that was reached in 1978, the German imports from France would have risen 0.5 percent, from England 0.2 percent and from the United States 0.33 percent. One can hardly measure the effect on the economic growth of the three countries that would have been induced by a German reflation; in the United States it would have been an increase of 0.007 percent! Certainly a deep economic disturbance in the Federal Republic — for instance, on account of a loss of competitive power through the development of wage costs and exchange rates — would probably provoke psychological feedback on the world economy, which is of greater importance than the marginal effect of increasing German imports.

It is our strong belief that it would be fatal to sacrifice our stable price policy for a higher economic growth in the short run, not only for our own economy but also for the world's economy. Our own experiences and those of others have sufficiently proved that in the medium term, inflation endangers full employment. For our business partners, too, a shortsighted easy money policy in Germany would not be a benefit. The German economy has not enough power to be the locomotive of the world business cycle, but it is important enough to push inflation in other countries, if the Federal Republic's prices should rise again.

The Federal Republic did all that could be done to prevent more international breakdowns in growth, by tolerating a strong revaluation of the deutsche mark. In 1978 our surplus on current account amounted to only 0.7 percent of the gross national product. Considering our close interdependence in foreign trade, this is by no means an abnormal figure. The surplus will probably decline in 1979.

Of extreme importance is the fact that the demands of the Third World will make it impossible for the Federal Republic (and other industrial countries) to deliberately renounce economic growth. We do not live on an island that allows us to enjoy the idyll of a pastoral life with few needs and less work. The new economic order aims to redistribute the wealth of the world. The developing countries' intention to increase their share of the world's national product from 10 percent today to 25 percent in the year 2000 may seem unrealistic. But we will not have time to discuss the adequacy of these demands. Worldwide poverty will not allow us to decide whether the increase of our productivity totally shall enlarge our consumption or enrich our quality of life. The situation requires that we raise our financial aid to developing countries. Our activities now amount to 0.21 percent of the gross national product, which is more than in Japan and in the United States, but far from the aim for 1980 (0.7 percent). We are conscious of the necessity of taking part in a remarkable transfer of resources.

The domestic political problems that are occasioned by this transfer — e.g., high taxes — can only be surmounted if the sacrifices can be offset by a satisfactory economic growth. The income transfer to the developing countries, in the form of credits and grants-in-aid, will not be the only sacrifice. We have to face a deterioration of the terms of trade caused by a rise in prices for raw materials. The Federal Republic, as a country that is highly industrialized but short of raw materials, will have to give a decisive portion of its aid in the form of higher prices for raw materials.

The Federal Republic should not neglect growth for another reason: the demands of the European Community. In the European Community, the transfer of resources has been a big problem not only for the new European monetary system. The question of admitting three Mediterranean countries (Greece, Spain, and Portugal) to the Community also involves the transfer problem. Common financial aid would help these poor countries to close the gap in their industrial development and will stabilize the democratic order in this region. The agricultural share of the gross national product in these countries is high. So the surpluses of farm production in the Community and the costs to finance the agrarian markets will increase.

Meanwhile, the responsibility for the European Community's budget has been taken over by the members of the European Parliament. This year, for the first time, they will be directly elected. They are accountable to the voters for all expenses and it will be difficult for them to give reasons for the continual growth of expenses. The Federal Republic has contributed to the European Community's budget (nearly 70 percent of the budget's total expenses — 32 billion deutsche mark — cover agrarian costs) about 10 billion deutsche mark, that is 5 percent of its own budget. Even taking into account the Community budget's reimbursement, the Federal Republic is already the biggest net payer. The cost to our country of cofinancing the European Community's budget will increase further. The Federal Republic can give more only if its future economic efficiency rises adequately. There are doubts whether the sharply growing expenses of the past few years (in the European Community, expenses have increased an average of 27 pecent per annum from 1971 to 1978) have been accompanied by an enlargement and a deepening of the Community, not to speak of the little response that the European Community's agricultural policy has found in the world. The time has come for reform.

Postulates

First, to abandon price stability would be a sacrifice that would bring about only short-term success. Although some growth is necessary to deal with domestic and foreign issues, it must not be achieved at the expense of price stability. The long-lasting periods of price increase have made clear the problem of creeping inflation and its damaging consequences. Today the United States' number one enemy is inflation. At the London summit in 1977, the government heads declared: "Inflation does not diminish unemployment. It is, on the contrary, one of its main causes."

I do not believe that low-level inflation is inevitable or that it contributes to economic growth; nor is it an unavoidable price for economic growth. Economic objections against inflation as a stimulus to growth are based on the experience — and the United States is proof of it — that inflation will lead to a deterioration of the balance of payments and the exchange rates. This would require restrictive measures to stop abruptly the rate of expansion.

The Federal Republic's development has proved that economic growth and relative full employment, combined with price stability, can be achieved and that, on the other hand, secure growth cannot be achieved in the long run without monetary stability. Checking inflation would at first inevitably lead to economic setback, but it would create a stable basis for a new upswing. Lasting economic growth presumes a high level of voluntary saving and an adequate use of capital. Both are diminished in a climate of inflation. Growth, connected with stable prices, demands that firms and trade unions develop a new attitude toward price and wage policies. The choice is between voluntary discipline (President Carter's remedy) or strong, direct government controls. In our interdependent world economy, severe problems are encountered if one country's economic expansion has priority above other goals (including price stability), and in other countries price stability is preferred.

Another demand, which one cannot acquiesce in, is no growth at the cost of the environment. If we do not want to aggravate inexcusably the future conditions of life, we have to observe the limits to growth that are set by the stability of the ecology. The environment can no longer be damaged free of cost. Those who cause damage have to be charged with the additional social costs. This will absorb resources that have formerly been used to produce goods and services. Thus it is economic growth that gives way for a responsible environment policy, because it creates the conditions for investments to protect the environment. The developing countries are not indifferent toward the industrial countries' environmental problems. But for them, protecting the environment is unimportant, as long as their few resources do not even suffice to cover the necessities of life.

> We do not ask ourselves if factories soil our environment, if they do give us work. We do not ask ourselves if insecticides are unhealthy, if they do prevent millions of people to die the gruesome death by starvation. We like the dirty air of industrial cities better than the pure air of the jungle, if it does shelter us from hunger, diseases and ignorance.[1]

I think developed countries have a pedagogical task of the greatest importance to prevent developing states from committing errors that now have to be corrected by industrial countries in their own regions.

A large increase in national debt in order to produce more growth would also sacrifice our future. We should not charge our descendants with the costs of today's continuous and adequate growth by transmitting to them the high interest and repayment charges of a fast-rising and lasting public debt. This would lead to unjust losses of wealth. These objections are not directed against temporarily higher public demand for credit for purposes of priming and increasing demand in a period of less than full employment. But as soon as the economy recovers and generates greater self-dynamics, which can be carried on by private consumption and investment, these "public crutches" have to be removed.

The Federal Republic's finance policy produced remarkable expansive impulses. Meanwhile it has reached the limits of what can be advocated from the economic and political aspects. The deficit of the total public budget—federal government, state, local, and social security budgets—amounts to 4 percent of the gross national product (2.7 percent in 1977). Even compared with other countries, this is a remarkable figure. In 1978 the net national debt in the United States amounted to only 0.75 percent of the gross national product. Continually financing the public budgets with high credits will affect economic growth, especially if the economy draws toward a state of normal employment. Private investors will be crowded out from capital markets. This problem has been discussed at length, even in the United States.

Increases in interest rates are also detrimental to future economic upswing. The scope for private activities becomes constrained and economic growth is decelerated.

Finally, we should not achieve higher economic growth at the cost of our liberal economic system. This demand holds true especially for foreign trade. The Federal Republic objects to all those tendencies, which have increased distinctly in recent years, that try to hinder or even stop free international trade by protectionist measures, in order to gain economic advantages. Even developing countries now are becoming more convinced of the value of free international exchange of goods. They are surprised to see industrial countries building up barriers against the imports of competitive developing countries, although they have praised the effects of free trade for years. The developing countries complain about the industrial nations' growing protectionism as another demonstration of their superior power.

Practice is proof that all countries benefit from a system of international division of labor and exchange of goods. Therefore, protectionism, as a stimulus to economic growth, is, in the long run, in the same way as self-defeating as sacrificing stability or environment. Last year, the European Community's heads of government called for an open system of world trade and the gradual abolition of protectionism. It has been pointed out that success in surmounting dirigistic and protectionist barriers is a condition of adequate economic growth and a decisive factor for the relationship among the European Community, the Western alliance, and the Third World.

It is the responsibility of all of us to help achieve economic growth — even if the necessary conditions for success have deteriorated in the Federal Republic — but this responsibility also forbids us to aim at illusory successes of economic growth, lest we fall victim to inflation, jeopardize the environment, waste raw materials, and invite excessive national debt and dirigisme.

Note

1. Quoted from the economics representative of the Embassy of Algeria in Bonn, November 28, 1978.

15

The Role of Germany in the Evolving International Economic System

J. Robert Schaetzel

I

There is considerable evidence that history tends to run in twenty-five–year cycles. Several years ago, a depressed Jean Monnet confessed in a conversation to bewilderment with contemporary developments and suggested that an era had ended.

That extraordinarily creative and fruitful quarter-century served Germany to a unique degree. On the foundation of American support and close German-American cooperation, Germany was the benefactor of that historic gesture from France: the Schuman Plan. NATO provided both security and the framework within which Germany could make its national contribution to the common defense. And finally, there came into being the network of international economic institutions — the World Bank, the International Monetary Fund, the OEEC and then the OECD, and the GATT. This offered Germany security (an invitation that Germany seized for its moral rebirth), economic rules, and an international system that allowed the full play of German resourcefulness and energy without alarm to friend or foe.

The end of this era came with the monetary crisis of 1971, the Yom Kippur War, and the oil embargo of 1973-1974. We are now well into a period of vast and uncertain change. The questions raised in European minds by SALT II portend the more difficult problems in so-called gray zone systems and efforts to get conventional arms control moving. The rapid growth of Soviet nuclear and conventional power creates doubts about the military balance. The new generation of Soviet leadership stirs up new worries. Will the post-Brezhnev leaders be pragmatists with a propensity for the consumer society or will they — untouched by the revolution, the purges of the 1930s, World War II, and the postwar agonies — see Russian military equality as an opportunity to exploit situations of weakness, whether in Africa, Asia, or even in Western Europe?

Politics has not been standing still. No one speaks today of a world Communist movement. The deep break between Peking and Moscow is now compounded by unprecedented Chinese initiatives in Western Europe, Japan, and the United States. The variety and differences among the Western European Communist parties offer Moscow small comfort. There remains the question of whether Communist experimentation with competition and market forces can be contained, or whether a bit of freedom can get out of hand.

Until the French elections in the spring of 1978, many observers anticipated that several Western European countries would shortly be experimenting with governing coalitions containing strong Communist components. Instead the political tide runs, at least for the moment, strongly to the Center and Right. Even socialist or labor governments behave with an economic orthodoxy that infuriates the outflanked Left.

Equally striking is the growing diversity among the Third World countries. An entirely new breed in economic terms — the advanced developing countries — looks more like the Western European than the United Nations Conference on Trade and Development (UNCTAD) prototype. Then there are the nouveaux riches, instantly wealthy from oil or raw materials, in a position to finesse the earlier stages of development as they attempt the leap into the industrial era. But there remain the impoverished, agricultural-based developing countries. This new diversity opens up the possibility of serious discussion and negotiation, rather than the past record of sterile collisions with the Group of 77, whose unity was preserved through the technique of nonnegotiable demands.

Overshadowing these phenomena are the basic changes taking place in economic behavior and performance. Few expect the industrial nations to resume the levels of real growth achieved in the last quarter-century. Slower growth and stubborn inflation have brought to the fore the heavy costs of social demands and programs. A central assumption of the international economic system, more dependent on growth and full employment than had been appreciated, was the adjustment process. Today the process has more doubters than believers, even in Japan. Economic stagnation, unemployment, and other forces have reduced the willlingness of democratic societies to transfer substantial resources to the more needy nations — or even to more needy regions within Western society itself. The oil crisis brought the industrial democracies face to face with a new and brutal truth: not merely their well-being but their sheer existence had fallen into the hands of states having different political, cultural, security, and strategic values. These forces of change are all at work within the international system — they make for instability.

II

The international economic institutions, become flaccid, have not adjusted to these changes. The postwar period amounted to a reaction against the excesses of nationalism and led to a willingness to experiment with the new international obligations and novel institutions. The real irony is that today, when everyone speaks of interdependence, the commitment to the international system falters.

United Nations agencies, especially the Economic and Social Council, the International Labor Organization (ILO), and the Food and Agriculture Organization (FAO), have fallen on hard times. The World Bank has carved out a special niche, helped by the fact that its activities do not involve it in those areas of monetary and trade policy that impinge on sensitive domestic political nerves. The IMF has not found a new role equal to that envisioned under the Bretton Woods system. The GATT has lost momentum and status; the OECD has failed to exploit the potential of its flexible charter.

Why this spotty and indifferent record? The mood of Dumbarton Oaks, Bretton Woods, and even Havana was that ahead lay a world to be constructed of order and progress. The public expected miracles that were not to be. Rather than converging, national interests diverged. The more than 150 nations have almost nothing in common. Quite apart from their deep conflict of interests, the sheer numbers become the enemy of efficiency. And finally there has been a failure of political leadership, a failure that has taken many forms. It shows up in indifference to the work of the international agencies, in the bypassing of agencies that have competence, in the appointment of representatives with dubious capability, in the refusal to live with the inevitable tedium and the inescapable costs of doing multilateral business. In short, there is no serious commitment on the part of any of the major leaders to strengthening and reforming the international economic system.

III

At a time when interdependence comes into full flower, that ultimate anachronism, nationalism, blossoms along with the decline in the strength and role of international institutions. This nationalistic fervor becomes the ultimate paradox: it occurs when almost all problems are multilateral. American embassies in the major capitals note that the only economic problems that are bilateral are the stubborn controversies over aviation agreements. Of course one reason for nationalism, apart from the excesses demanded by the ultra-Gaullists and the French Communists, is the desire to maintain full freedom for national social and economic planning. Britain finds itself inhibited by the European Commission in seeking to preserve, through subsidies, obsolete steel or shipbuilding facilities. Another paradox is the degree to which governments become aggressively nationalistic because they are weak. Dependent on the Gaullists, Valéry Giscard d'Estaing is severely limited in his freedom of action and frequently finds it prudent to join the Gaullist and Communist nationalistic parade. Similarly, the militant Left in Britain, the Tribune group, insists on absolute freedom for national action — or folly.

The next step in this degenerative process is rampant bilateralism and "ad hoc-ery." The unique postwar relationship between Bonn and Washington creates an almost irresistible temptation to contrive a kind of bilateral connection of economic strength and common economic principles. Several American economists have relished the thought of a kind of German-American "bigemony." The superficial plausibility of such an arrangement is seemingly strengthened by reference to the scale of the military contribution of the two to the NATO defense establishment.

There is an old Chinese proverb, "You can never swim in the same river twice; you change and the river changes." The extraordinary relationship between Germany and America that has existed for twenty-five years cannot be extended. Replacing the long German deferral to the United States, the present relationship is bound to evolve into more traditional patterns, similar to America's relations with its other major allies. Any effort to recapture or even refurbish a relationship born out of Adenauer's singlemindedness is bound to fail. Moreover, any form of "bigemony" would dismay Germany's neighbors, generating envy coupled with fear.

The future would seem to bring new tensions in the relations between Bonn and Washington. Only some elements of the confrontation over nuclear energy have been resolved. There remain Germany's commitment to the breeder reactor and the determination to sell this technology abroad. America's volatile policy with respect to fuel supply led Germany to join with the Dutch and British in a major isotopic separation program. Germany is now buying approximately 50 percent of its enriched material from the Soviet Union.

Assuming that SALT II negotiations are completed and eventually ratified — a bold assumption indeed — further arms control negotiations with the Soviet Union will inevitably create friction in German-American relations. This arena of controversy has produced a rash of episodes: the neutron bomb, cancellation of the B-1 bomber, the cruise missile, planned reduction of tactical nuclear weapons, and that intractable source of controversy — strategic doctrine. Long quiescent, military procurement also shows every sign of producing its own controversy.

Vastly different domestic energy situations put America and Germany on separate courses. Germany's dependence on them inevitably affects Bonn's strategy toward the Arab states, including investment in the area. It is by no means certain that the United States and Germany will react in similar ways to the competition each faces from the so-called advanced developing countries. Even in the area of trade, where common interests exist, Germany has been in the forefront of pushing for ever higher price levels for crucial commodities covered by the European Community's common agricultural policy.

IV

It may have been inevitable that these forces would draw the political leaders to that new form of collective activity, the economic summits. The attractions of this device are undeniable. Political egos are satisfied, a blaze of instant publicity produced — and all without any relinquishment of sovereignty. In these occasional affairs, the seven heads of government escape the boredom of meeting within the framework of established institutions. Undoubtedly, there are some tangible benefits. The mere fact of the now semiannual sessions forces the participants to concentrate for a few days on the larger issues within an international frame of reference. The process can generate a degree of peer pressure leading to commitments to future national action. In theory the summit technique can begin a process whereby the leaders instruct their subordinates to take action within existing international institutions.

But summitry is not without its costs, although they are generally ignored. As the economic summits become routine, inevitably there is a tendency to remove subjects from the competent agencies or the normal processes and bring them before the leaders. The established bureaucracies, already cursed by that endemic disease, caution, become more hesitant and less assertive, knowing that the nasty issues can be handed up to the top. A one- or two-day session is an impossible format for handling complex economic issues. Since success, progress, and agreement are the imperatives, the political leaders must develop a communiqué that presumably proves that these goals have been achieved. Despite the short life span of the economic summit technique, declining public interest and confidence are already evident. Given the low esteem in which political leadership is held today, a further shrinkage in this precious commodity is a high price to pay.

V

The intricate play of these forces, their impact on Germany, and the crucial role of the Federal Republic in their management can best be seen by close examination of two central issues: trade and trade policy, and the European Community. More than any other two countries, Germany and the United States share a commitment to the principle of a competitive, free market economy. This commitment leads naturally to a parallel belief in the indispensability of preserving and strengthening an open, liberal international economic system. Washington and Bonn both appreciate the merits of free capital movement and favor a sympathetic but moderate approach to the development problems of the poor nations of the southern hemisphere. And both countries suffer from occasional economic schizophrenia; for example, when farm politics prevails over the market philosophy, or when cartel arrangements or target prices are employed to moderate the disruptive forces of competition in steel products.

The trade problems lying ahead are formidable. The philosophical attack comes from many quarters, the common thread being to question the prevailing assumptions about the merit of the open, liberal competitive system. The Cambridge group in Britain argues for a closed, managed economy; labor in the United States cloaks the case for protectionism in the beguiling robes of fair trade. Democratic societies suffer from domestic pressure groups that insist on a wide range of social services and safeguards and put a premium on assured employment as against the dynamism and uncertainty of change in areas where the adjustment process for labor or industry works imperfectly. The adjustment process can all too easily misfire and lead to import restrictions as the easy political answer. The advanced countries are only beginning to feel the competition that will inexorably grow from the new industrial nations — Singapore, Brazil, Mexico. America moves to limit the flood of television sets from Japan only to find that an even larger torrent of sets flows in from Korea and Taiwan.

Assuming that the multilateral trade negotiations are brought to a successful conclusion and the results are accepted by the Congress, the world will still be left with an awesome agenda of problems. The codes being negotiated in Geneva will need to be translated into trade law. The technical problems are formidable, especially with respect to national subsidies that distort international trade. Definitional problems will be troublesome enough, but then there will come difficult questions of equity: How does one weigh national subsidies designed to enhance the competitiveness of high technology industries and assess claims that such subsidies are required to match the hidden assistance given to industries through military research and development and production contracts?

There is the enigma of the GATT. The codes amount to new contractual agreements and hence become the grounds for complaints about infractions. Processes will have to be devised and administered to determine the facts, doubly difficult in the nontariff barrier field. Dispute and settlement procedures will have to be improved. Traditional sanctions, such as the withholding of benefits, seem less than adequate to deal with offenses found under the new codes. This abbreviated catalog is presented merely to suggest the challenge the GATT faces.

It is not as though the organization were already bursting with health and efficiency. Sheer size of membership automatically reduces effectiveness. But a larger, more intractable problem is the degree to which the divergence of trade policy between the developed and the developing countries burdens the GATT. A conspiracy of silence has prevailed in the face of violations of GATT rules by the developing countries. While some officials and experts from the developing world recognize the intrinsic merit, to their own economic interests, of accepting the loose discipline of the Articles of Agreement, the squatter's rights of exception will be hard to give up.[1]

Over this range of problems hangs the cloud of rising protectionism. Although exhausted gratitude will attend the completion of the Tokyo round negotiation, success, if it can be called that, will have the side effect of removing the significant shield these negotiations have given governments in standing up to protectionist pressures. Each country, not least the United States with its more conservative Congress, will stand more exposed to demands of special interest groups for restrictive measures. An already weak international economic system can hardly withstand a trade battle in which the industrial democracies strike out at one another.

A disagreeable confluence of forces will emerge in the United States in 1979. The domestic preoccupations of the United States will be aggravated by the probable downturn in economic activity brought about by the Carter administration's antiinflation program. Inflation, mild recession, higher unemployment, and an austerity budget are an explosive protectionist mixture.

These problems are not unique to the United States. The common character of our problems can be seen in the similar difficulties of our steel, textiles, fibers, and petrochemical industries. In the latter field, both Germany and the United States increasingly feel the competitive pressures coming from Arab states.

The inescapable conclusion is that the merging trade problems cannot be solved within a bilateral context, or even on a regional basis. More effective international rules and institutions are essential. The charge is made that the call for an international regime is based on blind ideology when in fact it is a matter of elementary logic. A failure to institutionalize increasingly complex trade relations will lead directly to confrontation, dispute, and retaliation, and the adverse effects will not be restricted to matters of foreign trade. We have seen how America's trade imbalance with Japan has stimulated criticism about the minimal Japanese defense effort and raised questions as to why the United States should be asked to pay for the defense of the Japanese islands and interests. A working system of agreements and dispute management is the means of depoliticizing economic argument. One way governments can deflect the massive pressure from special interest groups is to make full use of international obligations and mechanisms.

International trade policy presents the advanced industrial democracies with the critical test. A failure to cope imaginatively with this range of issues surely will lead to failure in other fields — investment, North-South relations, and mutual security arrangements.

VI

The second case study, where the forces described also converge, is the process of European unity. It would be hard to overstate the importance of the European Community to the Federal Republic. A political framework that contributed in a basic way to Germany's metamorphosis, it also allowed and encouraged the country to European economic preeminence. The Community has become the major market for German goods.

Germany's broad interest in the process of European unity rests also on the kind of a Europe the Federal Republic wants, quite beyond important but narrow economic interests. Italy, a critical element to a stable Europe, has had a defined and consistent commitment to the Community as the means of tying itself to democratic, northern Europe. The nascent Mediterranean democracies — Greece, Spain, and Portugal — seek membership in the Community for political as much as economic reasons. This leads to the fundamental question for Germany: What kind of neighborhood does it wish to live in — one that is growing and slowly eliminating gross disparities in wealth, or one where the poor become desperate, where political instability presages collapse of Western Europe?

The year 1979 becomes critical for Europe. Will the Community be reborn, gaining a new dynamism from the European monetary system (EMS) and the direct election of the European Parliament? Or will Europe take the other road, opened up with the Luxembourg crisis of 1966 and the deliberate weakening of the Brussels institutions, and continue the slow but steady diminution of the authority of the Community?

The French and the British have set themselves against any evolution of the new directly elected Parliament in the direction of authentic legislative responsibilities. Entry of the three new members, unless accompanied by institutional and procedural reforms, can bring Community decision making to a halt. Economic summitry by France, Germany, Britain, and Italy has paid little attention to the effect this "exclusive club" has on the smaller Community members or on the Community institutions. If the European monetary system devolves into a bloc within a bloc and the commission is (almost absentmindedly) converted into an international secretariat rather than a novel executive body, then this road is likely to leave the Europeans finally with nothing more than a regional OECD.

VII

The pattern of these events, insofar as it can be gleaned, and the direction in which we are being moved are unclear. Indeed, one hallmark is pervasive, paradoxical behavior. The Chinese suddenly acquire a taste for democracy, Western technology, and the excitement of capitalist contracts with the industrial democracies. The socialist states of Eastern Europe experiment with profits and wage incentives. Prime Minister Raymond Barre launches an economic revolution in France that would turn French backs on Colbert and Napoleon with the goal of making his country more like Germany. James Callaghan turns out to be one of the best Tory prime ministers in twentieth-century Britain.

This is a time of destabilizing change. I have noted the rising doubts about the present relevance of the remarkably successful postwar combination of policies and institutions. If in this time of disillusionment a consensus should emerge that the postwar system is obsolete, then, unless we are prepared to accept the risks of international anarchy, we must face the problem of just what we wish to put in place of the old system.

One major factor seems clear: the center of gravity in international affairs is economics — trade, markets and competition, raw material availability and pricing, foreign investment, economic growth and full employment, and the adjustment process. Two examples may be used to illustrate this fact. First, whatever the prospects may be for stable political regimes in Africa, they will in good part be a function of whether the nations are to benefit from growth, including reasonably equitable internal economic conditions. Second, a viable Western defense, to be sought in considerable part in terms of a 3 percent annual increase in defense budgets (with the deflator), is manifestly dependent on adequate levels of economic growth. America is on the way to demonstrating the validity of this point. Despite the country's deep concern about Soviet arms and the president's commitment, the clamor has begun to ignore the 3 percent obligation.

VIII

Standing against these volatile and in some cases destructive forces are abiding common interests of Germany and America. The two countries all too easily can be led into the illusory comfort of ever closer bilateral arrangements. "Bigemony" is the next short step — not only bad policy but one that would launch the two nations on a dangerous adventure. After a quarter of a century of close, mutually beneficial relations, what would be more natural than for Americans to look across the Atlantic at Europe and see Germany — a German NATO army; a European currency, the deutsche mark; a European economic engine that is German.

The greater danger may lie in a different direction. Not sought by Germany, but arising out of the nation's strength and the sheer momentum of achievement, Germany could become the center and leader of Western Europe. There is a fine line between German leadership on behalf of Europe and leadership on behalf of Germany. Bonn has not entirely resisted the enticement of delivering lectures on prudent national economic behavior nor has it hidden its impatience with the excesses of less disciplined societies.

Another risk to Germany is the drift into self-pity. At a time of extraordinary economic well-being, internally and externally, a stubborn myth has been implanted that the Federal Republic has become the paymaster, the milk cow of Europe. If politicians insist on giving currency to this myth, it is no wonder the general public accepts the proposition as valid, and resents it. In view of the link between German stability and prosperity and European union, for German leaders to permit, even to encourage, this public disenchantment is an unforgivable error of policy.

IX

The pressing question for the Federal Republic is whether it will find the vision, the stamina, and the tenacity to assign its unique assets and national energy — its political stability, economic strength, and extensive national consensus, which runs across party lines — to the task of defining and creating a more effective international economic system.

The first step is to take advantage of the opportunities at hand to see that 1979 becomes a year of European renaissance. It will take clear, strategic thinking to insure that Chancellor Helmut Schmidt's initiative with respect to the European monetary system strengthens the European Community and its institutions. This is by no means assured. In fact the idea of an EMS working independently and quite outside the existing institutional framework of the Community would be sadly consistent with almost all recent European initiatives—the production of fissionable material, European energy programs, political cooperation, and so on.

It would mean, secondly, something other than the reiterated poor-mouthing of the European Commission, especially by the chancellor. The criticism has often had an eerie quality, almost as though the Community institutions had been imposed upon Germany by some alien force rather than by and at the will of the member states.

Third, the direct election of the European Parliament offers a special opportunity. It is within the power of the political leaders to determine the quality of the candidates who will stand for the June elections. If Germany indicates that the elections are to be taken seriously and that it is determined to field first-class candidates, this will strongly influence the decisions made by other member states. Further, Germany must take the lead in seeing that the new Parliament is in the midstream of Western parliamentary tradition; namely, that legislatures built on a popular mandate are responsible to the public constituency and such legislatures have a responsibility to assert themselves. The fears of the French Gaullists and Communists and the Left of the British Labor party and the extreme Right of the Tories should be proven correct by the emergence of a dynamic European Parliament. Germany is the only major member state with the internal political consensus that makes a firm, positive position on this issue possible.

If these efforts are mounted and are successful, Germany will also have the responsibility to insure that the revived Community looks outward and does not become an ironic monument to de Gaulle's dream of a European Europe. American tolerance for European developments is uncertain. Many of the uneasy reactions to the EMS stem from deep apprehension as to how many additional shocks the dollar can stand and a worry that Bonn and Paris may in fact have in mind a system that will be inner-oriented and work at cross-purposes to the dollar and the International Monetary Fund.

Germany's interest is in insuring that this does not happen. One sure way of disproving the skeptics is for Germany to take the lead, first within the European Community and then with the Community at the international level, to enlarge the areas of trade collaboration. This means that the German government must be acutely sensitive to the dangers inherent in assuming that with the conclusion of the present exhausting negotiations, trade matters for the time can be put aside. If the rules are to be elaborated and the GATT strengthened, leadership to this end can come only from Bonn. And if the Community is not prepared to take up this agenda, no new international effort is possible.

X

The world is once again at a historical crossroads. One distinct possibility is that the centrifugal, disintegrating forces will prevail, that one more attempt will be made to build a secure international order on the quicksand of nationalism. If, however, dangers are recognized and opportunities perceived, initiatives and leadership shown now could usher in another period of innovation and growth.

In this chemistry Germany is the unique element. No country has suffered more from the blind excesses of nationalism. No country has so benefited from the international procedures and structure that grew out of the genius of the postwar period. No country has the economic strength and internal political cohesion peculiar to Germany that can be brought to bear on the problems of the European and the international order.

Despite all the distractions confronting America today, the United States would no doubt react quickly and favorably to German initiatives that sought to limit the incipient chaos and strove to instill a degree of order into the international economic system.

Note

1. One interesting side note on this problem is the acute sensitivity of the Western Europeans and the Japanese to charges from the developing countries that "if the rich countries decide to organize among themselves to cope with a new range of trade problems this can only mean that they must be organizing against the developing world." There is similar unease in the face of resentment from the less-developed members of the GATT when suggestions are offered that the LDCs should begin to accept some discipline of agreed rules. This political nervousness among the advanced industrial countries will make reform of the GATT even more difficult.

16

The Prospects of German Foreign Policy

Hans J. Morgenthau

The broad outlines of the foreign policy of the Federal Republic of Germany are determined by three factors: the geopolitical position of the country, its aspirations with regard to other countries, and the aspirations of other countries with regard to it.

Since Germany's unification in 1870, Germany's position among the nations has been determined by two objective facts: the German people are by nature the most populous and disciplined people of Europe, and they have at their disposal the greatest industrial potential on the continent. In consequence, if nature were allowed to take its course, Germany would of necessity have become the master of Europe. It is this mastery that other European nations refuse to accept and that to prevent they have waged two world wars in one generation. This contradiction between the natural endowments of the German people and the political viability of the continent constitutes for the non-German world the German problem. How to reconcile these two elements of the contradiction has been the besetting issue for Germans and non-Germans alike.

Bismarck suffered from the *cauchemar des coalitions,* the fear that the great powers of Europe, especially France and Russia, would conclude a grand alliance in order to destroy the natural preeminence of Germany in Europe. On the other end of the political spectrum, Clemenceau confirmed Bismarck's fear when he declared that there were 20 million Germans too many. The division of Germany in consequence of the distribution of military power at the end of World War II and of the Yalta and Potsdam agreements similarly sought to reconcile German power and European freedom by cutting Germany down to size.

It is a testimony to the inherent strength of the German people that even the truncated Germany of today has again become the foremost industrial and military power on the continent. It is a testimony to the drastic changes that German power and foreign policy have undergone that the preeminence of Germany is no longer perceived by the other European nations as a threat to Europe. Three factors are responsible for that change.

The political balance of power that emerged from the distribution of military power at the end of World War II reduced all nations of Europe to the status of second or third rank powers, which to a greater or lesser extent had to lean, or were compelled to lean, for protection upon one or the other of the superpowers. The extent of that dependence determined the ability of those nations to pursue an independent foreign policy. Thus, the Federal Republic of Germany had to follow the American lead, as East Germany had to follow the Soviet lead.

This inability to pursue an independent foreign policy has been greatly enhanced by the stationing, in virtual permanence, of foreign troops in West and East Germany. This presence of foreign troops made it impossible for both Germanies to pursue, without the consent of the respective foreign powers, adventurous policies that might involve the nations concerned in international complications or even war.

Finally, a succession of West German governments and the electorate supporting them have drawn a lesson from Germany's defeats in two world wars and the human and material devastation accompanying those defeats. It is the same lesson Bismarck drew from the contemplation of Germany's geopolitical position, which became the basis of his foreign policy: the position of Germany in the center of Europe, surrounded by potentially hostile nations, makes it imperative for Germany to avoid a two-front confrontation. It requires either a Western or Eastern orientation.

This imperative of caution and self-restraint has been greatly enhanced by the geographical position of Germany between the two nuclear superpowers. A war between the United States and the Soviet Union would most likely be a nuclear war, and the two Germanies would hold the forward positions, inviting total destruction.

The Federal Republic of Germany has opted for the West for two basic reasons. Its eastern frontier follows the line of military demarcation established between the Red Army and the Western armies at the end of World War II. The military governments established in the Western zones of occupation considered it their main purpose to preserve the status quo of that de facto partition. That purpose was powerfully and in all probability decisively supported by the refusal of the German people—freely and clearly expressed in the West and mutedly in the East—to exchange the tyranny of the Nazis for that of the Communists.

That refusal, as applied to the German Democratic Republic, was expressed by the early West German governments through the Hallstein Doctrine, which denied the legitimacy of the East German government and assumed the representation of both Germanies by the government of the Federal Republic of Germany. By the same token, the Hallstein Doctrine proclaimed the illegitimacy of the partition of Germany and presented reunification of the two Germanies as the foremost aim of West German foreign policy.

This aim was essentially limited to rhetorical proclamations, since the Soviet Union was no more willing to relinquish its military hold upon East Germany than the Western powers were to relinquish theirs on West Germany. Unable to pursue its claim of exclusive representation with anything even approaching efficiency, and conscious of the permanent importance of West European and American support, the Federal Republic of Germany pursued in reality a policy of Western integration, as exemplified by the West German membership in the European Community and in NATO. Thus while West German rhetoric was turned to the East, the political and military realities pointed toward the West.

The treaties of 1970 with the Soviet Union and Poland, augmented by subsequent treaties with other Eastern bloc nations and the Final Act of Helsinki of 1975, mark a turning point in the foreign policy of the Federal Republic. They imply the recognition by the Federal Republic of the territorial status quo in Central and Eastern Europe and of the sovereignty of the East German government. They abolish for all practical purposes the Hallstein Doctrine. That, however, does not mean that reunification as a goal of the Federal Republic's foreign policy has also been abandoned. The Federal Republic still refuses to accept the partition of Germany as legitimate and, hence, definitive, but regards reunification impossible for the foreseeable future for reasons of ideology and the distribution of military and political power. When one considers the prospects of the Federal Republic's foreign policy, one must not lose sight of the possibility that reunification, now hardly anything more than a mirage on the distant horizon, might become a real goal of the Federal Republic's foreign policy.

The decline of American power and influence tilts the balance of power in favor of the Soviet Union and, in consequence, increases the insecurity of the nations of Western Europe. These nations—ambivalent toward the United States, whose support they need but resent—may then perceive themselves as having been abandoned by the United States and having to face, on their own, a Soviet Union unchallengeable in its military power. This state of mind would give the Soviet Union its long-sought-after opportunity to stabilize what it calls European security, which is in truth a euphemism for its own. Seen from the vantage point of the Kremlin, European security requires the reduction, if not the elimination, of American power on the continent, the consequent emasculation of NATO, and the isolation of the Federal Republic of Germany. The nations of Western Europe, isolated from each other and from the United States, would then no longer be able to maintain a viable balance of power vis-à-vis the Soviet

Union and would have to accommodate themselves to the Soviet hegemony over the Eurasian land mass.

This accommodation — were the Federal Republic of Germany to join in it — would signify a drastic change in the distribution of world power. The Western orientation of the Federal Republic has been derived from calculations of comparative political, military, and economic advantage. That orientation has not remained unchallenged from within the Federal Republic, even while rational calculation argued powerfully in its favor. If the development I have indicated above were to come to pass, rational arguments could indeed support an Eastern orientation. Traditionally fearful of the "Russian bear," a West Germany deprived of assured American protection would have to move into a neutral, if not friendly, political and military position vis-à-vis its towering neighbor to the east. That position would be greatly strengthened by the complementary relationship of the West German and Soviet economies. The Soviet Union has obviously decided to supplement its own efforts at industrial modernization with a massive influx of Western technology. The Federal Republic is one of the most highly developed industrial nations, dependent on large-scale exports for its prosperity. Once the political, military, and economic ties among the Western European nations and between them and the United States are loosened, the Soviet Union could offer a profitable alternative.

What argues against this possibility is not only the ideological cleavage between East and West and the distribution of military and political power, but also — and most emphatically — the interests of the Soviet Union, the Eastern bloc nations, and the Western powers. Even a truncated West Germany has become the most important economic and miliary power west of the Elbe River. Even this truncated West Germany is experienced by France, if not the other Western European nations, as a competitor, if not a threat. The Western military and economic integration of the Federal Republic has served to mitigate that competition and to stave off that threat. However, even in the organizations effecting that integration, the natural preeminence of Germany has made itself felt. NATO has become for all practical purposes an American-German alliance, and the German mark is, together with the Swiss franc, the strongest currency in Western Europe.

When, with all these factors in mind, one raises the question of the prospects for the foreign policy of the Federal Republic, one realizes how narrow the space is within which the foreign policy of the Federal Republic moves today and will be able to move in in the foreseeable future. The solution of the issue of reunification depends only remotely upon the Federal Republic and primarily upon the Soviet Union. The Soviet Union will not give up its hold upon the German Democratic Republic, a refusal that precludes reunification, unless it receives an equivalent. One could imagine an Eastern orientation of the Federal Republic in the sense of severing its intimate military and political ties with the West. Instead, a united Germany, the kingpin of the Finlandization of Western Europe, would maintain its formal independence, but lean politically and militarily upon the Soviet Union. There is very little likelihood that such a reorientation of the foreign policy of the Federal Republic will soon take place. But the history, first of Prussia and then of Germany, shows that the Eastern alternative has not been alien to Prussian and German statecraft and that it could materialize again as a viable option, given circumstances (especially in the nuclear field) favorable to it.

The Federal Republic, restrained in the East to relative immobility for the foreseeable future, must seek in continuing Western integration its main outlet for an active foreign policy. It must temper that activism with a considerable measure of self-restraint, always conscious of its preeminent power and the unaceptability of that preeminence to the other nations of Western Europe.

Thus the prospects for an active foreign policy of the Federal Republic are dim. That dimness results from the Eastern political situation in which the Federal Republic finds itself, from the restraints that its neighbors in the East and West impose upon it, and from the self-restraint that the Federal Republic has imposed upon itself and is likely to continue to practice in the future.